James Edmund Harting

The Birds of Shakespeare

Critically examined, explained, and illustrated

James Edmund Harting

The Birds of Shakespeare
Critically examined, explained, and illustrated

ISBN/EAN: 9783337058012

Printed in Europe, USA, Canada, Australia, Japan

Cover: Foto ©Thomas Meinert / pixelio.de

More available books at **www.hansebooks.com**

THE
BIRDS
OF
SHAKESPEARE.

CRITICALLY EXAMINED, EXPLAINED, AND ILLUSTRATED.

BY

JAMES EDMUND HARTING, F.L.S., F.Z.S.,

MEMBER OF THE BRITISH ORNITHOLOGISTS' UNION,
AUTHOR OF "THE BIRDS OF MIDDLESEX,"
ETC., ETC.

LONDON:
JOHN VAN VOORST, PATERNOSTER ROW.
MDCCCLXXI.

PREFACE.

OF no other author, perhaps, has more been written than of Shakespeare. Yet whatever other knowledge his commentators professed, few of them appear to have been naturalists, and none, so far as I am aware, have examined his knowledge of Ornithology.

An inquiry upon this subject, undertaken in the first instance for my own amusement, has resulted in the bringing together of so much that is curious and entertaining, that to the long list of books already published about Shakespeare, I have been bold enough to add yet another. In so doing, I venture to hope that the reader may so far appreciate the result of my labour as not to consider it superfluous.

As regards the treatment of the subject, a word or two of explanation seems necessary. In 1866, from the notes I had then collected, I contributed a series of articles on the birds of Shakespeare to *The Zoologist*. In these articles, I referred only to such birds as have a claim to be considered British, and omitted all notice of domesticated species. I had not then considered any special arrangement or grouping, but noticed each species *seriatim* in the order adopted by Mr. Yarrell in his excellent " History of British Birds." Since that date, I have collected so much additional information on the subject, that, instead of eighty pages (the extent of my first publication), three hundred have now passed through the printers' hands. With this large accession of material, it was found absolutely necessary to re-arrange and re-write the whole. The birds therefore have been now divided into certain natural groups, including the foreign and domesticated species, to each of which groups a chapter has been devoted ; and I have thought it desirable to give, by way of introduction, a sketch of Shakespeare's general knowledge of natural history and acquaintance with field-sports, as bearing more or less directly on his special knowledge of Ornithology, which I propose chiefly to consider.

After I had published the last of the series of articles referred to, I received an intimation for the first time, that, twenty years previously, a notice of the birds of Shakespeare had appeared in the pages of *The Zoologist*. I lost no time in procuring the particular number which contained the article, and found that, in December, 1846, Mr. T. W. Barlow, of Holmes Chapel, Cheshire, had, to a certain extent, directed attention to Shakespeare's knowledge as an Ornithologist. His communication, however, did not exceed half a dozen pages, in which space he has mentioned barely one-fourth of the species to which Shakespeare has referred. From the cursory nature of his remarks, moreover, I failed to discover a reference to any point which I had not already investigated. It would be unnecessary for me, therefore, to allude to this article, except for the purpose of acknowledging that Mr. Barlow was the first to enter upon what, as regards Shakespeare, may be termed this new field of research.

The labour of collecting and arranging Shakespeare's numerous allusions to birds, has been much greater than many would suppose, for not only have I derived little or no benefit from the various editions of his works which I have consulted, but reference to a glossarial index, or concordance, has, in nine cases out of ten, resulted in disappointment. It is due to Mr. Staunton, however, to state that I have found some of the foot-notes to his library edition of the Plays very useful.

Although oft-times difficult, it has been my endeavour, as far as practicable, to connect one with another the various passages quoted or referred to, so as to render the whole as readable and as entertaining as possible. With this view, many allusions have been passed over as being too trivial to deserve separate notice, but a reference to them will be found in the Appendix at the end of the volume,* where all the words quoted are arranged, for

---

* Such words are there enclosed in brackets [ ].

convenience, in the order in which they occur in the plays and poems.

In spelling Shakespeare's name, I have adopted the orthography of his friends Ben Jonson and the editors of the first folio.*

As regards the illustrations, it seems desirable also to say a few words.

In selecting for my frontispiece a portrait of Shakespeare as a falconer (a character which I am confident could not have been foreign to him), I have experienced considerable difficulty in making choice of a likeness.

Those who have made special inquiries into the authenticity of the various portraits of Shakespeare, are not agreed in the results at which they have arrived. This is to be attributed to the fact that, with the exception of the Droeshout etching, to which I shall presently state my objection, no likeness really exists of which a reliable history can be given without one or more missing links in the chain of evidence.

There are four portraits which have all more or less claim to be considered authentic. These are "the Jansen portrait," 1610; "the Stratford bust," prior to 1623; "the Droeshout etching," 1623; and "the Chandos portrait," of which the precise date is uncertain, but which must

* Amongst the entries in the Council Book of the Corporation of Stratford, during the period that John Shakespeare, the Poet's father, was a member of the Municipal body (he filled the office of Chamberlain in 1573), the name occurs one hundred and sixty-six times under fourteen different modes of spelling.

have been painted some years prior to 1616, the year of Shakespeare's death.

It would be impossible, within the compass of this preface, to review all that has been said for and against these four portraits. Neither will space permit me to give the history of each in detail. I can only briefly allude to the chief facts in connection with each, and state the reasons which have influenced me in selecting the Chandos portrait.

Mr. Boaden, who was the first to examine into the authenticity of reputed Shakespeare portraits,* has evinced a preference for the so-called "Jansen portrait," in the collection of the Duke of Somerset, considering it to have been painted by Cornelius Jansen, in 1610, for Lord Southampton, the great patron, at that date, of art and the drama.

The picture, indeed, bears upon the face of it an inscription—$\mathrm{\AE^{te}}\ 46 \atop 1610$—which gives much weight to the views expressed by Mr. Boaden.

It is certain that, in the year mentioned, Jansen was in England, and that he painted several pictures for Lord Southampton; it is equally true, that at that date Shakespeare was in his forty-sixth year. But Mr. Boaden fails to prove that this particular picture was painted by

* "An Inquiry into the Authenticity of various Pictures and Prints, which, from the decease of the Poet to our own times, have been offered to the public as Portraits of Shakespeare." By James Boaden. London, 1824.

Jansen, and that it was ever in the possession of Lord Southampton, or painted by his order.

As a fine head, and a work of art, it is the one of all others that I should like to think resembled Shakespeare, could its history be more satisfactorily detailed.

. Many regard as a genuine portrait, the Bust at Stratford-on-Avon, which is stated to have been executed by Gerard Johnson, and "probably" under the superintendence of Dr. John Hall. The precise date of its erection is not known, but we gather that it was previous to 1623, from the fact that Leonard Digges has referred to it in his Lines to the Memory of Shakespeare, prefixed to the first folio edition of the Plays published in that year. Mr. Wivell relies very strongly on the circumstance of its having been originally coloured to nature.* Hence tradition informs us that the eyes were hazel, the hair and beard auburn. It must be admitted, however, that a portrait after death can never be so faithful as a picture from the life, while no sculptor who examines this bust can maintain that it was executed from a cast.†

Those who approve of the Droeshout etching, published in 1623, as a frontispiece to the first folio, find a strong argument in favour of its being a likeness in the commendatory lines by Ben Jonson, which accompany it.

---

* "An Inquiry into the History, Authenticity, and Characteristics of the Shakespeare Portraits." By Abraham Wivell. London, 1827.

† The Stratford Portrait was doubtless painted from the bust, and probably about the time of the Garrick Jubilee, 1769.

Jonson knew Shakespeare well, and he says of this picture :—

> "This figure that thou here seest put,
> It was for gentle Shakespeare cut;
> Wherein the graver had a strife
> With Nature to outdoo the life.
> O, could he but have drawne his wit
> As well in brasse as he hath hit
> His face, the print would then surpasse
> All that was ever writ in brasse;
> But since he cannot, reader, looke
> Not on his picture, but his booke."

As a work of art it is by no means skilful, and is confessedly inferior not only to other engravings of that day, but also to other portraits by Martin Droeshout.

That it bore some likeness to Shakespeare *as an actor*, I do not doubt, but that it resembled him as a private individual when off the stage, I cannot bring myself to believe. The straight hair and shaven chin which are not found in other portraits having good claims to be considered authentic, and the unnaturally high forehead, which would be caused by the actor's wearing the wig of an old man partially bald, suggest at once that when the original portrait was taken, from which Droeshout engraved, Shakespeare was dressed as if about to sustain a part in which he was thought to excel as an actor.

Boaden has conjectured that this portrait represents Shakespeare in the character of old Knowell, in Ben

Jonson's *Every Man in his Humour*, a part which he is known to have played in 1598, and this would easily account for Ben Jonson's commendation.* This conjecture is so extremely probable, that I have no hesitation in endorsing it.

We come, then, now to "the Chandos portrait." With the longest pedigree of any, it possesses at least as much collateral evidence of probability, and is, moreover, important as belonging to the nation.† It has been traced back to the possession of Shakespeare's godson, William, afterwards Sir William, Davenant, and all that seems to be wanting materially, is the artist's name. The general opinion is, that it was painted either by Burbage or Taylor, both of whom were fellow-players of Shakespeare. It is styled the Chandos portrait from having come to the trustees of the National Portrait Gallery from the collection of the Duke of Chandos and Buckingham, through the Earl of Ellesmere, by whom it was purchased and presented. The history of the picture, so far as it can be ascertained, is as follows :—

It was originally the property of Taylor, the player

---

* Boaden adds: "Let it be remembered in aid of this inference that tradition has invariably assigned to him, as an actor, characters in the decline of life, and that one of his relatives is reported to have seen him in the part of old Adam, the faithful follower of Orlando, in that enchanting pastoral comedy *As You Like It*." Op. cit., p. 22.

† "Life Portraits of William Shakespeare," by J. Hain Friswell. London, 1864.

(our poet's Hamlet), by whom, or by Richard Burbage, it was painted.*

Taylor dying about the year 1653, at the advanced age of seventy,† left this picture by will to Davenant.‡ At the death of Davenant, who died intestate in 1663, it was bought, probably at a sale of his effects, by Betterton, the actor.

While in Betterton's possession, it was engraved by Van der Gucht, for Rowe's edition of Shakespeare, in 1709. Betterton dying without a will and in needy circumstances, his pictures were sold. Some were bought by Bullfinch, the printseller, who sold them again to a Mr. Sykes. The portrait of Shakespeare was purchased by Mrs. Barry, the actress, who afterwards sold it for forty guineas to Mr. Robert Keck, of the Inner Temple.

While in his possession, an engraving was made from it, in 1719, by Vertue, and it then passed to Mr. Nicholls, of Southgate, Middlesex, who acquired it on marrying the heiress of the Keck family.

The Marquis of Caernarvon, afterwards Duke of Chandos, marrying the daughter of Mr. Nicholls, it

---

* We have, unfortunately, no proof that Joseph Taylor, the player, ever painted portraits. There was a contemporary, however, named John Taylor, who was an artist, and it is possible that these two have been confounded.

Boaden refers the picture to Burbage, "who is known to have handled the pencil." Op. cit., p. 49.

† Taylor was thirty-three when Shakespeare died in 1616, and survived him thirty-seven years.

‡ This will, it appears, is not to be found (Wivell, Op. cit., p. 49), but it matters little, if we are assured that Davenant possessed the picture.

then became his Grace's property. When his pictures were sold at Stowe, in September, 1848, this portrait was purchased for three hundred and fifty-five guineas by the Earl of Ellesmere, who, in March, 1856, presented it to the Trustees of the National Portrait Gallery, in whose hands it still remains.

Notwithstanding this pedigree, the picture has been objected to on the ground that the dark hair and foreign complexion could never have belonged to our essentially English Shakespeare. Those who make this objection, seem to forget entirely the age of the portrait, and the fact that it is painted in oil and on canvas, a circumstance which of itself is quite sufficient, after the lapse of two centuries and a half, to account for the dark tone which now pervades it, to say nothing of the numerous touches and retouches to which it has been subjected at the hands of its various owners.

Notwithstanding the missing links of evidence, it seems to me that, having traced the picture back to the possession of Shakespeare's godson, we have gone far enough to justify us in accepting it as an authentic portrait in preference to many others. For we cannot suppose that Sir William Davenant would retain in his possession until his death a picture of one with whom he was personally acquainted, unless he considered that it was sufficiently faithful as a likeness to remind him of the original.

On the score of pedigree, then, and because I believe that the only well-authenticated portrait (*i.e.*, the Droeshout) represents Shakespeare as an actor, and not as a private individual, I have selected the Chandos portrait for my frontispiece.

By obtaining a reduced photograph of this *upon wood*, from the best engraving, and "vignetting" it, I have been enabled to place upon the left hand a hooded falcon, drawn by the unrivalled pencil of Mr. Wolf, and thus to entrust to the engraver, Mr. Pearson, a faithful likeness of man and bird.

As regards the other illustrations, my acknowledgments are due to Mr. J. G. Keulemans for the artistic manner in which he has executed my designs, and to Mr. Pearson for the careful way in which he has engraved them. .

With these observations, I conclude an undertaking which has occupied my leisure hours for six years, but which indeed has been, in every sense of the word, "a labour of love."

Should the reader, on closing this volume, consider its design but imperfectly executed, it is hoped that he will still have gleaned from it enough curious information to compensate him for the disappointment.

CONTENTS.

PAGE

INTRODUCTION.

SHAKESPEARE'S GENERAL KNOWLEDGE OF NATURAL HISTORY.

His Love of Sport.—Hawking.—Fishing.—Hunting.—Fowling.—Deer-Shooting.—Deer-Stealing.—"The Subtle Fox" and "Timorous Hare."—Coursing.—Coney-Catching.—Wild Animals mentioned by Shakespeare.—His Knowledge of their Habits.—Insects referred to in the Plays.—Shakespeare's Powers of Observation.—Practical Knowledge of Falconry.—Love of Birds 1

CHAPTER I.

THE EAGLE AND LARGER BIRDS OF PREY.

An "Eagle Eye."—Power of Flight.—A good Omen.—"The Bird of Jove."—The Roman Eagle.—The "Ensign" of the Eagle—Habits and Attitudes.—Eagles' Eggs.—Longevity of the Eagle: its Age computed.—The Eagle trained for Hawking.—The Vulture: its Repulsive Habits.—The Osprey: its Power over Fish.—The Kite.—The Kite's Nest.—The Buzzard 23

CHAPTER II.

HAWKS AND HAWKING.

Explanation of Hawking Terms.—The Falcon and Tiercel.—The Qualities of a good Falconer.—The "Lure" and its Use.—The "Quarry"—The Hawk's "Trappings."—Jesses, Bells, and Hood.—An Unmann'd Hawk.—The Cadge—The Hawk's Mew.—The Royal Mews.—Origin of the word "Mews."—Imping.—How to "Seel" a Hawk.—A Hawk for the

Bush.—Going "a-birding."—The "Stanniel" or Kestrel.—Origin of the Two Names.—The "Musket" or Sparrow-Hawk.—Hawk and Hernshaw.—Prices of Hawks.—Hawk's Furniture.—Hawk's Meat.—Falconer's Wages.—Sundries 49

CHAPTER III.

THE OWL AND ITS ASSOCIATIONS.

"The Bird of Juno."—"The Favourite of Minerva."—"The Bird of Wisdom."—Sacred to Proserpine.—Use in Medicine.—The Bird of Ill-Omen.—Its Appearance by Day.—Its Habits misunderstood.—Its Utility to the Farmer.—A Curious Tradition.—Its Note or Cry.—An Owl Robbing Nests.—Evidence not conclusive.—Its Retiring Habits.—Its "Five Wits."—Its Fame in Song.—The Owl's Good Night . . . 83

CHAPTER IV.

THE CROWS AND THEIR RELATIONS.

The Raven : a Bird of Ill Omen.—Its Supposed Prophetic Power.—Its Deep and Solemn Voice.—The Raven's Croak foreboding Death.—The "Night-Raven" and "Night-Crow."—The Raven's Presence on Battlefields.—Its alleged Desertion of its Young.—The Rook and Crow.—The Crow-Keeper, and "Scare-Crow."—The Chough.—Russet-pated Choughs.—The Daw, Magpie, and Jay 99

CHAPTER V.

THE BIRDS OF SONG.

The Nightingale.—"Lamenting Philomel."—Singing against a Thorn.—Erroneously supposed to Sing only by Night.—"Recording."—The Lark.—"The Herald of the Morn."—Singing at Heaven's Gate.—Song of the Lark.—Soaring and Singing.—Changing Eyes with Toad.—Lark-Catching.—The Common Bunting.—"The Throstle, with his Note so True."—Imitation of his Song.—The Ouzel-Cock.—The Robin-Redbreast, or Ruddock.—Covering the Dead with Leaves.—"Redbreast Teacher."—"The Wren with Little Quill."—Its Loud Song.—The Sparrow.—"Philip Sparrow."—Providence in the Fall of a Sparrow.—The Hedge-Sparrow and Cuckoo.—"The Cuckoo's Bird."—"Ungentle Gull."—"The Plain Song Cuckoo Gray."—The Song of the Cuckoo.—Cuckoo Songs.—The Wagtail, or Dishwasher.—Bird-catching.—Springes.—Gins.—Bat-fowling.—Its Two Significations.—Bird-Lime, Bird-Bolts, and Birding-Pieces 123

CONTENTS.

CHAPTER VI.

THE BIRDS UNDER DOMESTICATION.

Cock.—"Cock-Crow."—"Cock-shut-time."—"Cock-a-Hoop."—"Cock and Pye."—Cock-Fighting.—Ancestry of the Domestic Cock.—The Peacock. —Its Introduction into Europe, and Ancient Value.—In Request for the Table.—The Turkey.—Date of Introduction into England.—Shakespeare's Anachronism.—Pigeons.—First used as Letter-Carriers.—A Present of Pigeons.—Meaning of "Pigeon-Liver'd."—Pigeon-Post.—Mode of Feeding the Young.—The Barbary Pigeon.—The Rock-Dove.—Doves and Dovecotes.—The "Doves of Venus."—"The Dove of Paphos."—"As True as Turtle to her Mate:" "as Plantage to the Moon."—Mahomet's Dove.—A Dish of Doves.—The Goose.—"Green-Geese," and "Stubble-Geese."—"Cackling home to Camelot."—"The Wild-Goose Chase."—The Swan.—"The Bird of Apollo."—Song of the Swan.—Habits of the Swan.—The Swan's Nest.—As Soft as Swan's-down.—"Juno's Swans."—Cygnets 167

CHAPTER VII.

THE GAME-BIRDS AND "QUARRY" FLOWN AT BY FALCONERS.

Sporting in Shakespeare's Day.—The Pheasant.—Date of its Introduction into Britain.—Ancient Value of Game.—Game-Preserving.—Game-Laws.—Partridge-Hawking.—Anecdote of Charles I.—Quails.—Quail-Fighting.—The Lapwing.—Feigning to be Wounded.—Running as soon as Hatched.—The Heron, or Hernshaw.—Heron-Hawking.—Hawk and Hernshaw.—Heron at Table.—The Woodcock.—Springes for Woodcocks.—How to Make a Springe.—A Gin.—"The Woodcock's Head." —The Snipe 209

CHAPTER VIII.

WILD-FOWL AND SEA-FOWL.

"A Flight of Fowl."—Habit of Wounded Birds.—"Duck-Hunting."— Swimming "like a Duck."—Wild-fowling in Shakespeare's Day.— "The Stalking-Horse."—"The Caliver."—"The Stale."—Wild-Geese. —Sign of Hard Weather.—The Barnacle Goose.—Barnacles.—Wild Fowl.—Divers and Grebes.—The "Loon."—The "Di-dapper."—The Cormorant.—Its Voracity.—Fishing with Cormorants.—The King's Cormorants.—Their "Keep" at Westminster.—Fishing at Thetford.—The Master of the Cormorants.—Entries in State Papers.—The Home of the Cormorant.—The Sea-side.—Shakespeare's Sea-cliffs and "Sea-mells."—Gulls and Gull-Catchers 235

CHAPTER IX.

BIRDS NOT INCLUDED IN THE FOREGOING CHAPTERS.

The Parrot "clamorous against Rain."—Talking like a Parrot.—A rare "Parrot-Teacher."—The Popinjay.—The Starling.—Its Talking Powers.—The Kingfisher.—Halcyon Days.—Flight of the Kingfisher.—Estimated Speed.—The Swallow and "Martlet."—The Swallow's Herb and Swallow's Stone.—The "Ostridge."—"Eating Iron"—Bating with the Wind.—The Pelican.—Feeding its Young with its Blood.—Explanation of the Fable.—Former Existence of a Pelican in the English Fens.—Conclusion . . . 271

LIST OF ILLUSTRATIONS.

[THE HEAD AND TAIL PIECES FROM DESIGNS BY THE AUTHOR.]

	PAGE
WILLIAM SHAKESPEARE, adapted from the Chandos Portrait by J. Wolf, engraved by G. Pearson	*Frontis.*
Deer-Shooting, drawn by J. G. Keulemans, engraved by G. Pearson .	1
Rabbit and Beagle ,, ,, .	22
Goshawk and Hare ,, ,, .	23
White-tailed Eagle in Trap ,, ,, .	48
Falcon and Wild Duck ,, ,,	49
The Jesses ,, ,,	58
The Bells ,, ,,	60
The Hood ,, ,,	61
The Cadge ,, ,,	63
Imping ,, ,,	68
The Keeper's Tree ,, ,,	82
Owl Mobbed by Small Birds ,, ,,	83
Long-eared Owl ,, ,,	98
Rooks and Magpies ,, ,,	99
Jay Stealing Eggs ,, ,,	122
Blackbird, Thrush, Nightingale, and Wren ,, ,,	123
Bird-Trap ,, ,,	162
Birding-Piece of Prince Charles ,, ,,	165
Sparrow and Trap ,, ,, .	166
Turkey, Peacock, and Pigeon ,, ,,	167
Dog and Wounded Duck ,, ,, .	208
Pheasant and Partridges ,, ,, .	209
A Springe for Woodcocks ,, ,, .	229
Quails Fighting ,, ,, .	234
Wild-Fowl Alighting ,, ,, .	235
Caliver of the Sixteenth Century ,, ,, .	242
The Barnacle Goose ,, ,, .	247
The Barnacle Goose Tree. *From Aldrovandus* ,, ,, .	248
The Barnacle Goose Tree *From Gerard* ,, ,, .	250
Barnacles. *From Nature.* ,, ,, .	253
Black-headed Gull ,, ,, .	270
Kingfisher and Swallows ,, ,, .	271
Pelican and Young ,, ,, .	298

INTRODUCTION.

BEFORE proceeding to examine the ornithology of Shakespeare, it may be well to take a glance at his knowledge of natural history in general.

Pope has expressed the opinion that whatever object of nature or branch of science Shakespeare either speaks of or describes, it is always with competent if not with exclusive knowledge. His descriptions are always exact, his metaphors appropriate, and remarkably drawn from the true nature and inherent qualities of each subject. There can indeed be little doubt that Shakespeare must have derived the greater portion of his knowledge of nature from his own observation, and no one can fail to be delighted with the variety and richness of the images which he has by this means produced.

Whether we accompany him to the woods and fields, midst "daisies pied and violets blue," or sit with him "under the shade of melancholy boughs," whether we follow him to "the brook that brawls along the wood," or to that sea "whose rocky shore beats back the envious siege of watery Neptune," we are alike instructed by his observations, and charmed with his apt descriptions. How often do the latter strike us as echoes of our own experience, sent forth in fitter tones than we could find.

A sportsman is oft-times more or less a naturalist. His rambles in search of game bring him in contact with creatures of such curious structure and habits, with insects and plants of such rare beauty, that the purpose of his walk is for the time forgotten, and he turns aside from sport, to admire and learn from nature.

That Shakespeare was both a sportsman and a naturalist, there is much evidence to show. During the age in which he lived "hawking" was much in vogue. Throughout the Plays, we find frequent allusions to this sport, and the accurate employment of terms used exclusively in falconry, as well as the beautiful metaphors derived therefrom, prove that our poet had much practical knowledge on the subject. We shall have occasion later to discuss his knowledge of falconry at greater length. It will suffice for the present to observe that there are many passages in the Plays which to one unacquainted with the habits of animals and birds, or ignorant of hawking phraseology, would be wholly unintelligible, but which are otherwise found to contain the most beautiful and forcible metaphors. As instances of this may be cited that passage in *Othello* (Act iii. Sc. 3), where the Moor compares his suspected wife to a "haggard falcon," and the hawking scene in Act ii. of the Second Part of *King Henry VI.**

Shakespeare, although a contemplative man, appears to have found but little "recreation" in fishing, and the most enthusiastic disciple of Izaak Walton would find it difficult to illustrate a work on angling with quotations from Shakespeare. He might refer us to *Twelfth Night* (Act ii. Sc. 5), where Maria, on the appearance of Malvolio, exclaims, "Here comes the *trout* that must be caught with tickling;" and to the song of Caliban in *The Tempest* (Act ii. Sc. 2), "No more dams I'll make for fish." Possibly, by straining a point or two, he might ask with Benedick, in *Much Ado about Nothing* (Act i. Sc. 1), "Do you play the flouting Jack?"

But our poet seems to have considered—

"The pleasant'st angling is to see the fish
Cut with her golden oars the silver stream,
And greedily devour the treacherous bait."

Much Ado, Act iii. Sc. 1.†

---

* These passages will be found duly criticised in Chapter II.

† In the following passage from *The Tempest*, Shakespeare, *à propos* of fish, gives one of many proofs of his knowledge of human nature. Trinculo comes upon the strange form of Caliban lying flat on the sands :—"What have we here? A man, or a fish? dead or alive? A fish: he smells like a fish: a very ancient and fish-like smell; a kind of, not of the newest, poor-John. A strange fish! Were I in England now (as once I was), and had but this fish painted, not a holiday fool there but would give a piece of silver: there would this monster make a man :

His forte lay more in hunting and fowling than in fishing,* and in all that relates to deer-stalking (as practised in his day, when the deer was killed with cross-bow or bow and arrow), to deer-hunting with hounds, and to coursing, we find him fully informed.

In the less noble art of bird-catching † he was probably no mean adept, while the knowledge which he displays of the habits of our wild animals, as the fox, the badger, the weasel, and the wild cat, could only have been acquired by one accustomed to much observation by flood and field.

On each of these subjects a chapter might be written, but it will suffice for our present purpose to draw attention only to some of the more remarkable passages in support of the assertions above made.

Deer-shooting was a favourite sport of both sexes in Shakespeare's day, and to enable the ladies to enjoy it in safety, "stands," or "standings," were erected in many parks, and concealed with boughs. From these the ladies with bow and arrow, or cross-bow, shot at the deer as they were driven past them by the keepers.

---

any strange beast there makes a man : when they will not give a doit to relieve a lame beggar, they will lay out ten to see a dead Indian !"—*Tempest,* Act ii. Sc. 2.

* The author of " The Treatyse of Fysshynge wyth an Angle, 1496," makes the following quaint remarks on the superiority of " Fysshynge" over " Huntynge" :— "For huntynge, as to myn entent, is too laboryous, for the hunter must alwaye renne and followe his houndes : traueyllynge and swetynge full sore. He blowyth tyll his lyppes blyster. And when he weenyth it be an hare, full oft it is an hegge hogge. Thus he chasyth and wote not what."

† The subject of Bird-catching will be fully discussed in a subsequent chapter.

Queen Elizabeth was extremely fond of this sport, and the nobility who entertained her in her different progresses, made large hunting parties, which she usually joined when the weather was favourable. She frequently amused herself in following the hounds. "Her Majesty," says a courtier, writing to Sir Robert Sidney, "is well and excellently disposed to hunting, for every second day she is on horseback, and continues the sport long."* At this time Her Majesty had just entered the seventy-seventh year of her age, and was then at her palace at Oatlands. Often, when she was not disposed to hunt herself, she was entertained with a sight of the sport. At Cowdray Park, Sussex, then the seat of Lord Montagu (1591), Her Majesty one day after dinner saw "sixteen bucks, all having fayre lawe, pulled downe with greyhounds in a laund or lawn."†

No wonder, then, that the ladies of England, with the royal example before their eyes, found such delight in the chase during the age of which we speak, and not content with being mere spectators, vied with each other in the skilful use of the bow.

To this pastime Shakespeare has made frequent allusion.

In *Love's Labour's Lost*, the first scene of the fourth act is laid in a park, where the Princess asks,—

---

* Letter from Rowland White to Sir Robert Sidney, dated 12th Sept. 1600.
† Nichols' "Progresses, Processions, and Magnificent Festivities of Queen Elizabeth," vol. iii. p. 90. (1788—1805.)

"Then, forester,* my friend, where is the bush
    That we must stand and play the murtherer in?"

To which the forester replies,—

"Hereby, upon the edge of yonder coppice;
    A 'stand' where you may make the fairest shoot."

And in *Henry VI.* Part III. Act iii. Sc. 1,—

"Under this thick-grown brake we'll shroud ourselves;
    For through this laund anon the deer will come;
    And in this covert will we make our 'stand,'
    Culling the principal of all the deer."

Again, in *Cymbeline* (Act iii. Sc. 4), "When thou hast ta'en thy 'stand,' the elected deer before thee." Other passages might be mentioned, but it will be sufficient to refer only to *The Merry Wives of Windsor* (Act v. Sc. 5), and to the song in *As You Like It* (Act iv. Sc. 2), commencing "What shall he have that kill'd the deer?"

Deer-stealing in Shakespeare's day was regarded only as a youthful frolic. Antony Wood ("Athen. Oxon." i. 371), speaking of Dr. John Thornborough, who was admitted a member of Magdalen College, Oxford, in 1570, at the age

---

* "A forester is an officer of the forest sworn to preserve the vert and venison therein, and to attend the wild beasts within his bailiwick, and to watch and endeavour to keep them safe, by day and night. He is likewise to apprehend all offenders in vert and venison, and to present them to the Courts of the Forest, to the end they may be punished according to their offences."—*The Gentleman's Recreation*. 1686.

of eighteen, and who was successively Bishop of Limerick and Bishop of Bristol and Worcester, informs us, that he and his kinsman, Robert Pinkney, " seldom studied or gave themselves to their books, but spent their time in the fencing schools, and dancing schools, in stealing deer and conies, in hunting the hare and wooing girls."

Shakespeare himself has been accused of this indiscretion. The story is first told in print by Rowe, in his " Life of Shakespeare " :—" He had, by a misfortune common enough to young fellows, fallen into ill company, and amongst them some that made a frequent practice of deer-stealing engaged him more than once in robbing a park that belonged to Sir Thomas Lucy of Charlecote, near Stratford. For this he was prosecuted by that gentleman, as he thought somewhat too severely ; and in order to revenge that ill-usage, he made a ballad upon him. And though this, probably the first essay of his poetry, be lost, yet it is said to have been so very bitter, that it redoubled the prosecution against him to that degree, that he was obliged to leave his business and family in Warwickshire, for some time, and shelter himself in London."

Mr. Staunton, in his library edition of Shakespeare's Plays, says : " What degree of authenticity the story possesses will never probably be known. Rowe derived his version of it no doubt through Betterton ; but Davies makes no allusion to the source from which he drew his information, and we are left to grope our way, so far as this important incident is concerned, mainly by the light of collateral circumstances. These, it must be admitted, serve in some respects to confirm the tradition. Shakespeare certainly quitted Stratford-upon-Avon when a young man, and it could have been no ordinary impulse which drove him to leave wife, children, friends, and occupation, to take up his abode among strangers in a distant place.

"Then there is the pasquinade, and the unmistakable identification of Sir Thomas Lucy as Justice Shallow, in the Second Part of *Henry IV.*, and in the opening scene of *The Merry Wives of Windsor*. The genuineness of the former may be doubted; but the ridicule in the Plays betokens a latent hostility to the Lucy family, which is unaccountable, except upon the supposition that the deerstealing foray is founded on facts."

The more legitimate sport in killing deer was by means of blood-hounds, and in *The Midsummer Night's Dream* we are furnished with an accurate description of the dogs in most repute:—

"My hounds are bred out of the Spartan kind,
So flew'd, so sanded; and their heads are hung
With ears that sweep away the morning dew;
Crook-knee'd, and dew-lapp'd like Thessalian bulls;
Slow in pursuit, but match'd in mouth like bells,

Each under each. A cry more tuneable
Was never holla'd to, nor cheer'd with horn."

Act. iv. Sc. 1.

In the *Comedy of Errors* (Act iv. Sc. 2), Dromio of Syracuse alludes to "a hound that runs counter, and yet draws dry foot well," and in the *Taming of the Shrew* we have the following animated dialogue :—

"*Lord.* Saw'st thou not, boy, how Silver made it good
At the hedge-corner, in the coldest fault?
I would not lose the dog for twenty pound.
Huntsman. Why, Belman is as good as he, my lord;
He cried upon it at the merest loss,
And twice to-day pick'd out the dullest scent:
Trust me, I take him for the better dog."

Many more such instances might be adduced, but the reader might perhaps be tempted to exclaim, with Timon of Athens :—

"Get thee away, and take thy beagles with thee."

Act iv. Sc. 3.

We will therefore only glance at that amusing scene in the *Merry Wives of Windsor* (Act v. Sc. 5), where Falstaff appears in Windsor Forest, disguised with a buck's head on. "Divide me," says he, "like a brib'd-buck, each a haunch: I will keep my sides to myself, my shoulders for the fellow of this walk, and my horns I bequeath your husbands."

We have here an allusion to the ancient method of "breaking up" a deer.* "The fellow of this walk" is the forester, to whom it was customary on such occasions to present a shoulder. Dame Juliana Berners, in her "Boke of St. Albans," 1496, says,—

> "And the right shoulder, wheresoever he be,
> Bere it to the *foster*, for that is fee."

And in Turbervile's "Book of Hunting," 1575, the distribution of the various parts of a deer is minutely described.

The touching description of a wounded stag, in *As You Like It*, can scarcely escape notice. Alluding to "the melancholy Jaques," one of the lords says,—

> "To-day my lord of Amiens and myself
> Did steal behind him, as he lay along
> Under an oak, whose antique root peeps out
> Upon the brook that brawls along this wood;
> To the which place a poor sequestred stag,
> That from the hunters' aim had ta'en a hurt,
> Did come to languish; and, indeed, my lord,
> The wretched animal heav'd forth such groans,
> That their discharge did stretch his leathern coat

' "We say the deer is '*broken up*,' the fox and hare are '*cased.*'"—*The Gentleman's Recreation*. 1686.

From this ancient practice, too, is derived the phrase, "to eat humble pie," more correctly written "*umble pie*." This was a venison pasty, made of the umbles (heart, liver, and lungs), and always given to inferiors, and placed low down on the table when the squire feasted publicly in the hall.

Almost to bursting; and the big round tears
Cours'd one another down his innocent nose
In piteous chase; and thus the hairy fool,
Much marked of the melancholy Jaques,
Stood on th' extremest verge of the swift brook,
Augmenting it with tears."   Act ii. Sc. 1.

Although the deer, as the nobler animal, has received more attention from our poet than the fox and the hare, yet the two last-named are by no means forgotten :—

" The fox [who] barks not when he would steal the lamb "
(*Henry VI.* Part II. Act iii. Sc. 1);

who, when he "hath once got in his nose," will "soon find means to make the body follow" (*Henry VI.* Part III. Act iv. Sc. 7); and—

" Who ne'er so tame, so cherish'd and lock'd up,
Will have a wild trick of his ancestors "
(*Cymbeline,* Act v. Sc. 2);

receives his share of notice, although it is not always in his praise, and "subtle as the fox" has become a proverb (*Cymbeline,* Act iii. Sc. 3).

From the "subtle fox" to the "timorous hare," the transition is easy. What "more a coward than a hare"? (*Twelfth Night,* Act iii. Sc. 5.)

In Roxburgh and Aberdeen, as we learn from Jamieson's "Scottish Dictionary," a hare is termed "a bawd," and the knowledge of this fact enables us to understand the dialogue in *Romeo and Juliet*, which would otherwise be unintelligible :—

> "*Mercutio.* A bawd, a bawd, a bawd ! So ho !
> *Romeo.* What hast thou found ?
> *Mercutio.* No hare, sir." Act ii. Sc. 4.

That coursing was in vogue in Shakespeare's day, and practised in the same way as at present, we may infer from such expressions as "a good hare-finder" (*Much Ado*, Act i. Sc. 1), " Holla me like a hare" (*Coriolanus*, Act i. Sc. 8), and "I see you stand like greyhounds in the slips, straining upon the start" (*Henry V.* Act iii. Sc. 1).

Rabbits were taken, and no doubt poached, in the same way then as now; for we read of the coney * "that you see dwell where she is kindled" (*As You Like It*, Act iii. Sc. 2) struggling "in the net." (*Henry VI.* Part III. Act i. Sc. 4.)

The Brock† or Badger (*Twelfth Night*, Act ii. Sc. 5) ;

---

* "The coney is called the first year 'a rabbet,' and afterwards 'an old coney.' He is a beast of the warren, and not a beast of venery."—*The Gentleman's Recreation.* 1686.

† *Brock* is the old name for badger, and we still find the word occurring in many names of places, possibly thereby indicating localities where the badger was formerly common. Of these may be mentioned, Brockhurst in Shropshire, Brockenhurst in Kent, Brockenborough in Wiltshire, Brockford in Suffolk, Brockhall in Northampton, Brockhampton in Oxford, Dorset, Gloucester, and Herefordshire, Brockham Green in Surrey, Brockholes in Lancashire and Yorkshire, Brock-le-bank in Cumberland, Brocklesby in Lincolnshire, Brockley in Somersetshire, Brockley in Suffolk, Brockley Hill in Kent, Brockley Hill in Hertfordshire, Brockmoor in Staffordshire, Brockworth in Gloucestershire.

the Wild Cat who "sleeps by day" (*Merch. of Venice*, Act ii. Sc. 5, and *Pericles*, Act iii. Intro.); "the quarrelous Weasel" (*Cymbeline*, Act iii. Sc. 4, and *Henry IV*. Part I. Act ii. Sc. 3); "the Dormouse of little valour" (*Twelfth Night*, Act iii. Sc. 1); "the joiner Squirrel" (*Romeo and Juliet*, Act i. Sc. 4), whose habit of hoarding appears to have been well known to Shakespeare (*Midsummer Night's Dream*, Act iv. Sc. 2); and "the blind Mole," who "casts copp'd hills towards heaven" (*Pericles*, Act i. Sc. 1); "—all these are mentioned in their turn, while the Bat "with leathern wing,"† "the venom Toad," "the thorny Hedgehog,"‡ "the Adder blue," and the "spotted Snake with double tongue," are all called in most aptly by way of simile or metaphor.

We cannot forget Titania's directions to her fairies in regard to Bats:—

"Some war with *rear mice* § for their leathern wings,
 To make my small elves coats"

(*Midsummer Night's Dream*, Act ii. Sc. 2);

* See also *Winter's Tale*, Act iv. Sc. 3.
† In the Midland Counties, the bat is often called leathern-wings. Compare the high German "*leder-maus*."
‡ . . . . "hedgehogs which
Lie tumbling in my bare-foot way, and mount
Their pricks at my footfall."   *Tempest*, Act ii. Sc. 2.
§ "*Rere-mouse*" from the old English "*hrere-mus*," literally a raw mouse. The adjective "rere" is still used in Wiltshire for "raw." The bat is also known as the "rennie-mouse" or "reiny-mouse," although Miss Gurney, in her "Glossary of Norfolk Words," gives "ranny" for the shrew-mouse. The old name of "flittermouse," "fluttermouse," or "fliddermouse," from the high German, "*fledermaus*," does not appear in Shakespeare's works.

nor the comfortable seat which Ariel appears to have found " on the bat's back" (*Tempest*, Act v. Sc. 1).

The following striking passage must also be familiar to readers of Shakespeare :—

> " Ere the bat hath flown
> His cloister'd flight ; ere, to black Hecate's summons,
> The shard-borne beetle, with his drowsy hums,
> Hath rung night's yawning peal,
> There shall be done a deed of dreadful note."
>
> *Macbeth*, Act iii. Sc. 2.

In a printed broadside of the time of Queen Anne, in the collection of the Society of Antiquaries of London, is the following curious fable relating to the Bat :—

"615. THE BIRDS AND BEASTS. A Fable.

" Once the Birds and Beasts strove for the prerogative : the neuter Batt, seeing the Beasts prevail, goes to them and shows them her large forehead, long ears, and teeth : afterwards, when the Birds prevail'd, the Batt flies with the Birds, and sings chit, chit, chat, and shows them her wings.

" Hence Beakless Bird, hence Winged Beast, they cry'd ; Hence plumeless wings ; thus scorn her either side.

" LONDON. PRINTED FOR EDW. LEWIS, FLOWER-DE-LUCE COURT, FLEET STREET. 1710. '

In alluding to the "venom toad" as "mark'd by the destinies to be avoided," Shakespeare probably only treated it as other writers had done before him, and, without any personal investigation of the matter, ranked it with the viper and other poisonous reptiles, when in fact it is perfectly harmless.

The habit which the snake has, in common with other reptiles, of periodically casting its skin or slough, is frequently alluded to in the Plays, where that covering is sometimes called "the enamell'd skin" (*Midsummer Night's Dream*, Act ii. Sc. 1); at other times the "casted slough" (*Henry V.* Act iv. Sc. 1, and *Twelfth Night*, Act iii. Sc. 4); and the "shining checker'd slough" (*Henry VI.* Part II. Act iii. Sc. 1).

It is difficult to say why the Adder is supposed to be deaf, unless because it has no visible ears—but then the term would apply to other reptiles. Shakespeare has several times alluded to this. In the Second Part of *King Henry VI.* Act iii. Sc. 2, Queen Margaret asks the King,—

"What, art thou, like the adder, waxen deaf?"

And in *Troilus and Cressida*, Act ii. Sc. 2, Hector says to Paris and Troilus,—

"Pleasure and revenge
Have ears more deaf than adders to the voice
Of any true decision."

Again, in Sonnet CXII., "the adder's sense" is referred to in such a way as to leave no doubt of the poet's impression that adders do not hear.

> "*Caliban.*	Sometime am I
> All wound with adders, who, with cloven tongues
> Do hiss me into madness."
>
> *Tempest*, Act ii. Sc. 2.

The "eyeless venom'd worm" referred to in *Timon of Athens*, Act iv. Sc. 3, is of course the Slow-worm (*Anguis fragilis*).

The observant naturalist must doubtless have remarked the partiality evinced by snakes and other reptiles for basking in the sun. Shakespeare has noticed that—

> "The snake lies rolled in the cheerful sun."
>
> *Titus Andronicus*, Act ii. Sc. 3.

And—

> "It is the bright day that brings forth the adder;
> And that craves wary walking."
>
> *Julius Cæsar*, Act ii. Sc. 1.

In *Macbeth*, Act iii. Sc. 2, allusion is made to the wonderful vitality which snakes possess, and to the popular notion that they are enabled, when cut in two, to reunite the dissevered portions and recover:—

> "We have scotch'd the snake, not kill'd it;
> She'll close and be herself."

Passing to the insect world, we may well be astonished at the number of species to which Shakespeare has alluded. Although the same attention has not been given to the insects as to the birds, the following have, nevertheless, been noted. Many others, doubtless, have been overlooked.

The Beetle (*Macbeth*, Act iii. Sc. 2; *King Lear*, Act iv. Sc. 6; *Measure for Measure*, Act iii. Sc. 1). The Grasshopper (*Romeo and Juliet*, Act i. Sc. 4). The Cricket, (*Pericles*, Act iii. Introduction; *Winter's Tale*, Act ii. Sc. 1; *Romeo and Juliet*, Act i. Sc. 4; *Cymbeline*, Act ii. Sc. 2). The Glowworm (*Hamlet*, Act i. Sc. 5); and the Caterpillar (*Richard II.* Act ii. Sc. 4; *Henry VI.* Part II. Act iii. Sc. 1; *Twelfth Night*, Act ii. Sc. 1; *Romeo and Juliet*, Act. i. Sc. 1). The Butterfly (*Troilus and Cressida*, Act iii. Sc. 3; *Midsummer Night's Dream*, Act iii. Sc. 1); and Moth (*Merchant of Venice*, Act ii. Sc. 9; *King John*, Act iv. Sc. 1). The House-fly (*Titus Andronicus*, Act iii. Sc. 2). The small Gilded-fly (*King Lear*, Act iv. Sc. 6). The Blow-fly (*Love's Labour's Lost*, Act v. Sc. 2; *Tempest*, Act iii. Sc. 1); and the Gad-fly, or Brize (*Troilus and Cressida*, Act i. Sc. 3). The Greycoated Gnat (*Romeo and Juliet*, Act i. Sc. 4; *Comedy of Errors*, Act ii. Sc. 2; the Wasp (*Taming of the Shrew*, Act ii. Sc. 1; *Two Gentlemen of Verona*, Act i. Sc. 2; *Henry VIII.* Act iii. Sc. 2); the Drone (*Henry V.* Act i. Sc. 2); and the Honey-bee (numerous passages).

To three only of these shall we direct further attention:

firstly, because a more extended notice of all would be beyond the limits of the present work; and, secondly, because the Entomology of Shakespeare has been already dealt with elsewhere.*

These three are the Bee, the Drone, and the Fly, and we select quotations in reference to these in order to illustrate Shakespeare's knowledge of the subject on which he wrote; the lessons to be learnt from his allusions; and the sympathy which he has manifested for all living creatures.

What better picture of the interior of a hive can be found than the following? How well are the duties of the inmates described!

> " For so work the honey bees,
> Creatures that, by a rule in nature, teach
> The act of order to a peopled kingdom.
> They have a king, and officers of sorts:
> Where some, like magistrates, correct at home;
> Others, like merchants, venture trade abroad;
> Others, like soldiers, armed in their stings,
> Make boot upon the summer's velvet buds;
> Which pillage they with merry march bring home
> To the tent-royal of their emperor;
> Who, busied in his majesty, surveys
> The singing masons building roofs of gold,
> The civil citizens kneading-up the honey;

---

* "The Natural History of the Insects mentioned in Shakspeare's Plays," by Robert Patterson, 12mo. Lond. 1841.

The poor mechanic porters crowding in
  Their heavy burdens at his narrow gate ;
  The sad-ey'd justice, with his surly hum,
  Delivering o'er to executors pale
  The lazy yawning drone.   I this infer,—
  That many things, having full reference
  To one consent, may work contrariously ;
  As many arrows, loosed several ways,
  Come to one mark ; as many ways meet in one town ;
  As many fresh streams meet in one salt sea ;
  As many lines close in the dial's centre ;
  So may a thousand actions, once afoot,
  End in one purpose, and be all well borne
  Without defeat."

Henry V. Act i. Sc. 2.

"The lazy yawning drone" is frequently alluded to as the type of idleness and inactivity (*Pericles*, Act ii. Sc. 1 ; *Henry VI*. Part II. Act iii. Sc. 2).

And we are counselled—

  "Not to eat honey, like a drone,
     From others' labours."

Pericles, Act i. Sc. 4.

Who does not remember the scene in which Titus Andronicus reproves his brother Marcus for killing a fly at dinner?—

"*Marcus.* Alas, my lord, I have but kill'd a fly.
Titus. But how if that fly had a father and mother?
How would he hang his slender gilded wings,
And buzz lamenting doings in the air!
Poor harmless fly!
That, with his pretty buzzing melody,
Came here to make us merry! and thou hast
kill'd him."

Titus Andronicus, Act iii. Sc. 2.

This is but one of the many lessons taught us by Shakespeare in his allusions to the animal world, and the kindly spirit which characterizes all his dealings with animals is frequently exemplified throughout the Plays; perhaps nowhere so clearly as in *Measure for Measure*, Act iii. Sc. 1, where we are told—

"The sense of death is most in apprehension;
And the poor beetle that we tread upon,
In corporal sufferance finds a pang as great
As when a giant dies."

Probably enough has been said to show the reader that Shakespeare's knowledge of natural history was by no means slight, and if it be thought to have been only general, it was, at all events, accurate. The use which he has made of this knowledge, throughout his works, in depicting virtue and vice in their true colours, in pointing out lessons of industry, patience, and mercy, and in showing the profit to be derived from a study of natural objects, is everywhere apparent.

The words of the banished Duke, in *As You Like It* (Act ii. Sc. 1), seem to no one so applicable as to Shakespeare himself. He—

> "Finds tongues in trees, books in the running brooks,
> Sermons in stones, and good in everything."

But to come to the Ornithology. The accurate observations on this subject, the apt allusions, and the beautiful metaphors to be met with throughout the Plays, may be said to owe their origin mainly to three causes. Firstly, Shakespeare had a good practical knowledge of Falconry, a pastime which, being much in vogue in his day, brought under his notice, almost of necessity, many wild birds, exclusive of the various species which were hawked at and killed. Secondly, he was a great reader, and, possessing a good memory, was enabled subsequently to express in verse ideas which had been suggested by older authors. Thirdly, and most important of all, he was a genuine naturalist, and gathered a large amount of information from his own practical observations. In all his walks, he evidently did not fail to note even the most trivial facts in natural history, and these were treasured up in his memory, to be called forth as occasion required, to be aptly and eloquently introduced into his works.

Apart from the consideration that a poet may be expected, almost of necessity, to invoke the birds of song, Shakespeare has gone further, and displays a greater knowledge of ornithology, and a greater accuracy in his statements, than is generally the case with poets. How far we shall succeed in proving this assertion, it will be for the reader of the following pages to determine.

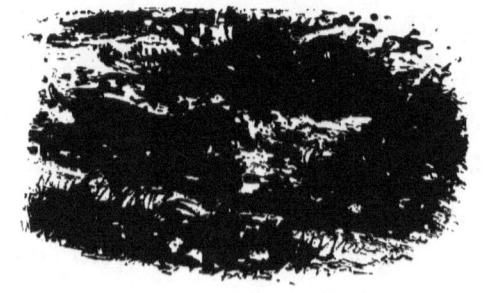

CHAPTER I.

THE EAGLE AND THE LARGER BIRDS OF PREY.

AT the head of the diurnal birds of prey, most authors have agreed in placing the Eagles. Their large size, powerful flight, and great muscular strength, give them a superiority which is universally admitted. In reviewing, therefore, the birds of which Shakespeare has made mention, no apology seems to be necessary for commencing with the genus *Aquila*.

Throughout the works of our great dramatist, frequent allusions may be found to an eagle, but the word "eagle" is almost always employed in a generic sense, and in a few instances only can we infer, from the context, that a particular species is indicated. Indeed, it is not improbable that in the poet's opinion only one species of eagle existed. Be this as it may, the introduction of an eagle and his attributes, by way of simile or metaphor, has been accomplished by Shakespeare with much beauty and effect. Considered as the emblem of majesty, the eagle has been variously styled "the king of birds," "the royal bird," "the princely eagle," and "Jove's bird," while so great is his power of vision, that an "eagle eye" has become proverbial.

> " Behold, his eye,
> As bright as is the eagle's, lightens forth
> Controlling majesty."
>
> *Richard II.* Act iii. Sc. 3.

The clearness of vision in birds is indeed extraordinary, and has been calculated, by the eminent French naturalist Lacépède, to be nine times more extensive than that of the farthest-sighted man. The opinion that the eagle possessed the power of gazing undazzled at the sun, is of great antiquity. Pliny relates that it exposes its brood to this test as soon as hatched, to prove if they be genuine or not. Chaucer refers to the belief in his "Assemblie of Foules":—

> "There mighten men the royal egal find,
> That with his sharp look persith the sonne."

So also Spenser, in his "Hymn of Heavenly Beauty,"—

> "And like the native brood of eagle's kind,
> On that bright sun of glory fix their eyes."

It is not surprising, therefore, that Shakespeare has borrowed the idea:—

"Nay, if thou be that princely eagle's bird,
Show thy descent by gazing 'gainst the sun."
Henry VI. Part III. Act ii. Sc. 1.

Again—

" What peremptory eagle-sighted eye
Dares look upon the heaven of her brow,
That is not blinded by her majesty ? "
Love's Labour's Lost, Act iv. Sc. 3.

But in the same play and scene we are told—

" A lover's eyes will gaze an eagle blind."

And in this respect Paris was said to excel :—

" An *eagle*, madam,
Hath not so green, so quick, so fair an eye,
As Paris hath."
Romeo and Juliet, Act iii. Sc. 5.

The supposition that the eye of the eagle is green must be regarded as a poetic license. In all the species of this genus with which we are acquainted, the colour of the iris is either hazel or yellow. But it would be absurd to look for exactness in trifles such as these.

The power of flight in the eagle is no less surprising than his power of vision. Birds of this kind have been killed which measured seven or eight feet from tip to tip of wing, and were strong enough to carry off hares, lambs, and even young children. This strength of wing is not unnoticed by Shakespeare :—

> "This was but as a fly by an eagle."
>
> *Antony and Cleopatra*, Act ii. Sc. 2.

And—

> "An eagle flight, bold, and forth on,
> Leaving no track behind."
>
> *Timon of Athens*, Act i. Sc. 1.

This last line recalls to mind the following allusion to the flight of the Jerfalcon :—"Then prone she dashes with so much velocity, that the impression of her path remains on the eye, in the same manner as that of the shooting meteor or flashing lightning, and you fancy that there is a torrent of falcon rushing for fathoms through the air."*

Spenser, in the fifth book of his "Faerie Queene" (iv. 42), has depicted the grandeur of an eagle on the wing :—

> "Like to an eagle in his kingly pride
> Soring thro' his wide empire of the aire
> To weather his brode sailes."

But notwithstanding his great powers of flight, we are reminded that the eagle is not always secure. Guns, traps, and other engines of destruction are directed against him, whenever and wheresoever opportunity occurs :—

* Mudie, "Feathered Tribes of the British Islands," i. p. 82.

A GOOD OMEN.

> " And often, to our comfort, shall we find
> The sharded beetle in a safer hold
> Than is the full-wing'd eagle."
>
> *Cymbeline*, Act iii. Sc. 3.

With the Romans, the eagle was a bird of good omen. Josephus, the Jewish historian, says the eagle was selected for the Roman legionary standard, because he is the king of all birds, and the most powerful of them all, whence he has become the emblem of empire, and the omen of victory.*

Accordingly, we read in *Julius Cæsar*, Act v. Sc. 1 :—

> " Coming from Sardis, on our former ensign
> Two mighty eagles fell ; and there they perch'd,
> Gorging and feeding from our soldiers' hands."

This incident is more fully detailed in North's "Plutarch," as follows :—" When they raised their campe, there came two eagles, that flying with a marvellous force, lighted upon two of the foremost ensigns, and alwaies followed the souldiers, which gave them meate and fed them, untill they came neare to the citie of Phillipes ; and there one day onely before the battell, they both flew away."

The ensign of the eagle was not peculiar, however, to the Romans. The golden eagle, with extended wings, was borne by the Persian monarchs,† and it is not impro-

---

* "De Bello Judico," iii. 5.   † Xenophon, "Cyropædia," vii.

bable that from them the Romans adopted it; while the
Persians themselves may have borrowed the symbol from
the ancient Assyrians, on whose banners it waved until
Babylon was conquered by Cyrus.

As a bird of good omen, the eagle is often mentioned
by Shakespeare:—

"I chose an eagle, and did avoid a puttock."

Cymbeline, Act i. Sc. 2.

The name "Puttock" has been applied both to the
Kite and the Common Buzzard, and both were considered
birds of ill omen.

In Act iv. Sc. 2, of the same play, we read,—

"I saw Jove's bird, the Roman eagle, wing'd
From the spungy south to this part of the west,
There vanish'd in the sunbeams."

This was said to portend success to the Roman host.
In Izaak Walton's "Compleat Angler," we are furnished
with a reason for styling the eagle "Jove's bird." The
falconer, in discoursing on the merits of his recreation with
a brother angler, says,—"In the air my troops of hawks
soar upon high, and when they are lost in the sight of
men, then they attend upon and converse with the gods;
therefore I think my eagle is so justly styled Jove's
servant in ordinary."

"For the Roman eagle,
From south to west on wing soaring aloft,

Lessen'd herself, and in the beams o' the sun
So vanish'd : which foreshadow'd our princely eagle,
The imperial Cæsar, should again unite
His favour with the radiant Cymbeline,
Which shines here in the west."

Cymbeline, Act v. Sc. 5.

In a paper "On the Roman Imperial and Crested Eagles," * Mr. Hogg says,—"The Roman Eagle, which is generally termed the Imperial Eagle, is represented with its head *plain*, that is to say, *not crested*. It is in appearance the same as the attendant bird of the 'king of gods and men,' and is generally represented as standing at the foot of his throne, or sometimes as the bearer of his thunder and lightning. Indeed he also often appears perched on the top of his sceptre. He is always considered as the attribute or emblem of 'Father Jove.'"

A good copy of this bird of Jupiter, called by Virgil and Ovid "Jovis armiger," from an antique group, representing the eagle and Ganymedes, may be seen in Bell's "Pantheon," vol. i. Also "a small bronze eagle, the ensign of a Roman legion," is given in Duppa's "Travels in Sicily" (2nd ed., 1829, tab. iv.). That traveller states, that the original bronze figure is preserved in the Museum of the Convent of St. Nicholas d'Arcun, at Catania. This Convent is now called Convento di S. Benedetto, ac-

* "Annals and Magazine of Natural History." June, 1864.

cording to Mr. G. Dennis, in his "Handbook of Sicily," (p. 349); and he mentions this ensign as "a Roman legionary eagle in excellent preservation."

From the second century before Christ, the eagle is said to have become the sole military ensign, and it was mostly small in size, because Florus (lib. 4, cap. 12) relates that an ensign-bearer, in the wars of Julius Cæsar, in order to prevent the enemy from taking it, pulled off the eagle from the top of the gilt pole, and hid it by placing it under cover of his belt.

In later times, the eagle was borne with the legion, which, indeed, occasionally took its name, "*aquila.*" This eagle, which was also adopted by the Roman emperors for their imperial symbol, is considered to be the *Aquila heliaca* of Savigny (*imperialis* of Temminck), and resembles our golden eagle, *Aquila chrysaëtos*, in plumage, though of a darker brown, and with more or less white on the scapulars. It differs also in the structure of the foot. It inhabits Southern Europe, North Africa, Palestine, and India. Living examples of this species may be seen at the present time in the Gardens of the Zoological Society.

Sicilius, in *Cymbeline* (Act v. Sc. 4), speaking of the apparition and descent of Jupiter, who was seated upon an eagle, says,—

"The holy eagle
Stoop'd, as to foot us: his ascension is
More sweet than our blest fields: his royal bird

Prunes the immortal wing, and cloys his beak,
As when his god is pleas'd."

"*Prune*" signifies to clean and adjust the feathers, and is synonymous with *plume*. A word more generally used, perhaps, than either, is *preen*.

Cloys is, doubtless, a misprint for *cleys*, that is, *claws*. Those who have kept hawks must often have observed the habit which they have of raising one foot, and whetting the beak against it. This is the action to which Shakespeare refers. The same word occurs in Ben Jonson's "Underwoods," (vii. 29) thus :—

"To save her from the seize
Of vulture death, and those relentless *cleys*."

The verb " to cloy " has a very different signification, namely, " to satiate," " choke," or " clog up." Shakespeare makes frequent use of it.

In "Lucrece" it occurs :—

"But poorly rich, so wanteth in his store,
That, *cloy'd* with much, he pineth still for more."

And again, in *Richard II.* (Act i. Sc. 3) :—

"O, who can hold a fire in his hand,
By thinking on the frosty Caucasus?
Or *cloy* the hungry edge of appetite,
By bare imagination of a feast?"

See also *Henry V.* Act ii. Sc. 2.

Sometimes the word was written "accloy;" as, for instance, in Spenser's "Faerie Queene" (ii. 7)—

"And with uncomely weeds the gentle wave *accloyes*."

And in the same author's "Shepheard's Calendar" (February," 135)—

"The mouldie mosse which thee *accloyeth*."

It is clear, therefore, that the word occurring in the fourth scene of the fifth act of *Cymbeline*, should be written *cleys*, and not *cloys*.

But to return from this digression; there is a passage in the first act of *Henry V.* Sc. 2, which seems to deserve some notice while on the subject of eagles, *i. e.* :—

"For once the eagle England being in prey,
 To her unguarded nest the weasel Scot
 Comes sneaking, and so sucks her princely eggs."

That the weasel sucks eggs, and is partial to such fare, is very generally admitted. Shakespeare alludes to the fact again in *As You Like It* (Act ii. Sc. 5), where Jaques says:—"I can suck melancholy out of a song, as a weasel sucks eggs." But whether the weasel has ever been found in the same situation or at such an altitude as the eagle, is not so certain. A near relative of the weasel, however, namely, a marten-cat, was once found in an eagle's nest. "The forester, having reason to think that the bird was sitting hard, peeped over the cliff into the eyrie. To his amazement, a marten was suckling her kittens in comfortable enjoyment."*

The allusion above made to the "princely eggs," reminds us of the princely bird which laid them, and those who have read the works of Shakespeare—and who has not?—must doubtless remember the beautiful simile uttered by Warwick when dying on the field of Barnet:—

"Thus yields the cedar to the axe's edge,
Whose arms gave shelter to the *princely* eagle."

Henry VI. Part III. Act v. Sc. 2.

The conscious superiority of the eagle is depicted by Tamora, who tells us :—

"The eagle suffers little birds to sing,
And is not careful what they mean thereby,
Knowing that with the shadow of his wing
He can at pleasure stint their melody."

Titus Andronicus, Act iv. Sc. 4.

The great age to which this bird sometimes attains has been remarked by most writers on Ornithology. The Psalmist has beautifully alluded to it where he says of the righteous man,—"His youth shall be renewed like the eagle's." A golden eagle, which had been nine years in the possession of Mr. Owen Holland, of Conway, lived thirty-two years with the gentleman who made him a

* Colquhoun, "The Moor and the Loch," p. 330. And this is not an isolated instance. *See* Newton, "Ootheca Wolleyana," Part I. p. 11.

present of it, but what its age was when the latter received it from Ireland is unknown.* Another, that died at Vienna, was stated to have lived in confinement one hundred and four years.† A white-tailed eagle captured in Caithness, died at Duff House in February, 1862, having been kept in confinement, by the late Earl of Fife, for thirty-two years. But even the eagle may be outlived. Apemantus asks of Timon :—

"Will these moss'd trees,
That have outliv'd the eagle, page thy heels,
And skip when thou point'st out?"

Timon of Athens, Act. iv. Sc. 3.

The old text has "moyst trees." The emendation, however, which was made by Hanmer, is strengthened by the line in *As You Like It* (Act iv. Sc. 3) :—

"Under an oak, whose boughs were *moss'd* with age."

In an old French "riddle-book," entitled "Demands Joyous," which was printed in English by Wynkyn de Worde in 1511 (a single copy only of which is said to be extant), is the following curious "demande" and "response." It is here transcribed, as bearing upon the subject of the age of an eagle :—

"*Dem*. What is the age of a field-mouse?

Res. A year. And the life of a hedge-hog is three

---

* Pennant, "British Zoology."   † Yarrell, "History of British Birds."

times that of a mouse; and the life of a dog is three times that of a hedge-hog; and the life of a horse is three times that of a dog; and the life of a man is three times that of a horse; and the life of a goose is three times that of a man; and the life of a swan is three times that of a goose; and the life of a swallow is three times that of a swan; *and the life of an eagle is three times that of a swallow;* and the life of a serpent is three times that of an eagle; and the life of a raven is three times that of a serpent; and the life of a hart is three times that of a raven; and an oak groweth 500 years, and fadeth 500 years."

The Rev. W. B. Daniel alludes[*] to "the received maxim that animals live seven times the number of years that bring them to perfection," upon which computation the average life of an eagle would be twenty-one years. But this maxim is founded on a misconception. Fleurens, in his treatise "De la Longévité Humaine," says that the duration of life in any animal is equal to five times the number of years requisite to perfect its growth, and that the growth has ceased when the bones have finally consolidated with their *epiphyses*, which in the young are merely cartilages.

Like many other rapacious birds, eagles are very fond of bathing, and it has been found essential to supply them with baths when in confinement, in order to keep them

[*] "Rural Sports," vol. i. p. 246.

in good health. The freshness and vigour which they thus derive is alluded to in *Henry IV.* (Part I. Act iv. Sc. 1):—

"*Hotspur.* Where is his son,
  The nimble-footed mad-cap Prince of Wales,
  And his comrades? . . . . . .
Vernon. All furnish'd, all in arms; . .
  Like eagles having lately bath'd."

The larger birds of prey are no less fond of washing, though they care so little for water to drink, that it has been erroneously asserted that they never drink. "What I observed," says the Abbé Spallanzani,[*] "is, that eagles, when left even for several months without water, did not seem to suffer the smallest inconvenience from the want of it, but when they were supplied with water, they not only got into the vessel and sprinkled their feathers like other birds, but repeatedly dipped the beak, then raised the head, in the manner of common fowls, and swallowed what they had taken up. Hence it is evident that they drink."

In Persia, Tartary, India, and other parts of the East, the eagle was formerly, and is still to a certain extent, used for hunting down the larger birds and beasts. In the thirteenth century, the Khan of Tartary kept upwards of two hundred hawks and eagles, some of which had been trained to catch wolves; and such was the boldness and

[*] "Dissertations," vol. i. p. 173.

power of these birds, that none, however large, could escape from their talons.*

Burton, in his "Anatomy of Melancholy,"† quoting from Sir Antony Shirley's "Travels," says: "The Muscovian Emperours reclaim eagles, to let fly at hindes, foxes, &c., and such a one was sent for a present to Queen Elizabeth."

A traveller to the Putrid Sea, in 1819, wrote: "Wolves are very common on these steppes; and they are so bold that they sometimes attack travellers. We passed by a large one, lying on the ground with an eagle, which had probably attacked him, by his side. Its talons were nearly buried in his back; in the struggle both had died." ‡

Owing to the great difficulty in training them, as well as to the difficulty in obtaining them, eagles have rarely been trained to the chase in England. Some years since, Captain Green, of Buckden, in Huntingdonshire, had a fine golden eagle, which he had taught to take hares and rabbits; § and this species has been found to be more tractable than any other.

Whether Shakespeare was aware of the use of trained eagles or not, we cannot say, but he has in

---

* See Pennant's "Arctic Zoology," ii. p. 195; Sir J. Malcolm's "Sketches of Persia;" Johnston's "Sketches of Indian Field Sports;" Atkinson's "Travels in Oriental and Western Siberia," and Burton's "Falconry in the Valley of the Indus."
† Folio, 1676. Part ii. p. 169.
‡ "Memoirs of Stephen Grellet," i. p. 459.
§ See "The Naturalist" for May, 1837.

many cases employed hawking terms in connection with this bird:—

> "That hateful duke,
> Whose haughty spirit, winged with desire,
> Will cost my crown, and, like an empty eagle,
> *Tire* on the flesh of me and of my son!"
>
> *Henry VI.* Part III. Act i. Sc. 1.

The meaning of the word *tire* is thus explained by falconers. When a hawk was in training, it was often necessary to prolong her meal as much as possible, to prevent her from gorging; this was effected by giving her a tough or bony bit to *tire on;* that is, to tear, or pull at.

> "Even as an empty eagle, sharp by fast,
> *Tires* with her beak on feathers, flesh, and bone,
> Shaking her wings, devouring all in haste,
> Till either gorge be stuff'd, or prey be gone."
>
> *Venus and Adonis.*

So also, in *Timon of Athens* (Act iii. Sc. 6), one of the lords says:—

"Upon that were my thoughts *tiring* when we encounter'd."

In the following passage, two hawking terms are used in connection with the eagle:—

> "Know, the gallant monarch is in arms,
> And, like an eagle o'er his aiery, *towers*,
> To *souse* annoyance that comes near his nest."
>
> *King John*, Act v. Sc. 2.

This passage has been differently rendered, by removing the punctuation between "aiery" and "towers," and reading the former "airey" or "airy," and making "towers" a substantive. But the meaning of the passage, as it stands above, seems to us sufficiently clear.

"Aiery" is equivalent to "eyrie," the nesting-place. The word occurs again in *Richard III.* (Act i. Sc. 3) :—

"Our *aiery* buildeth in the cedar's top ;"
and,
"Your *aiery* buildeth in our *aiery's* nest."

The verb "to tower," in the language of falconry, signifies "to rise spirally to a height." Compare the French "*tour*." As a further argument, too, for reading "towers" as a verb, and not as a substantive, compare the following passage from *Macbeth*, which plainly shows that Shakespeare was not unacquainted with this word as a hawking term :—

"A falcon *towering* in her pride of place."
Macbeth, Act ii. Sc. 4.

The word "souse," above quoted, is likewise borrowed from the language of falconry, and, as a substantive, is equivalent to "swoop." It would seem to be derived from the German "sausen," which signifies to rush with a whistling sound like the wind ; and this is certainly expressive of the "whish" made by the wings of a falcon when swooping on her prey.

There is a good illustration of this passage in Drayton's

"Polyolbion," Song xx., where a description of hawking at wild-fowl is given. After the falconers have put up the fowl from the sedge, the hawk, in the words of the author, having previously "towered," "gives it a souse." Beaumont and Fletcher also make use of this word as a hawking term in *The Chances*, iv. 1; and it occurs in Spenser's "Faerie Queene," Book iv. Canto v. 30.

A notice of the various hawks made use of by falconers, and mentioned by Shakespeare, might be here properly introduced, but it will be more convenient to reserve this notice for a separate chapter, and confine our attention for the present to the larger diurnal birds of prey which, like the eagles, are seldom, if ever, reclaimed by man.

Of these, excluding the eagle, Shakespeare makes mention of four—the Vulture, the Osprey, the Kite, and the Buzzard.

Those who are acquainted with the repulsive habits of the Vulture, led as he is by instinct to gorge on carrion, will best understand the allusions to this bird which are to be met with in the works of Shakespeare.

What more forcible expression can be found to indicate a guilty conscience than "the gnawing vulture of the mind"? (*Titus Andronicus*, Act v. Sc. 2.)

"There cannot be
That vulture in you, to devour so many."
Macbeth, Act iv. Sc. 3.

When King Lear would denounce the unkindness of a

daughter, which he could never forget, laying his hand upon his heart, he exclaims :—

"O Regan, she hath tied
Sharp-tooth'd unkindness, like a vulture, here."

King Lear, Act ii. Sc. 4.

One of the worst wishes to which Falstaff could give vent when in a bad humour, was :—

"Let vultures gripe thy guts!"

Merry Wives of Windsor, Act i. Sc. 3.

And the same idea is expressed in *Henry IV*. (Part II. Act v. Sc. 4) :—

"Let vultures vile seize on his lungs also!"

Occasionally we find the word "vulture" employed as an adjective :—

"Her sad behaviour feeds her vulture folly."

Lucrece.

And—

"Whose vulture thought doth pitch the price so high."

Venus and Adonis.

The structure of the Osprey is wonderfully adapted to his habits, and an examination of the feet of this bird will prove how admirably contrived they are for grasping and holding a slippery fish. Mr. St. John, who had excellent opportunities of studying the Osprey in his native haunts, says :*—"I generally saw the osprey fishing about the lower pools of the rivers near their mouths; and a

* "Tour in Sutherland," vol. i. p. 113.

beautiful sight it is. The long-winged bird hovers (as a kestrel does over a mouse), at a considerable distance above the water, sometimes on perfectly motionless wing, and sometimes, wheeling slowly in circles, turning his head and looking eagerly down at the water. He sees a trout when at a great height, and suddenly closing his wings, drops like a shot bird into the water, often plunging completely under, and at other times appearing scarcely to touch the water, but seldom failing to rise again with a good-sized fish in his talons. Sometimes, in the midst of his swoop, the osprey stops himself suddenly in the most abrupt manner, probably because the fish, having changed its position, is no longer within range. He then hovers, again stationary, in the air, anxiously looking below for the re-appearance of the prey. Having well examined one pool, he suddenly turns off, and with rapid flight takes himself to an adjoining part of the stream, where he again begins to hover and circle in the air. On making a pounce into the water, the osprey dashes up the spray far and wide, so as to be seen for a considerable distance."

After this description, it is easy to understand the allusion of Aufidius, who says :—

"I think he'll be to Rome,
As is the osprey to the fish, who takes it
By sovereignty of nature."

Coriolanus, Act iv. Sc. 7.

Mr. Staunton thinks that the image is founded on the fabulous power attributed to the osprey of fascinating the fish on which he preys. In Peele's play of *The Battle of Alcazar*, 1594 (Act i. Sc. 1), we read :—

" I will provide thee of a princely osprey,
That, as he flieth over fish in pools,
The fish shall turn their glistering bellies up,
And thou shalt take thy liberal choice of all."

Another of the birds of prey mentioned by Shakespeare is "the lazar Kite" (*Henry V.* Act ii. Sc. 1). Although a large bird, and called by some the royal Kite (*Milvus regalis*), it has not the bold dash of many of our smaller hawks in seizing live and strong prey, but glides about ignobly, looking for a sickly or wounded victim, or for offal of any sort.

" And kites
Fly o'er our heads, and downward look on us,
As we were sickly prey."

Julius Cæsar, Act v. Sc. 1.

" Ere this
I should have fatted all the region kites
With this slave's offal."

Hamlet, Act ii. Sc. 2.

" A prey for carrion kites."

Henry VI. Part II. Act v. Sc. 2.

From the ignoble habits of the bird, the name "kite" became a term of reproach:—

" You kite ! "

Antony and Cleopatra, Act iii. Sc. 13.

And—

" Detested kite ! "

King Lear, Act i. Sc. 4.

When pressed by hunger, however, the kite becomes more fearless; and instances have occurred in which a bird of this species has entered the farmyard and boldly carried off a chicken.

" Wer 't not all one, an empty eagle were set
To guard the chicken from a hungry kite,
As place Duke Humphrey for the king's protector ? "

Henry VI. Part II. Act iii. Sc. 1.

The synonym "puttock" is sometimes applied to the kite, sometimes to the common buzzard. In the following passage, where reference is made to the supposed murder of Gloster by Suffolk, it evidently has reference to the former bird :—

" Who finds the partridge in the puttock's nest,
But may imagine how the bird was dead,
Although the kite soar with unbloodied beak ? "

Henry VI. Part II. Act iii. Sc. 2.

With the ancients the kite appears to have been a bird of ill-omen. In *Cymbeline* (Act. i. Sc. 2), Imogen says :—

"I chose an eagle, and did avoid a puttock."

And the superiority of the eagle is again adverted to by Hastings, in *Richard III.* (Act i. Sc. 1):—

"More pity that the eagle should be mew'd,
While kites and buzzards prey at liberty."

The intractable disposition of the kite is thus noticed:—

"Another way I have to man my haggard,
To make her come, and know her keeper's call;
That is, to watch her, as we watch these kites,
That bate, and beat, and will not be obedient."
Taming of the Shrew, Act iv. Sc. 1.

A wild hawk was sometimes tamed by watching it night and day, to prevent its sleeping. In "An approved treatyse of Hawks and Hawking," by Edmund Bert, Gent., which was published in London in 1619, the author says:—"I have heard of some who watched and kept their hawks awake seven nights and as many days, and then they would be wild, rammish, and disorderly." This practice is often alluded to by Shakespeare:—

"You must be *watch'd* ere you be made tame, must you?"
Troilus and Cressida, Act iii. Sc. 2.

"I'll *watch* him tame."
Othello, Act iii. Sc. 3.

> "But I will *watch* you from such *watching* now."
>
> *Romeo and Juliet*, Act iv. Sc. 4.

The habit which the kite has, in common with other rapacious birds, of rejecting or disgorging the undigested portions of its food, such as bones and fur, in the shape of pellets, was apparently well known to Shakespeare, for he says:—

> "If charnel-houses and our graves must send
> Those that we bury back, our monuments
> Shall be the maws of kites."
>
> *Macbeth*, Act iii. Sc. 4.

And again,—

> "Thou detestable maw . . .
> Gorg'd with the dearest morsel of the earth."
>
> *Romeo and Juliet*, Act v. Sc. 3.

Another curious fact in the natural history of the kite is adverted to in the *Winter's Tale* (Act iv. Sc. 2). It is there said,—

> "When the kite builds, look to lesser linen."

This line may be perhaps best illustrated by giving a description of a kite's nest which we have seen, and which was taken many years ago in Huntingdonshire. The outside of the nest was composed of strong sticks; the lining consisted of small pieces of linen, part of a saddle-girth, a bit of a harvest glove, part of a straw bonnet, pieces of paper, and a worsted garter. In the midst of this singular collection of materials were deposited two eggs. The kite is now almost extinct in England, and a kite's nest, of course, is a great rarity. The Rev. H. B. Tristram, speaking of the habits of the Egyptian kite (*Milvus Ægyptius*), says :*—" Its nest, the marine storeshop of the desert, is decorated with whatever scraps of bournouses and coloured rags can be collected ; and to these are added, on every surrounding branch, the cast-off coats of serpents, large scraps of thin bark, and perhaps a bustard's wing."

We have alluded to the Buzzard (*Buteo vulgaris*) in the passage above quoted from *Richard III.*, and also to the synonym " puttock," which was sometimes applied to this bird, as well as to the kite.

Mr. St. John, who was well acquainted with the common buzzard, thought that in all its habits it more nearly resembled the eagle than any other kind of hawk.†

In the following passage, it seems probable, as suggested by Mr. Staunton, that a play upon the words is intended, and that " buzzard " in the second line means a beetle, so called from its buzzing noise :—

" O, slow-wing'd turtle ! shall a buzzard take thee ?
Ay, for a turtle, as he takes a buzzard."
Taming of the Shrew, Act ii. Sc. 1.

* " The Great Sahara," p. 392.   † " Tour in Sutherland," vol. i. p. 121.

Neither the kite nor the buzzard were ever trained for hawking, being deficient both in speed and pluck.

The former, however, was occasionally "flown at" by falconers, although oftener for want of a better bird, than because he showed much sport.

Both are now far less common than in Shakespeare's day. The increased number of shooters, and the war of extermination which is carried on by gamekeepers, inevitably seal their doom.

CHAPTER II.

HAWKS AND HAWKING.

TO those who have ever taken part in a hawking excursion, it must be a matter of some surprise that so delightful a pastime has ceased to be popular. Yet, at the present day, perhaps not one person in five hundred has ever seen a trained hawk flown. In Shakespeare's time things were very different. Every one who could afford it kept a hawk, and the rank of the owner was indicated by the species of bird which he carried. To a king belonged the gerfalcon; to a prince, the falcon gentle; to an earl, the peregrine; to a lady, the merlin; to a young squire, the hobby; while a yeoman carried a goshawk; a priest, a sparrowhawk; and a knave, or servant, a kestrel. But the sport was attended with great expense, and much time and attention were required of the falconer before his birds were perfectly trained, and he himself a proficient.

This, combined with the increased enclosure and

cultivation of waste lands, has probably contributed as much as anything to the decline of falconry in England.

During the age in which Shakespeare lived, the sport was at its height, and it is, therefore, not surprising that he has taken much notice of it in his works, and has displayed a considerable knowledge on the subject.

In the second part of *King Henry VI.* Act 2, we find a scene laid at St. Alban's, and the King, Queen, Gloster, Cardinal, and Suffolk appearing, with falconers halloaing. We quote that portion of the scene which refers more particularly to the sport :—

" *Queen.* Believe me, lords, for *flying at the brook*,
   I saw not better sport these seven years' day:
   Yet, by your leave, the wind was very high;
   And, ten to one, old Joan* had not gone out.
King. But what a *point*, my lord, your falcon made,
   And what a *pitch* she flew above the rest!—
   To see how God in all his creatures works!
   Yea, man and birds are fain of climbing high.
Suff. No marvel, an it like your majesty,
   My lord protector's hawks do *tower* so well;
   They know their master loves to be aloft,
   And bears his thoughts above his falcon's *pitch*.
Glo. My lord, 'tis but a base ignoble mind
   That mounts no higher than a bird can *soar*.

---

* The name, no doubt, of a favourite falcon.

Card. I thought as much; he'd be above the clouds.

  * * * * *

> Believe me, cousin Gloster,
> Had not your man put up the fowl so suddenly,
> We had had more sport."

"Flying at the brook" is synonymous with "hawking by the river," and shows us that the party were in pursuit of water-fowl. Chaucer speaks of

> "Ryding on, hawking by the river,
> With grey goshawk in hand."

"*Point.*"—The fluttering or hovering over the spot where the "quarry" has been "put in."

"*Pitch.*"—The height to which a hawk rises before swooping.

> "How high a *pitch* his resolution soars!"
>
> *Richard II.* Act i. Sc. 1.

"*Tower.*"—A common expression in falconry, signifying to rise spirally to a height. Compare the French "*tour.*" The word occurs again in *Macbeth*, Act ii. Sc. 4, with reference to a fact which we might well be excused for doubting, did we not know that it was related as an unusual circumstance:—

> "On Tuesday last,
> A falcon, *tow'ring* in her pride of place,
> Was by a mousing owl hawk'd at and kill'd."

Many of the incidents connected with Duncan's death are not to be found in the narrative of that event, but are taken from the chronicler's account of King Duffe's murder. Among the prodigies there mentioned is the one referred to by Shakespeare. "Monstrous sightes also, that were scene without the Scottishe kingdome that year, were these. .... There was a sparhauke also strangled by an owle." We have known a Tawny Owl to kill and devour a Kestrel which had been kept in the same aviary with it.

By "tow'ring in her pride of place," is here understood to mean circling at her highest point of elevation. So in Massinger's play of *The Guardian*, Act i. Sc. 2:—

> "Then for an evening flight
> A tiercel gentle which I call, my masters,
> As he were sent a messenger to the moon,
> In such a *place*, flies, as he seems to say
> See me or see me not."

By the falcon is always understood the female, as distinguished from the tercel, or male, of the peregrine or goshawk. The latter was probably called the tercel, or tiercel, from being about *a third* smaller than the falcon. Some authorities, however, state that of the three young birds usually found in the nest of a falcon, two of them are females and *the third* a male; hence the name of tercel.*

* Tardif, "Treatise on Falconry."

By others, again, the term is supposed to have been derived from the French *gentil*, meaning neat or handsome, because of the beauty of its form.

There appears to be a great deal of confusion in the nomenclature of the hawks used in falconry. The same name has been applied to two distinct species, and the same species, in different states of plumage, has received two or more names. With regard to the "tercel," as distinguished from the "tercel-gentle," it would appear that the former name was given to the male goshawk, and the latter to the male peregrine; for the peregrine being a long-winged hawk, and the more *noble* of the two, the word "gentle," or "gentil," was applied to it with that signification.

In this view we are supported to some extent by quaint old Izaak Walton. In his "Compleat Angler," there is an animated conversation between an angler, a hunter, and a falconer, each of whom in turn commends his own recreation. The falconer gives a list of his hawks, and divides them into two classes, viz.: the long-winged and short-winged hawks. In enumerating each species in pairs, he gives first the name of the female, and then that of the male: among the first class we find—

> The gerfalcon and jerkin,
> The falcon and tercel-gentle, &c.

In the second class we have—

> The eagle and iron,*
> The goshawk and tercel, &c.

From this we may conclude that the name tercel-gentle was applied to the male peregrine, a long-winged hawk, to distinguish it from the tercel, or male goshawk, a short-winged hawk.

The female falcon, from her greater size and strength, was always considered superior to the male—stronger in flight :—

> "As confident as is the falcon's flight
> Against a bird."
> *Richard II.* Act i. Sc. 3.

And possessing more powerful talons :—

> "So doves do peck the falcon's piercing talons."
> *Henry VI.* Part III. Act i. Sc. 4.

She was more easily trained, and capable of being flown at larger game. Hence Shakespeare asserts—

> "The falcon as the tercel, for all the ducks i' the river."
> *Troilus and Cressida*, Act iii. Sc. 2.

Sometimes we find the word "tercel" written "tassel," as in *Romeo and Juliet* (Act ii. Sc. 2) :—

> "O, for a falconer's voice,
> To lure this *tassel-gentle* back again!"

---

* No doubt a corruption of "erne," a name which is still given to the sea eagle (*Aquila albicilla*).

Spenser almost invariably spells the word in this way.* To understand the allusion to the falconer's voice, it should be observed that after a hawk had been flown, and had either struck or missed the object of her pursuit, the "lure" (which we shall presently describe) was thrown up to entice her back, and at the same time the falconer shouted to attract her attention.

Professor Schneider, in a Latin volume published at Leipsic, in 1788,† thus enumerates the qualities of a good falconer: "Sit mediocris staturæ; sit perfecti ingenii; bonæ memoriæ; levis auditu; acuti visûs; *homo magnæ vocis;* sit agilis et promptus; sciat natare," &c. &c.

Each falconer had his own particular call, but it was generally somewhat like—

"Hillo, ho, ho, boy! come, bird, come!"

Hamlet, Act i. Sc. 5.

The "lure" was of various shapes, and consisted merely of a piece of iron or wood, generally in the shape of a heart or horseshoe, to which were attached the wings of some bird, with a piece of raw meat fixed between them. A strong leathern strap, about three feet long, fastened to it with a swivel, enabled the falconer to swing it round his head, or throw it to a distance. With high-flying hawks,

---

* See his "Faerie Queene," Book III. Canto 4.

† This scarce volume, of which we are fortunate enough to possess a copy, contains the work of the Emperor Frederic II., "De arte venandi cum avibus;" Albertus Magnus, "De Falconibus;" as also a digest of Hubner's work, "Sur le vol des oiseaux de proie," and other ancient and rare works on Falconry.

however, it was often found necessary to use a live pigeon, secured to a string by soft leather jesses, in order to recall them.*

The long-winged hawks were always brought to the lure, the short-winged ones to the hand :—

" As falcon to the lure, away she flies."
Venus and Adonis.

The game flown at was called in hawking parlance the "quarry," and differed according to the hawk that was used. The gerfalcon and peregrine were flown at herons, ducks, pigeons, rooks, and magpies; the goshawk was used for hares and partridges; while the smaller kinds, such as the merlin and hobby, were trained to take blackbirds, larks, and snipe. The French falconers, however, do not appear to have been so particular :—

" We 'll e'en to 't like French falconers, fly at anything we see."—*Hamlet*, Act ii. Sc. 2.

The word " quarry " occurs in many of the Plays.

" This ' quarry ' cries on havoc."†
Hamlet, Act v. Sc. 2.

---

* Salvin and Brodrick, "Falconry in the British Islands," pp. 38, 39.

† To "cry on" anything was a familiar expression formerly. In *Othello* (Act v. Sc. 1), we read—

"Whose noise is this that ' cries on ' murder?"

And in *Richard III.* (Act v. Sc. 3), Richmond says :—

"Methought, their souls, whose bodies Richard murder'd,
Came to my tent, and ' cried on ' victory."

To "cry havoc" appears to have been a signal for indiscriminate slaughter.

In the language of the forest, "quarry" also meant a heap of slaughtered game. So, in *Coriolanus* (Act iii. Sc. 1), Caius Marcius says:—

"And let me use my sword, I'd make a 'quarry'
With thousands of these quarter'd slaves."

The beauty of the following passage, from its being clothed in technicalities, will be likely to escape the notice of those who are not conversant with hawking phraseology; but an acquaintance with the terms employed will elicit admiration at the force and beauty of the metaphor.

Othello, mistrusting the constancy of Desdemona towards him, and comparing her to a hawk, exclaims:—

"If I do prove her *haggard*,
Though that her *jesses* were my dear heart-strings,
I'd whistle her off, and let her down the wind,
To prey at fortune."

Othello, Act iii. Sc. 3.

By "haggard" is meant a wild-caught and unreclaimed mature hawk, as distinguished from an "eyess," or nestling; that is, a young hawk taken from the "eyrie" or nest.

The expression, "Cry havoc, kings!" occurs in *King John*, Act ii. Sc. 2; and again in *Julius Cæsar*, Act iii. Sc. 1 :—

"Cry havoc, and let slip the dogs of war."

In *Coriolanus* (Act iii. Sc. 1), Menenius says—

"Do not cry *Havoc*, where you should but hunt
With modest warrant."

I

"There is, sir, an aiery of children, little eyases, that cry out."

Hamlet, Act ii. Sc. 2.

By some falconers "haggards" were also called "passage hawks," from being always caught when in that state, at the time of their periodical passage or migration. As will be seen hereafter, the word "haggard" occurs frequently throughout the Plays.

The "jesses" were two narrow strips of leather, fastened one to each leg, the other ends being attached to a swivel, from which depended the "leash." When the hawk was flown, the swivel and leash were taken off, the jesses and bells remaining on the bird.

Some of the old falconers' directions on these points are very quaint. Turbervile, in his "Book of Falconrie," 1575, speaking of the trappings of a hawk, says:—" Shee must haue jesses of leather, the which must haue knottes at the ende, and they should be halfe a foote long, or there about; at the least a shaftmeete betweene the hoose of the jesse, and the knotte at the ende, whereby you tye the hauke."

In the modern "jesse," however, there are no knots. It is fastened in this wise. The leg of the hawk is placed against the "jesse," between the slits A and B. The end A is then passed through the slit B, and the end C in turn through the slit A. The swivel, with its dependent leash, is then attached to slit C; and the same with the other leg.

Othello says:—

"I'd whistle her off, and let her down the wind,
  To prey at fortune."

Falconers always flew their hawk *against* the wind. If flown *down* the wind, she seldom returned. When, therefore, a useless bird was to be dismissed, her owner flew her "down the wind;" and thenceforth she shifted for herself, and was said "to prey at fortune."

The word "haggard," as before observed, is of frequent occurrence throughout the Plays of Shakespeare. In the *Taming of the Shrew* (Act iv. Sc. 2), Hortensio speaks of Bianca as "this proud disdainful *haggard*." In *Much Ado about Nothing* (Act iii. Sc. 1), Hero, alluding to Beatrice, says—

"I know, her spirits are as coy and wild
  As *haggards* of the rock."

In *Twelfth Night* (Act iii. Sc. 1), Viola says of the Clown:—

"This fellow's wise enough to play the fool;
  And to do that well craves a kind of wit:

> He must observe their mood on whom he jests,
> The quality of persons, and the time;
> And, *like the haggard*, check at every feather
> That comes before his eye."

To "check" is a term used in falconry, signifying to "fly at," although it sometimes meant to "change the bird in pursuit."* The word occurs again in the same play (Act ii. Sc. 4), and in *Hamlet*, Act iv. Sc. 7.

Besides the "jesses," the "bells" formed an indispensable part of a hawk's trappings. These were of circular form, from a quarter to a full inch in diameter, and made of brass or silver, and were attached, one to each leg of the bird, by means of small slips of leather called "bewits." The use of bells was to lead the falconer by their sound to the hawk when in a wood, or out of sight.

* Salvin and Brodrick, "Falconry in the British Islands."

"As the ox hath his bow,* sir, the horse his curb, and the *falcon her bells*, so man hath his desires."—*As You Like It*, Act iii. Sc. 3.

So in *Henry VI.* Part III. Act i. Sc. 1—

"Nor he that loves him best,
The proudest he that holds up Lancaster,
Dares stir a wing, if Warwick *shake his bells.*"

Again—

"Harmless Lucretia, marking what he tells
With trembling fear, *as fowl hears falcon's bells.*"
Lucrece.

The "hood," too, was a necessary appendage to the trained falcon. This was a cap or cover for the head, which was not removed until the "quarry" was started, in order to prevent the hawk from flying too soon.

* His "bow," that is, his "yoke." Some editions read "low;" an evident mistake.

The Constable of France, speaking of the valour of the Dauphin, says:—

"'Tis a *hooded* valour, and when it appears it will *bate*."
Henry V. Act iii. Sc. 7.

The allusion is to the ordinary action of a hawk, which, when unhooded, *bates*, or flutters. But a quibble may be here intended between "bate," the hawking technical, and "bate," to dwindle or abate. The word occurs again in *Romeo and Juliet* (Act iii. Sc. 2)—

"*Hood* my unmann'd blood, *bating* in my cheeks."

And to those not conversant with the terms employed in falconry, this line would be unintelligible. An "unmanned" hawk was one not sufficiently reclaimed to be familiar with her keeper, and such birds generally "bated," that is, fluttered or beat their wings violently in their efforts to escape.

Petruchio, in *The Taming of the Shrew*, gives us a lesson in reclaiming a hawk when speaking thus of Catherine:—

" My falcon now is sharp, and passing empty,
  And, till she *stoop*, she must not be full-gorg'd,
  For then she never looks upon her *lure*.
  Another way I have to *man* my *haggard*,
  To make her come, and know her keeper's call,
  That is, to watch her, as we watch these kites

That *bate*, and beat, and will not be obedient.
She eat no meat to-day, nor none shall eat;
Last night she slept not, nor to-night she shall not."
Taming of the Shrew, Act iv. Sc. 1.

The word "stoop," sometimes written "stoup" (Spenser's "Faerie Queene," Book I. Canto XI. 18), and "swoop" (*Macbeth*, "at one fell swoop"), signifies a rapid descent on the "quarry." It occurs again in *Henry V*. Act iv. Sc. 1:—

"And though his affections are higher mounted than ours, yet, when they *stoop*, they *stoop* with the like wing."

The hawks, when carried to the field, were borne on "the cadge," as shown in the engraving; the person carrying it being called "the cadger." The modern word "cad," now generally used in an opprobrious sense, is in all probability an abbreviation of "cadger," and therefore synonymous with "servant" or common fellow.

Florizel, addressing Perdita, in the *Winter's Tale* (Act iv. Sc. 3), says,—

"I bless the time
When my good falcon made her flight across
Thy father's ground;"

for this was the occasion of his first meeting her.

In the following passage from *Measure for Measure*, (Act iii. Sc. 1), there occurs a word in connection with falconry, which requires some explanation,—

"This outward-sainted deputy,
Whose settled visage and deliberate word
Nips youth i' th' head, and follies doth *enmew*
As falcon doth the fowl."

The verb "to mew," or "enmew," signifies to enclose or shut up, owing its origin to the word "mews," the place where the hawks were confined :—

"To-night she's *mew'd* up."
Romeo and Juliet, Act iii. Sc. 4.

Gremio, speaking of Bianca to Signor Baptista, says,—

"Why, will you *mew* her?"
Taming of the Shrew, Act i. Sc. 1.

A question presently solved by Tranio, who says :—

> "And therefore has he closely *mew'd* her up,
> Because she will not be annoy'd with suitors."

The word "mew," derived from the old French "*mue*," signifies a change, or moult, when birds and other animals cast their feathers, hair, or horns. Hence Latham observes that "the mew is that place, whether it be abroad or in the house, where you set down your hawk during the time she raiseth or reproduceth her feathers."

It was necessary to take great care of a hawk in her mewing time. In "The Gentleman's Academie," edited by Gervase Markham, 1595, there are several sections on the mewing of hawks, from one of which it may be learnt that the best time to commence is in the beginning of Lent; and if well kept, the bird will be mewed, that is, moulted, by the beginning of August.

> "Forthcoming from her darksome *mew*."
>
> *Faerie Queene*, Book I. Canto v. 20.

The Royal hawks were kept at the mews at Charing Cross during many reigns (according to Stowe, from the time of Richard II., in 1377), but they were removed by Henry VIII., who converted the place into stables. The name, however, confirmed by the usage of so long a period, remained to the building, although, after the hawks were withdrawn, it became inapplicable. But, what is more curious still, in later times, when the people of London began to build ranges of stabling at the back of their streets and houses, they christened those places " mews," after the old stabling at Charing Cross.

The word " enmew," quoted above in the passage from *Measure for Measure*, would seem rather to signify here, " to seize upon," or " to disable." It is sometimes written " enewe." In Nash's " Quaternio ; or, a Fourefold Way to a Happie Life," published in 1633, it occurs in a spirited description of hawking at water-fowl :—" And to hear an accipitary relate againe how he went forth in a cleare, calme, and sunshine evening, about an houre before the sunne did usually maske himselfe, unto the river, where finding of a mallard, he whistled off* his falcon, and how shee flew from him as if shee would never have turned head againe, yet presently upon a shoote came in ; how then by degrees, by little and little, by flying about and about, shee mounted so high, until shee had lessened herselfe to the view of the beholder to the shape of a pigeon or partridge, and had made the height of the moon the place† of her flight ; how presently, upon the landing of the fowle, shee came downe like a stone and *enewed* it, and suddenly got up againe, and suddenly upon a second landing came down againe, and missing of it, in the

---

* Compare, *ante*, pp. 57–59. " I'd whistle her off," &c.

† Compare, *ante*, p. 52, " A falcon tow'ring in her pride of place," &c.

downe course recovered it beyond expectation, to the admiration of the beholder at a long flight."

Another method of spelling the same word may be instanced by the following quotation from Turbervile's "Book of Falconrie," 1575 :—

"And if shee misse, to mark her how shee then gets up amaine,
For best advantage, to *eneaw* the springing fowle againe."

In the days of falconry* a peculiar method of repairing a broken wing-feather was known to falconers by the term "imping." The verb "to imp," appears to be derived from the Anglo-Saxon "impan," signifying to graft, or inoculate; and the mode of operation is thus described in a scarce pamphlet by Sir John Sebright, entitled "Observations on Hawking":—

"When any of the flight or tail-feathers of a hawk are accidentally broken, the speed of the bird is so injured, that the falconer finds it necessary to repair them by an expedient called 'imping.'

"This curious process consists in attaching to the part that remains an exact substitute for the piece lost. For this purpose the falconer is always provided with pinions (right and left) and with tail-feathers of hawks, or with

---

* It will be observed that, in these pages, falconry is treated as a thing of the past, as indeed it is a sport now almost obsolete, and but few comparatively are acquainted with its technicalities.

the feathers separated from the pinion carefully preserved and numbered, so as to prevent mistake in taking a true match for the injured feather. He then with a sharp knife gently parts the web of the feather to be repaired at its thickest part, and cuts the shaft obliquely forward, so as not to damage the web on the opposite edge. He next cuts the substitute feather as exactly as possible at the corresponding point and with the same degree of slope.

"For the purpose of uniting them, he is provided with an iron needle with broad angular points at both ends, and after wetting the needle with salt-and-water, he thrusts it into the centre of the pith of each part, as truly straight and as nearly to the same length in each as may be.

"When this operation has been skilfully performed, the junction is so neat, that an inexperienced eye would hardly discern the point of union, and as the iron rusts from having been wetted with brine, there is little or no danger of separation."

After this explanation, the meaning of the following lines is clear :—

"If then we shall shake off our slavish yoke,
  Imp out our drooping country's *broken wing.*"
                              Richard II. Act ii. Sc. 1.

Passages such as this are likely enough to be overlooked by the majority of readers, but it is in such chiefly that the ornithologist sees a proof that Shakespeare, for the age in which he lived, possessed a surprising knowledge of ornithology.

Besides "imping," there was another practice in use, now happily obsolete, termed "seeling," to which we find several allusions in the Plays. It consisted in sewing a thread through the upper and under eyelids of a newly-caught hawk, to obscure the sight for a time, and accustom her to the hood.

Turbervile, in his "Book of Falconrie," 1575, gives the following quaint directions "how to seele a hawke":—
"Take a needle threeded with untwisted thread, and (casting your Hawke) take her by the beake, and put the needle through her eye-lidde, not right against the sight of the eye, but somewhat nearer to the beake, because she may see backwards. And you must take good heede that you hurt not the webbe, which is under the eye-lidde, or on the inside thereof. Then put your needle also through that other eye-lidde, drawing the endes of the thread together, tye them over the beake, not with a straight knotte, but cut off the threedes endes neare to the knotte, and twist them together in such sorte, that the eye-liddes

may be raysed so upwards, that the Hawke may not see at all, and when the threed shall ware loose or untyed, then the Hawke may see somewhat backwardes, which is the cause that the threed is put nearer to the beake. For a Sparrow-hawke should see somewhat backwardes, and a Falcon forwardes. The reasõ is that if the Sparrow-hawke should see forwardes, shee would beate off her feathers, or break them when she bateth upon the fist, and seeing the companie of men, or such like, she would bate too much."

In *Antony and Cleopatra* (Act iii. Sc. 13) we read—

"The wise gods *seel* our eyes."

And in the same play (Act v. Sc. 2) Seleucus says:—

"Madam,
I had rather *seel* my lips, than, to my peril,
Speak that which is not."

In his beautiful soliloquy on sleep, Henry IV., addressing the fickle goddess, exclaims,—

"Wilt thou upon the high and giddy mast
Seel up the ship-boy's eyes, and rock his brains
In cradle of the rude imperious surge?"

Henry IV. Part II. Act iii. Sc. 1.

The word occurs again in *Othello* (Act i. Sc. 3)—

"When light-wing'd toys
Of feather'd Cupid *seel* with wanton dulness," &c.

And in the same play (Act iii. Sc. 3)—

"She that, so young, could give out such a seeming,
To *seel* her father's eyes up close as oak."

In the last line it is more probable, considering the use of the technical term "seel," above explained, that Shakespeare wrote "close as hawk's."

Sir Emerson Tennant, in his "Sketches of the Natural History of Ceylon," speaking of the goshawk (p. 246), says:—"In the district of Anarajapoora, where it is trained for hawking, it is usual, in lieu of a hood, to darken its eyes by means of a silken thread passed through holes in the eyelids." This practice of "seeling" appears to be of some antiquity, but has happily given way, to a great extent, to the more merciful use of the hood.

The old treatises on falconry contain numerous quaint recipes for the various ailments to which hawks are subject. From one of these we learn that petroleum is nothing new, as some people now-a-days would have us believe. Turbervile, writing in 1575, says, in his "Booke of Falconrie":—"An other approued medecine is to annoint the swelling of your hawkes foot with *Oleum petrœlium* (which is the oyle of a rocke) and with oyle of white Lillies, taking of each of these like quantity, the blood of a pigeon, and the tallow of a candle, heating all these together a little at the fire. This unguent wil throughly resolue the mischief."—P. 258.

Hawking was sometimes called "birding." In the *Merry Wives of Windsor* (Act iii. Sc. 3), Master Page says,—

"I do invite you to-morrow morning to my house to breakfast; after, we'll *a-birding* together; I have a fine hawk for the bush."

This was probably a goshawk, for, being a short-winged hawk and of slower flight, this species was considered the best for a woody district, or, as Shakespeare terms it, "the bush."

In the same play (Act iii. Sc. 5) Dame Quickly, referring to Mistress Ford, says,—"Her husband goes this morning *a-birding;*" and Mistress Ford, herself, says (Act iv. Sc. 2),—"He's *a-birding*, sweet Sir John."

But it seems that birding was not always synonymous with hawking, for, later on in the last-mentioned scene, we read as follows :—

"*Falstaff.* What shall I do? I'll creep up into the chimney.

Mrs. Ford. There they always use to discharge their *birding-pieces.*"

The word "hawk," as in the case of the eagle, is almost invariably employed by Shakespeare in its generic sense :—

"Dost thou love hawking? thou hast hawks will soar
    Above the morning lark."

                Taming of the Shrew, Induction, Sc. 2.

In *Henry V.* (Act iii. Sc. 7), the Dauphin, when speaking in praise of his horse, says,—

"When I bestride him, I soar, I am a hawk."

And in the first part of *Henry VI.* (Act ii. Sc. 4), the Earl of Warwick boasts that

"Between two hawks, which flies the higher pitch;
. . . . .
I have perhaps some shallow spirit of judgment."

Again,—
"Twenty crowns!
I'll venture so much of my hawk or hound,
But twenty times so much upon my wife."
Taming of the Shrew, Act v. Sc. 2.

In two instances only does Shakespeare allude to a particular species of hawk. These are the Kestrel and Sparrowhawk.

When Malvolio, in *Twelfth Night* (Act ii. Sc. 5), finds the letter which Maria has purposely dropt in his path, Sir Toby Belch, looking on from ambush, exclaims, in sporting terms :—

"And with what wing the *stanniel* checks at it!"

Here *stanniel* is a corruption of *standgale*, a name for the kestrel hawk, and Malvolio is said to "check at" the letter, just as a kestrel hovers over a mouse or other object which has suddenly attracted its attention.

It is true that the reading of the folios here is *stallion;* but the word *wing*, and the falconers' term *checks*, abundantly prove that a bird must be meant. Sir Thomas Hanmer, therefore, proposed this correction, which all subsequent editors have received as justifiable.

The origin of the word "kestrel" is somewhat uncertain. By some it is derived from "coystril," a knave or peasant, from being the hawk formerly used by persons of inferior rank, as we learn from Dame Juliana Berners, in her "Boke of St. Albans." This opinion is strengthened by the reading "coystril," in *Twelfth Night* (Act i. Sc. 3), and "coistrel," in *Pericles* (Act iv. Sc. 6). A different spelling again occurs in "The Gentleman's Recreation," by Ric. Blome (folio, London, 1686), where the word is written "castrell."

The sparrowhawk is only mentioned once by Shakespeare, and the passage is one which might be very easily overlooked by any one not conversant with the language of falconry. In the *Merry Wives of Windsor*, Mrs. Ford addresses Falstaff's page with—

"How now, my *eyas-musket?*"

"Musket"* was the name given by the falconers of old

* The weapon of this name, the most important of small fire-arms, is said to have borrowed its title from this the most useful of small hawks, in the same way that other arms—as the falcon, falconet, and saker—have derived their names from larger and more formidable birds of prey. Against this view it is asserted that the musket was invented in the fifteenth century by the Muscovites, and owes its name to its inventors. See Bescherelle, "Dict. Nat.," and "The Target· a Treatise upon the Art Military," 1756.

to the male sparrowhawk; "eyas" or "eyess," as before explained, signifying a nestling, or young bird from the eyrie or nest. In the above speech, Mrs. Ford probably intended to imply no more than we should now-a-days mean by the expression "a perky little fellow."

The words of Hamlet with reference to a hawk must be familiar to all readers of Shakespeare, the more so, possibly, because the passage in question appears to have puzzled many commentators :—

"I am but mad north-north-west: when the wind is southerly, I know a *hawk* from a *handsaw*."

Hamlet, Act. ii. Sc. 2.

The explanation is simple enough. The last word should be "hernshaw," the old name for the heron. It is not every one who knows a hawk from a heron when he sees it, although it is scarcely possible to conceive two birds more unlike in appearance. Hamlet's statement, then, is simply to the effect that he only feigned madness when it suited his purpose; at other times he could even outwit the many, and see a distinction where they, from ignorance, would fail.

The ingenuity which has been exercised in a laudable endeavour to interpret this passage is really surprising. "An ingenious friend," says the *Athenæum*,* "suggests the following explanation :—'Among the ancient Ægyp-

---

* December 30th, 1865.

tians, the hawk signified the Etesian, or northerly wind (which, in the beginning of summer, drives the vapour towards the south, and which, covering Ethiopia with dense clouds, there resolves them into rains, causing the Nile to swell), because that bird follows the direction of that wind (Job xxxix. 26). The heron, hern, or hernshaw signified the southerly wind, because it takes its flight from Ethiopia into Upper Egypt, following the course of the Nile as it retires within its banks, and living on the small worms hatched in the mud of the river. Hence the heads of these two birds may be seen surmounting the *canopi* used by the ancent Ægyptians to indicate the rising and falling of the Nile respectively. Now Hamlet, though feigning madness, yet claims sufficient sanity to distinguish a hawk from a hernshaw when the wind is southerly; that is, in the time of the migration of the latter to the north, and when the former is not to be seen. Shakespeare may have become acquainted with the habits of these migrating birds of Egypt through a translation of Plutarch, who gives a particular account of them, published in the middle of the sixteenth century by Thomas North.'"

The present chapter, embodying, as it does, a treatise on hawking, illustrated by quotations from Shakespeare, would scarcely be complete without some reference to the prices paid for hawks, and to the expenses of keeping them, at the period at which Shakespeare lived. These particulars may be gleaned from scattered entries in certain "Household Books" and "Privy Purse Accounts" of noble owners, which the invaluable labours of antiquaries have placed within reach of the curious.

We have been at some pains to collect and arrange the following entries, believing that the information which they supply will be far more interesting to the reader if allowed to remain in the form in which we have found it :—

PRICES OF HAWKS.

Itm̃ the viij daye paied to Walshe for so moche money by him layed out for one goshawke and ij fawcons . iij li.

Itm̃ the xv daye paied for v fawcons and a tarsell . . . : viij li.

Itm̃ the iij daye paied in rewarde to Sr Richard Sandes s'vñt for the bringing of a saker to the king at hampton courte . . . v s̃.

Itm̃ the same daye paied for fyve ffawcons vij li. vj s̃. viij d.

Itm̃ the iij daye paied to a stranger called Jasper, fawconer, for vj sakers and v sakeretts at viij corons a pece which amot^s to $_{iiij}^{xx}$ viij corons . . xx li. x s̃. viij d.

Itm̃ the viij daye paied to maister Walshe for so much money by him paied for goshawks the which the king's grace bought upon the cage . iij li.

Itm̅ to iij of maister Skevington's s'vn̅ts
in rewarde for bringing iij hobbyes
to the king's grace .   .   . iij li.
Itm̅ the xj daye paied to a s'vn̅t of
Maister Saint John in rewarde for
bringing a caste of hawks . .   xx s̅.
Itm̅ the viij daye paied to a s'vn̅t of
the duc of Ferrers in rewarde for
bringing of a caste of fawcons to
the king's grace at Westm . . xxiij li. vj s̅. viij d.
Itm̅ the xix daye paid to a s'vn̅t of
Maister Walshe's for bringing of a
caste of Lancretts to the king's
grace in rewarde .   .   .   x s̅.
Itm̅ the xxvij daye paied to the Abbot
of Tewxbury s'vn̅t in rewarde for
bringing a caste of Launners to the
king's grace   .   .   .   xx s̅.
Itm̅ the xvj daye paied to Augustyne
the fawconer for viij hawks at vj
Angells a pece, whiche amounteth to xviij li.

HAWKS' FURNITURE.

Itm̅ the iiij daye paied for ij dousin of
hawks' hoods at iij s̅. iiij d. le dousin   vj s̅. viij d.
Itm̅ the same daye paied for iij hawks'
gloves at vj s̅. viij d. le glove .   xx s̅.

Itm̃ the same day paied for vj dousin
gilte bells at iij corons le dousin   xliij s̃.

HAWKS' MEAT.

Itm̃ the xx daye paied to Philip Clampe
for the mete of ij hawks after the
rate of ij d. by the daye from the
xx daye of Aprill unto the xviij
day of Novembre . .   xxv s̃.

Itm̃ the xxj daye paied to James the
henne taker for hawks' mete .   x s̃.

Itm̃ the xj daye paied to Hans the
fawconer for hawks' mete   xiiij s̃. iiij d.

Itm̃ to the same Hugh paied the same
daye for the mete of v hawks by
the same space that is to saye for
one quarter of a yere; ev̄y hawke
at one penny by the daye .   xxxviij s̃. vj d.

Itm̃ the xvj daye to maister Hennage
for the birds' mete . . .   xij d.

Itm̃ the v day to Nicholas Clampe for
the mete of iiij hawks fro the x
daye of Maye unto the xxiij daye
of June after one peny a daye for
a hawke . . .   xv s̃.

Itm̃ to the same John Evans for the
mete of iiij hawks by the space of

lxxxxvij dayes for evy hawke one
penny by the daye . . xxxij s. iiij d.

FALCONERS' WAGES.

Itm the vij daye paied to John Evans
for his bourde wages for one quarter
due at our Lady daye laste paste . xxx s. v d.

Itm the ix daye paied to the same John
Evans for his bourde wages fro
Mydsom tyll Michelmas after iiij d.
by the daye . . . xxx s. v d.

Itm the xxvj daye paied to Nicholas
Clampe one of the fawconers for
his wages due for one quarter ended
at Easter laste paste . l s.

Itm the same daye paied to the same
Clampe for his bourde wages from
the xxv daye of Decembre unto
the laste daye of this monethe the
which amounts to cxxvij dayes, at
iiij d. by the daye. xlij s. iiij d.

SUNDRIES.

Itm the vth daye paied to old Hugh in
rewarde when his hawks went to
the mewe . . . . . xl s.

Itm the xxv daye paied to Walter in
rewarde for a Jerfawcon that dyed . xl s.

SUNDRIES.

Itm̃ the same daye paied to one that toke up a Lanner that had been lacking a hole yere. . . . x s̃.

Itm̃ the laste daye paied unto Nicholas Clampe for keeping of a lanneret called 'Cutte' for one hole yere at j d. a daye . . . . xxx s̃. v d.

Itm̃ the xxvij daye paied to a s'vñt of my lorde Brayes in rewarde for taking up of a fawcon of the kings in Bedfordshire . . . . vj s̃. viij d.

Itm̃ the xvij daye paied to one Richard Mason for taking up of a fawcon of the kings besides Hartford . . vj s̃. viij d.

Itm̃ the xiij daye paied to a s'vñt of my lorde Darcys in rewarde for taking up of a hawke of the kings and bringing hir to Yorke place vij s̃. vi d.

Itm̃ the xiij daye paied to Iohn Weste of the garde to ryde into the contry for an hawke by the kings comande^t . . . . . xx s̃.

Itm̃ the xxviij daye paid to Willm Tyldesley, grome of the Chambre, for lying oute to take hawkes by the kings comande^t. . . x s̃.

Itm̃ the xiiij paied to a s'vñt of maister

M

Skevingtons in rewarde for bringing hawkes out of Irlande . .	xl š.
Itm̃ the x daye paied to Garard the fawconer in rewarde for taking of a fawcon and a tarsell .	lvj š.
Itm̃ the xj daye of Marche paied to Garrat and Richard the fawconers in rewarde for finding the Herons .	x š.

The interest which attaches to these curious extracts must excuse us with the reader for their length.

We cannot peruse them without being carried back, in spirit, to an age in which, for all that concerns sport, we would fain have lived to bear a part. Alas! that so delightful a pastime as hawking should have declined, and that we should live to see our noble falcons gibbeted, like thieves, upon "the keeper's tree."

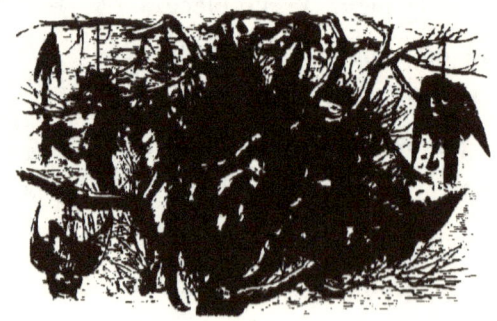

CHAPTER III.

THE OWL AND ITS ASSOCIATIONS.

AS Jove assumed the shape of an Eagle, so Juno selected that of an Owl, for, as Aldrovandus tells us, it was not decorous that the queen of heaven should take on herself the likeness of any small or vulgar bird, but rather that she should be embodied in one whose reign by night was equal with that of the eagle by day. The owl has usually been regarded as a bird of ill omen, and superstitiously considered a messenger of woe. The Athenians alone among the ancients seem to have been free from this popular prejudice, and to have regarded the owl with veneration rather than abhorrence, considering it as the favourite of Minerva, and the image of wisdom. The Romans viewed the owl with detestation and dread. By them it was held sacred to Proserpine : its appearance foreboded unfortunate events, and, according to Pliny, the city of Rome underwent a solemn lustration in consequence of an owl having accidentally strayed into the Capitol.

In the ancient pharmacopœia, which savoured not a little of magic, the owl appears to have been "great medicine." Ovid tells us that this bird was used wholesale in the composition of Medea's gruel:—

"Et strigis infames ipsis cum carnibus alas."

While, according to Horace, the old witch Canidia made use of the feathers in her incantations:—

"Plumamque nocturnæ strigis."

The "owlet's wing" was an ingredient of the cauldron wherein the witches prepared their "charm of powerful trouble" (*Macbeth*, Act iv. Sc. 1); and, with the character assigned to it by the ancients, Shakespeare, no doubt, felt that the introduction of an owl in a dreadful scene of a tragedy would help to make the subject come home more forcibly to the people, who had, from early times, associated its presence with melancholy, misfortune, and death. Accordingly, we find the unfortunate owl stigmatized at various times as the "obscure," "ominous," "fearful," and "fatal" "bird of night." Its doleful cry pierces the ear of Lady Macbeth while the murder is being done:—

"Hark!—Peace! It was the owl that shriek'd,
The fatal bellman which gives the stern'st good night."

Macbeth, Act ii. Sc. 1.

And when the murderer rushes in immediately afterwards, exclaiming,—

"I have done the deed. Didst thou not hear a noise?"
She replies,—

"I heard the owl scream."

And later on—

"The *obscure bird* clamour'd the live-long night."
Macbeth, Act ii. Sc. 2.

The awe, no doubt, with which this bird is regarded by the superstitious, may be attributed in some measure to the fact of its flying by night.

"Deep night, dark night, the silent of the night,
. . . . .
The time when screech-owls cry and ban-dogs howl."
Henry VI. Part II. Act i. Sc. 4.

And yet, strange to say, the appearance of an owl by day is by some considered equally ominous :—

"The owl by day,
If he arise, is mocked and wondered at."
Henry VI. Part III. Act v. Sc. 4.

"For night-owls shriek, where mounting larks should sing."
Richard II. Act iii. Sc. 3.

Should an owl appear at a birth it is said to forbode ill-luck to the infant. King Henry VI., addressing Gloster, says,—

"The owl shriek'd at thy birth, an evil sign."
Henry VI. Part III. Act v. Sc. 6.

While upon any other occasion its presence was supposed to predict a death, or at least some dire mishap :—

"The screech-owl, screeching loud,
Puts the wretch, that lies in woe,
In remembrance of a shroud."
Midsummer Night's Dream, Act v. Sc. 2.

When Richard III. is irritated by the ill-news showered thick upon him, he interrupts the third messenger with—

"Out on ye, owls! nothing but songs of death?"
Richard III. Act iv. Sc. 4.

It is curious how wide-spread is the superstition regarding certain birds, and particularly the owl. Even amongst the Land Dayaks of Borneo, the owl is considered a bird of ill omen. Mr. Spenser St. John, in his "Life in the Forests of the Far East," observes with regard to omens (vol. i. p. 202) :—

"If a man be going on a war expedition, and has a slip during his first day's journey, he must return to his village, especially if by the accident blood be drawn, for then, should he proceed, he has no prospect but wounds or death. If the accident occur during a long expedition, he must return to his last night's resting place. In some tribes, if a deer cry near a party who are setting out on a journey, they will return. When going out at night to the jungle, if the scream of a hawk, or an owl, or of a small kind of frog be heard, it is a sign that sickness will follow if the design be pursued; and again, if the screech of the two former be heard in front of a party on the war-path, it is an evil sign, and they must return. Omens derived from the cry of birds are always sought previously to setting out on a journey, and before fixing on a spot to build new houses, or to prepare their farms."

Far from bringing any ill-luck to our dwellings, owls are really of the greatest service to us in destroying great numbers of vermin. A Swiss naturalist, speaking of the quantity of field-voles which are annually destroyed by owls and buzzards, says:*—

"C'est un fait curieux que l'homme s'acharne tout particulièrement à detruire ses meillures amis, et qu'il poursuive de ses malédictions les êtres qui le servent le mieux. Je joindrai donc ma faible voix à celle de bien d'autres naturalistes pour demander que l'on protége les premières de ces bêtes.

"Les hibous et les chouettes, bien loin de jeter de mauvais sorts sur nos demeures, prennent au contraire, un grand soin de nos intérêts. Ces oiseaux exterminent, en effet, bien plus de souris que n'en pourront prendre jamais les meilleurs taupiers. Les buses n'ont nulle-

---

* Victor Fatio, "Les Campagnols du Bassin du Léman." Bale, Génève, et Paris. 1867. P. 16.

ment mérité leur place sur la porte de nos granges, et plutôt que de les tuer, l'on ferait bien mieux d'établir chez nous, comme cela s'est fait avec succès dans certaines localités, de hauts perchoirs dans nos campagnes pour attirer ces oiseaux bienfaisants."

Among the many curious legends which exist with reference to this bird, we may mention one to which Shakespeare has alluded in Hamlet:—

" They say the owl was a baker's daughter."

Hamlet, Act iv. Sc. 5.

Mr. Staunton, in his edition of Shakespeare's Plays, says this has reference to a tradition still current in some parts of England. " Our Saviour went into a baker's shop where they were baking, and asked for some bread to eat. The mistress of the shop immediately put a piece of dough into the oven to bake for him, but was reprimanded by her daughter, who, insisting that the piece of dough was too large, reduced it considerably in size. The dough, however, immediately afterwards began to swell, and presently became of an enormous size. Whereupon the baker's daughter cried out, ' Wheugh! wheugh! wheugh!' which owl-like noise, it is said, probably induced our Saviour, for her wickedness, to transform her into that bird."

Mr. Douce represents this story as still current amongst the common people in Gloucestershire.* According to

---

* " Illustrations of Shakespeare, and of Ancient Manners." 1807.

Nuttall, the north country nurses would have it that the owl was a daughter of Pharaoh, and when they heard it hoot on a winter's night, they sang to the wondering child—

> "Oh! ŏ ŏ ŏ, ō ō;
>
> I once was a king's daughter, and sat on my father's knee,
> But now I'm a poor hoolet, and hide in a hollow tree."

There is much difference of opinion amongst naturalists as to whether the power of hooting and shrieking is possessed by the same species. In the following passage from *Julius Cæsar* (Act i. Sc. 3), both sounds are attributed to the same bird:—

> "Yesterday the *bird of night* did sit,
> Even at noonday, upon the market-place,
> Hooting and shrieking."

It is generally supposed that the common barn or white owl does not hoot, but only shrieks, and is, in fact, the bird always alluded to as the "screech-owl," while the brown owls (*Strix otus, brachyotus,* and *aluco*) are the hooters—

> "The clamorous owl, that nightly hoots."
> *Midsummer Night's Dream*, Act ii. Sc. 2.

But Mr. Colquhoun, speaking of the white or barn owl, says,* "It does hoot, but very rarely. I heard one six times in succession, and then it ceased." Sir William

---

* "The Moor and the Loch."

Jardine once shot a white owl in the act of hooting; and Mr. Boulton, of Beverley, Yorkshire, describes * the note of one of these birds which he had reared from the nest, and kept in confinement for fifteen months, as follows :—" It does hoot exactly like the long-eared owl, but not so frequently. I use the term 'hoot' in contradistinction to 'screech,' which it often does when irritated."

In Gardiner's " Music of Nature " the note of the brown owl is thus rendered :—

Mr. Colquhoun, to whom allusion has just been made, says, that the music of the white or barn owl is a little different from that of the brown owls. It is only one prolonged cadence, lower and not so mournful as that of the tawny fellow.

It would appear that owls do not keep to one note. A friend of Gilbert White's remarked that most of his owls hooted in B flat, but that one went almost half a note below A. The pipe by which he tried their notes was a common half-crown pitchpipe. A neighbour, also, of the Selborne naturalist, who was said to have a nice ear, remarked that the owls about Selborne hooted in three different keys: in G flat (or F sharp), in B flat, and A

* "The Zoologist" for 1863, p. 8,765.

flat. He heard two hooting to each other, the one in A flat, the other in B flat.

It did not appear, however, whether the sounds proceeded from different species of brown owls, or from different individuals of the same species.

Another question in the life-history of the owl is raised by the following passage from *Macbeth* (Act iv. Sc. 2) :—

" For the poor wren,
The most diminutive of birds, will fight,
Her young ones in her nest, against the owl."

This defence of their young by birds has often been noticed by Shakespeare :—

" Unreasonable creatures feed their young ;
And though man's face be fearful to their eyes,
Yet, in protection of their tender ones,
Who hath not seen them (even with those wings
Which sometimes they have us'd with fearful flight)
Make war with him that climb'd unto their nest,
Off'ring their own lives in their young's defence ? "

Henry VI. Part III. Act ii. Sc. 2.

We are not aware, however, that an owl has ever been caught in the act of robbing a nest, and, indeed, it would not be easy to detect him, from the fact of his preying by night. Nevertheless, there is presumptive evidence to support the charge. A writer in *The Field*, of 29th June, 1867, says :—" Standing in my garden in Bedford Park, Croydon, an evening or two since, I saw a white owl fly to a sparrow's nest lodged on a water-spout under the roof of the house, and as though that visit was not successful, he repeated it, and then went to a nest on the next house, in the same way. It was too dark for me to see if he succeeded in his marauding expedition against the poor sparrows. Is it a common occurrence for an owl to go robbing nests? I never saw it done before, though I have lived all my life in the country, and of course seen this favourite bird skimming over the water meadows for its supper." To this communication the editor adds the following note :—" This fact is extremely interesting, and, we think, generally unknown. It would, however, have added much to the interest, had the robbery actually been proved; it does not seem quite certain that this was the owl's object in visiting the roof."

Some years ago, having made the discovery that some stock-doves were building in the wooden spire of our village church, we commissioned the parish clerk to secure a pair of young birds as soon as they were ready to fly. He made several attempts for this purpose, paying occasional visits to see how the young birds were getting on, when, on going to the nest, as he supposed for the last time, to carry them off, he found it empty. This happened three or four times, and he was much puzzled to account for it. The birds could not have flown—they were not old enough. No one else could have taken them, for the church could not be entered without the key, which he always kept. Had rats carried them off? The clerk said there were none. Had there been any, he must have heard or seen them on one or other of his many visits to the church, or at least have found signs of their presence. But this was never the case. He stated, however, that a pair of barn owls lived in the same spire, and he thought that they were the culprits, taking the young ones, as he said, as soon as they were fat enough, to save themselves the trouble of hunting out of doors. Be this as it may, we feel bound to say, on behalf of the owls, they were never caught in the fact, and that the parent stock-doves were not deterred from laying again and again, and at length rearing a brood. Charles Waterton, whose name will be familiar to all naturalists, argues strongly against the notion of the barn owl robbing dove-cotes. He says*:—" When farmers complain that the barn owl destroys the eggs of their pigeons, they lay the saddle on the wrong horse. They ought to put it on the rat.

" Formerly, I could get very few young pigeons till the rats were excluded effectually from the dove-cot. Since that took place, it has produced a great abundance every year, though the barn owls frequent it, and are encouraged all around it. The barn owl merely resorts to it for repose and concealment. If it were really an enemy to

* " Essays on Natural History," 1st Series, p. 14.

the dove-cot, we should see the pigeons in commotion as soon as it begins its evening flight, but the pigeons heed it not; whereas if the sparrowhawk or hobby should make its appearance, the whole community would be up at once—proof sufficient that the barn owl is not looked upon as a bad or even a suspicious character by the inhabitants of the dove-cot."

Its habit of breeding in retired situations is alluded to in *Titus Andronicus*, Act ii. Sc. 3 :—

> " Here never shines the sun ; here nothing breeds,
> Unless the nightly owl."

And Shakespeare has truly characterized the appearance of this bird on the wing, when he speaks of

> " The night-owl's lazy flight."
> *Henry VI.* Part III. Act ii. Sc. 1.

Why the owl has been called the "bird of wisdom" it is not easy to determine. Possibly because it can see in the dark, and is the only bird which looks straightforward. Shakespeare frequently alludes to its "five wits," and the readers of Tennyson's poems will no doubt remember the lines :—

> " Alone, and warming his *five wits*,
> The white owl in the belfry sits."

With our early writers the five senses appear to have been generally called the "five wits." Chaucer, in the

"Parsone's Tale," says:—"Certes delites been after the appetites of the 'five wittes;' as sight, hereing, smelling, savouring, and touching." But it is not clear how this proverbial phrase became connected with the owl, nor what is the origin of "warming" the wits.

"*Petruchio.* Am I not *wise?*
Katharine. Yes, keep you *warm.*"
Taming of the Shrew, Act ii. Sc. 1.

"If he have *wit* enough to keep himself *warm.*"
Much Ado, Act i. Sc. 1.

"Bless thy *five wits.*"
King Lear, Act iii. Sc. 4, and Act iii. Sc. 6.

The allusion above made to Tennyson's well-known poem, reminds us of the quaint and characteristic song in the last scene of *Love's Labour's Lost:*—

III.

"When icicles hang by the wall,
  And Dick the shepherd blows his nail,
And Tom bears logs into the hall,
  And milk comes frozen home in pail;
When blood is nipp'd, and ways be foul,
Then nightly sings the staring owl,
  To-who;
Tu-whit, to-who, a merry note,
While greasy Joan doth keel the pot.

IV.

When all aloud the wind doth blow,
  And coughing drowns the parson's saw,
And birds sit brooding in the snow,
  And Marian's nose looks red and raw ;
When roasted crabs hiss in the bowl,
Then nightly sings the staring owl,
    To-who ;
Tu-whit, to-who, a merry note,
While greasy Joan doth keel the pot."

Nor do we forget Ariel's song in *The Tempest* (Act v. Sc. 1)—

"Where the bee sucks, there lurk I ;
In a cowslip's bell I lie,
There I couch when owls do cry."

Amongst the fairies, at least, the owl seems to have found friends, and is generally represented as a companion in their moonlight gambols :—

"This is the fairy land !—O, spite of spites !—
We talk with goblins, owls, and elvish sprites."
                                Comedy of Errors, Act ii. Sc. 2.

The folio of 1623 omits "elvish," but the folio of 1632 has "elves," which Rowe changed to "elvish."

The following quotation we have some hesitation in introducing, for there appears to be a difference of reading, which quite alters the sense :—

"No, rather, I abjure all roofs, and choose

. . . .

To be a comrade with the wolf and owl,—
Necessity's sharp pinch."

King Lear, Act ii. Sc. 4.

Mr. Collier, taking into consideration the last line, reads :—

"To be a comrade with the wolf, and howl
Necessity's sharp pinch."

And this seems more likely to be the correct reading. Albeit, in support of the former version, the following passage in *Lucrece* has been adduced :—

"No noise but owls' and wolves' death-boding cries."

It is not to be supposed that Shakespeare was always a firm believer in the popular notions respecting animals and birds to which he has made allusion. In many cases he had a particular motive in introducing such notions, although possibly aware of their erroneous nature, and he evidently adopted them only to impart an air of reality to the scenes which he depicted, and to bring them home more forcibly to the impressionable minds of his auditors, to whom such "folks-lore" would be familiar. This is notably the case as regards the owl, and no one can read the first scene in the second act of *Macbeth*, or the fourth scene in the first act of *Henry VI.* (Part II.), without feeling the impressive effect produced by the introduction of a bird which is held in such detestation by the ignorant, but which naturalists have shown to be not only harmless, but useful.

But—

" The owl, night's herald, shrieks,—'tis very late."

Venus and Adonis.

And, therefore, with Boyet, in *Love's Labour's Lost* (Act iv. Sc. 1), we will say :—

" Good night, my good owl."

CHAPTER IV.

THE CROWS AND THEIR RELATIONS.

TO a superficial observer of nature, there may appear to be a much greater resemblance between the Raven, the Crow, the Rook, and the Jackdaw, than we find to be actually the case. At the same time, so different to them in outward appearance are the Jay and Magpie, that it may appear extraordinary to class them all together. Nevertheless, while each, of course, has its distinguishing characters, all are included in the first section of the family of crows.

The Raven (*Corvus corax*), from his size and character, naturally takes the lead. Go where we will over the face of the wide world, the well-known hoarse croak of the raven is still to be heard. He was seen perched on the bare rocks, looking over the dreary snows of the highest points visited in the Arctic Expeditions. Under the burning sun of the equator he enjoys his feast of carrion. He was discovered in the islands of the Pacific Ocean by Captain

Cook; and in the lowest Southern or Antarctic regions, other travellers have found him pursuing his cautious predatory life, just as in England.*

From the earliest times the raven, with his deep and solemn voice, has always commanded attention, and superstitious people have become impressed with the idea that there is something unearthly in his nature and ominous in his voice.† By the Romans this bird was consecrated to Apollo, and regarded as a foreteller of good or evil. Through a long course of centuries this character has clung to him; and even to this day, there are many who believe that the raven's croak predicts a death.

No wonder, then, that Shakespeare has taken advantage of this wide-spread belief, and has introduced the raven into many of the solemn passages of his Plays, to carry conviction to the minds of the people, and render his images the more impressive. He frequently alludes to "the ill-boding raven:"

" It comes o'er my memory,
As doth the raven o'er the infectious house,
Boding to all."

Othello, Act iv. Sc. 1.

Thersites, in *Troilus and Cressida* (Act v. Sc. 2), says,—

* Stanley's " Familiar History of Birds," p. 179.
† An excellent dissertation on the organ of voice in the raven will be found in the second volume of Yarrell's " British Birds," 3rd ed. p. 72

"Would I could meet that rogue Diomed; I would croak like a raven; I would bode, I would bode."

In the play of *Henry VI.* Suffolk vainly endeavours to cheer up the King, who has swooned on hearing of Gloster's death, saying:—

"Comfort, my sovereign! gracious Henry, comfort!"

But the King, likening his message to the ill-boding note of a raven, replies:—

"What, doth my lord of Suffolk comfort me?
Came he right now to sing a raven's note,
Whose dismal tune bereft my vital powers;
And thinks he that the chirping of a wren,
By crying comfort from a hollow breast,
Can chase away the first-conceived sound?"

Henry VI. Part II. Act iii. Sc. 2.

After Balthazar has sung his well-known song, "Sigh no more, ladies," (*Much Ado*, Act ii. Sc. 3,) Benedick observes to himself, "An he had been a dog that should have howled thus, they would have hanged him: and I pray God his bad voice bode no mischief. I had as lief have heard the night-raven, come what plague could have come after it."

Willughby thought that the so-called "night-raven" was the bittern. Speaking of the curious noise produced by the latter bird, he says:—"This, I suppose, is the bird which the vulgar call the night-raven, and have a great dread of."*

The bittern was one of the very few birds which Goldsmith, in his "Animated Nature," described from personal observation, and he, too, calls it the "night-raven." Its hollow boom, he says, caused it to be held in detestation by the vulgar. "I remember, in the place where I was a boy, with what terror the bird's note affected the whole village; they considered it as the presage of some sad event, and generally found, or made one to succeed it. If any person in the neighbourhood died, they supposed it could not be otherwise, for the night-raven had foretold it; but if nobody happened to die, the death of a cow or a sheep gave completion to the prophecy."

Sometimes it was called the *night-crow*—

"The night-crow cried, aboding luckless time."

Henry VI. Part III. Act v. Sc. 6.

Shakespeare has introduced an allusion to the raven with much effect, in the fifth scene of the first act in *Macbeth*, where an attendant enters the chamber of Lady Macbeth to announce—

"The king comes here to-night.
Lady M.   Thou 'rt mad to say it!—
Is not thy master with him? who, were't so,
Would have informed for preparation.

---

* Willughby's "Ornithology," folio, 1678. Book I. p. 25.

Attend. So please you, it is true :—our thane is coming :
   One of my fellows had the speed of him ;
   Who, almost dead for breath, had scarcely more
   Than would make up his message.
Lady M.   Give him tending ;
   He brings great news.   [*Exit Attendant.*
                     The raven himself is hoarse
   That croaks the fatal entrance of Duncan
   Under my battlements."

On this passage Johnson remarks : " The messenger, says the servant, had hardly breath to make up his message ; to which the lady answers mentally, that he may well want breath ; such a message would add hoarseness to the raven. That even the bird whose harsh voice is accustomed to predict calamities, could not croak the entrance of Duncan but in a note of unwonted harshness."

The preference which the raven evinces for " sickly prey," or carrion, is not unnoticed by the poet :—

   " Now powers from home, and discontents at home,
      Meet in one line ; and vast confusion waits,
      As doth a raven on a sick-fallen beast,
      The imminent decay of wrested pomp."
                  King John, Act iv. Sc. 3.

And again—

> "Ravens
> Fly o'er our heads, and downward look on us,
> As we were sickly prey."
>
> *Julius Cæsar*, Act v. Sc. 3.

In *Henry V.* (Act iv. Sc. 2) we have a graphic picture of a distressed army followed by ravens on the look-out for corpses :—

> "Yond island *carrions*, desperate of their bones,
> Ill-favour'dly become the morning field :
> Their ragged curtains poorly are let loose,
> And our air shakes them passing scornfully.
> And their executors, the knavish crows,
> Fly o'er them all, impatient for their hour."

It is most probable that the supposed prophetic power of the raven, respecting battles and bloodshed, originated in its frequent presence on these occasions, drawn to the field of slaughter by an attractive banquet of unburied bodies of the slain. Hence poets have described this bird as possessing a mysterious knowledge of these things. The Icelanders, notwithstanding their endeavours to destroy as many as they can, yet give them credit for the gift of prophecy, and have a high opinion of them as soothsayers. And the priests of the North American Indians wear, as a distinguishing mark of their sacred profession, two or three raven skins, fixed to the girdle behind their back, in such a manner that the tails stick out horizontally from the body. They have also a split raven skin on the head, so fastened as to let the beak project from the forehead.*

The solitary habits of this bird during the nesting season are thus alluded to:—

"A barren detested vale, you see, it is;
The trees, though summer, yet forlorn and lean,
O'ercome with moss and baleful misseltoe:
Here never shines the sun; here nothing breeds,
Unless the nightly owl or fatal raven."

Titus Andronicus, Act ii. Sc. 3.

And a curious belief is mentioned with regard to the rearing of its young:—

"Some say that ravens foster forlorn children,
The whilst their own birds famish in their nests."

Titus Andronicus, Act ii. Sc. 3.

It would appear, from some passages in the sacred Scriptures, that the desertion of their young had not escaped the observation of the inspired writers. It was certainly a current belief in olden times, that when the raven saw its young ones newly hatched, and covered with down, it conceived such an aversion that it forsook them, and did not return to the nest until a darker plumage had shown itself. And to this belief commentators suppose the Psalmist alludes when he says:—"He

* Stanley's "Familiar History of Birds," p. 188.

giveth to the beast his food, and to the young ravens which cry." (Psalm cxlvii. 9.) And again, in Job, "*Who provideth for the raven his food? When his young ones cry unto God, they wander for lack of meat.*" (Job xxxviii. 41.)

In Batman "upon Bartholome his book, 'De proprietatibus Rerum,' folio, 1582," we find the following passage bearing upon the question :—" The raven is called *Corvus* of Corax. It is said that ravens birdes (*i.e.*, young ravens) be fed with deaw of heaven all the time that they have no black feathers by benefite of age." (Lib. xii. c. 10.)

Izaak Walton, in his "Compleat Angler," speaking of fish without mouths, which "are nourished and take breath by the porousness of their gills, man knows not how," observes that "this may be believed if we consider that when the raven hath hatched her eggs, she takes no further care, but leaves her young ones to the care of the God of nature, who is said in the Psalms (Psal. cxlvii. 9) 'to feed the young ravens that call upon him.' And they be kept alive, and fed by a dew or worms that breed in their nests ; or some other ways that we mortals know not."

Shakespeare, no doubt, had the words of the Psalmist in his mind when he wrote—

"And He that doth the ravens feed,
Yea, providently caters for the sparrow,
Be comfort to my age !"

As You Like It, Act ii. Sc. 3.

We read in the First Book of Kings, xvii. 4, that when the prophet Elijah fled from the tyranny of King Ahab, and concealed himself by the brook Cherith, God commanded the ravens to feed him there. The remembrance of this passage may have been in our poet's mind when he penned the following lines in the *Winter's Tale*. Antigonus, ordered by Leontes to expose the infant Perdita to death, says, with a touch of pity :—

" Come on, poor babe :
Some powerful spirit instruct the kites and ravens
To be thy nurses ! "
Winter's Tale, Act ii. Sc. 3.

As in the case of the owl, it appears that ravens' feathers were employed by the witches of old in their incantations ; for it was believed that the wings of this bird carried contagion with them wherever they appeared. Marlowe, in his *Jew of Malta*, speaks of—

. . " the sad presaging raven, that tolls
The sick man's passport in her hollow beak,
And in the shadow of the silent night
Doth shake contagion from her sable wings."

Hence the curse which Shakespeare puts into the mouth of Caliban :—

" As wicked dew as e'er my mother brush'd
With raven's feather from unwholesome fen,
Drop on you both ! "
Tempest, Act i. Sc. 2.

Here "wicked" may be taken to mean pernicious or destructive—the antonym being "virtuous," as in the expression "the virtuous properties of plants." A bad sore is described, in an old tract on hawking (Harl. MS. 2,340), as "a wykked felone."

As the type of blackness, both as regards colour and character, we find the raven frequently contrasted with the white dove, the emblem of all that is pure and gentle.

"Who will not change a raven for a dove?"
Midsummer Night's Dream, Act ii. Sc. 2.

"I'll sacrifice the lamb that I do love,
To spite a raven's heart within a dove."
Twelfth Night, Act v. Sc. 1.

"Beautiful tyrant! fiend angelical!
Dove-feather'd raven!
. . . . .
Just opposite to what thou justly seem'st."
Romeo and Juliet, Act iii. Sc. 2.

The quarto (1599) and folio here read, "ravenous, dove-feather'd raven," &c.

As colour is intensified by contrast, so we read—

"Whiter than snow upon a raven's back."

So the undated quarto. Other editions have the emendation—

"Whiter than new snow on a raven's back."
Romeo and Juliet, Act iii. Sc. 2.

We have seen a variety of the jackdaw of a dirty yellowish-white colour; it could scarcely be called "amber-colour'd." No doubt other members of the genus *Corvus* have occasionally been observed to vary quite as much in their plumage. Shakespeare says,—

"An amber-colour'd raven was well noted."
Love's Labour's Lost, Act iv. Sc. 3.

No doubt it was; quite as much as a white blackbird. This apparent contradiction of terms is in reality no myth. We have seen three or four albino varieties of the blackbird, and could give a tolerably long list of dark-plumaged birds of which pure white, or almost pure white, varieties have been found. This may be the result of disease, or of old age, drying up the animal secretions, and causing the absence of colour which we call white. According to ancient authors, ravens were formerly white, but were changed to black for babbling. The great age to which the raven sometimes attains has been alluded to in the first chapter, where some reference is made to "ancient" eagles, and tame ravens have been known to outlive several masters who owned them successively. But birds, like all things else, succumb to time. Shakespeare tells us,—

> "Time's glory is to calm contending Kings, ...
> To fill with worm-holes stately monuments, . . .
> To pluck the quills from ancient ravens' wings."
>
> *Lucrece.*

Next to the raven, the Carrion-Crow (*Corvus corone*) claims our attention, from his close relationship to his larger congener. So closely, indeed, does he resemble the raven upon a slightly modified scale, that we might also fancy him—

> "A crow of the same nest."
>
> *All's Well that Ends Well*, Act iv. Sc. 3.

Like him, he leads a predatory life, carrying off young game-birds, chickens, and eggs; and where he cannot obtain a fresh meal, he has no objection to carrion and offal of all kinds. Should a sheep die in the field, the crows of the neighbourhood are sure to be attracted to it.

> "The fold stands empty in the drowned field,
> And crows are fatted with the murrain flock."
>
> *Midsummer Night's Dream*, Act. ii. Sc. 1.

Gamekeepers, knowing this propensity, and having an eye to the better preservation of pheasants' eggs for the future, avail themselves of the opportunity, when a sheep dies, to place a little strychnine in the mouth and eyes, and on a second visit they are seldom disappointed in finding two or three dead crows.

Throughout the Plays we meet with frequent allusions to the crow, and its partiality for carrion. In the fifth act of *Cymbeline* a scene is laid in a field between the British and Roman camps, where the following dialogue takes place :—

" *British Captain.*   Stand ! who's there ?
  Posthumus. A Roman,
    Who had not now been drooping here, if seconds
    Had answer'd him.
  British Captain.   Lay hands on him ; a dog !
    A leg of Rome shall not return to tell
    What crows have peck'd them here."
Cymbeline, Act. v. Sc. 3.

Again—

" *Boy.* Mine host Pistol, you must come to my master,—and you, hostess ;—he is very sick, and would to bed. . . .
  Host. By my troth, he'll yield the crow a pudding one of these days."
Henry V. Act ii. Sc. 1.

The Duke of York, on the field of St. Albans, boasting of his victory over Lord Clifford, says, in reply to the Earl of Warwick :—

" The deadly-handed Clifford slew my steed,
  But match to match I have encounter'd him,

>   And made a prey for carrion kites and crows
>   Even of the bonny beast he lov'd so well."
>
> *Henry VI.* Part II. Act v. Sc. 2.

Cassius, on the eve of battle, augured a defeat because, as he said,—

> "Crows
> Fly o'er our heads, and downward look on us,
> As we were sickly prey; their shadows seem
> A canopy most fatal, under which
> Our army lies, ready to give up the ghost."
>
> *Julius Cæsar,* Act v. Sc. 1.

In the third act of *Cymbeline* (Sc. 1), when Caius Lucius, the Roman Ambassador, comes to demand tribute from the British King, he is met with a flat refusal, and Cloten, one of the lords in waiting, deriding his threat of war, says:—

"His Majesty bids you welcome. Make pastime with us a day or two, or longer: if you seek us afterwards in other terms, you shall find us in our saltwater girdle: if you beat us out of it, it is yours; if you fall in the adventure, *our crows shall fare the better for you;* and there's an end."

Alexander Iden, addressing the lifeless body of Jack Cade, whom he had just slain, exclaims:—

> "Hence will I drag thee headlong by the heels
> Unto a dunghill, which shall be thy grave,

And there cut off thy most ungracious head ;
Which I will bear in triumph to the king,
Leaving thy trunk *for crows to feed upon.*"
Henry VI. Part II. Act iv. Sc. 10.

Many similar instances might be brought forward.

As in the case of the raven, we find the crow, as the emblem of blackness, contrasted with the white dove :—

" With the dove of Paphos might the crow
Vie feathers white."
Pericles, Act iv. Introd.

Again—

" Lawn as white as driven snow ;
Cyprus black as e'er was crow."
Winter's Tale, Act iv. Sc. 3.

Here we have not only the crow contrasted with snow, but also cyprus, a thin transparent black stuff, somewhat like crape, placed in contradistinction with lawn, which is a white material, like muslin.*

" So shows a snowy dove trooping with crows,
As yonder lady o'er her fellows shows."
Romeo and Juliet, Act i. Sc. 5.

---

* Compare, " A *cyprus*, not a bosom, hides my heart."
Twelfth Night, Act iii. Sc. 1.

> "Compare her face with some that I shall show,
> And I will make thee think thy swan a crow."
>
> *Romeo and Juliet*, Act i. Sc. 2.

Beatrice says (*Much Ado about Nothing*, Act i. Sc. 1),—"I had rather hear my dog bark at a crow than a man swear he loves me;" but then this was meant to be personal, for Benedick, whom she addressed, was not a favoured suitor. She might have added, with Dromio, in the *Comedy of Errors*, Act iii. Sc. 1 :—

> "We'll pluck a crow together."

This saying appears to be of some antiquity, but the origin of it is not very clear.

The custom of protecting newly sown wheat from the birds by keeping a lad to shout, or putting up a "scarecrow," is no doubt an old one. Shakespeare makes allusion to both methods :—

> "That fellow handles his bow like *a crow-keeper*."
>
> *King Lear*, Act iv. Sc. 6.

That is like a boy employed to keep the crows from the corn. So again—

> "Scaring the ladies like a *crow-keeper*."
>
> *Romeo and Juliet*, Act i. Sc. 4.

The rustic, although entrusted with a bow and arrows, was not expected to have much skill in archery, and

Roger Ascham, in his "Toxophilus," when speaking of a clumsy archer, has a similar comparison to that in the passage just quoted :—" Another coureth downe and layeth out his buttockes, as though hee should shoote at crowes."

" We must not make a *scare-crow* of the law,
Setting it up to fear * the birds of prey,
And let it keep one shape, till custom make it
Their perch, and not their terror."
Measure for Measure, Act ii. Sc. 1.

Lord Talbot relates that, when a prisoner in France, he was exhibited publicly in the market-place :—

" Here, said they, is the terror of the French,
The *scare-crow* that affrights our children so."
Henry VI. Part I. Act i. Sc. 4.

And Falstaff, alluding to his recruits on the march to Shrewsbury, says of them :—

" No eye hath seen such *scare-crows*."
Henry IV. Part I. Act iv. Sc. 2.

Associated with the crow by many of the poets is the Red-legged Crow, or Chough—the Cornish Chough, as it is sometimes called, from its being considered a bird peculiar to the south-west coast of England. Since this last name was applied to it, the study of ornithology has

---

* "To fear,' that is, "to frighten."

become so universally courted, that it can scarcely be necessary to show that the geographical distribution of the species is much wider than was formerly supposed.

The old song of "The Chough and Crow" will probably be remembered as long as the English language lasts.

Shakespeare has introduced both these birds in a fine description of Dover Cliff. It is not improbable that the chough, which affects precipices and sea-cliffs, may once have frequented the cliffs at Dover; but whatever may have been the case formerly, this haunt, if it ever was one, has long since been deserted. Shakespeare, at all events, has placed this bird in a situation most natural to it :—

"Come on, sir; here's the place :—stand still.—How fearful
And dizzy 't is, to cast one's eyes so low!
The *crows* and *choughs*, that wing the midway air,
Show scarce so gross as beetles : half way down
Hangs one that gathers samphire,—dreadful trade !
Methinks he seems no bigger than his head :
The fishermen, that walk upon the beach,
Appear like mice ; and yond tall anchoring bark,
Diminish'd to her cock ; her cock, a buoy
Almost too small for sight : the murmuring surge,
That on the unnumber'd idle pebbles chafes,
Cannot be heard so high.—I 'll look no more,

Lest my brain turn, and the deficient sight
Topple down headlong."

King Lear, Act iv. Sc. 6.

The chough is easily tamed, and a prettier sight than three or four of these birds, with their bright red legs and bills, strutting about on a well-mown lawn, can scarcely be conceived.

It is to be regretted that the species is not more plentiful and more generally domesticated.

Instances, we believe, are on record of choughs being taught to speak, but Shakespeare appears to have entertained no great opinion of their talking powers. He speaks of

"Chough's language, gabble enough, and good enough."

All's Well that Ends Well, Act iv. Sc. 1.

And probably there was a good deal more chattering than talking, as we understand the term.

"There be . . .   .
. . . lords that can prate
As amply and unnecessarily
As this Gonzalo; I myself could make
A chough of as deep chat."

Tempest, Act ii. Sc. 1.

In *Henry IV.*, in the scene where Falstaff, with the

Prince and Poins, meet to rob the travellers at Gadshill, Falstaff calls the victims "fat chuffs," probably from their strutting about with much noise.

In the *Winter's Tale*, the rogue Autolycus appears as a pedlar, and while drawing the attention of those around him to his wares, he takes the opportunity to pick their pockets. His power of persuasion was so great that, as he himself said,—

"They throng who should buy first, as if my trinkets had been hallowed, and brought a benediction to the buyer: by which means I saw whose purse was best in picture; and what I saw, to my good use I remembered."

He proceeds to compare them to choughs whom he had allured by his chaff, and says :—

"In this time of lethargy, I picked and cut most of their festive purses; and had not the old man come in with a whoobub against his daughter and the king's son, and scared my choughs from the chaff, I had not left a purse alive in the whole army."—*Winter's Tale*, Act iv. Sc. 3.

The word "chough," it appears, was not always intended to refer to the bird with red legs and bill, as we may infer from the following passage in O'Flaherty's "West or H'Iar Connaught, 1684," p. 13 :—" I omit other ordinary fowl and birds, as bernacles, wild geese, swans, cocks-of-the-wood, woodcocks, *choughs*, rooks, *Cornish choughs, with red legs and bills*," &c. Here the first-mentioned choughs were in all probability jackdaws.

Shakespeare alludes to—

"Russet-pated choughs, many in sort,
Rising and cawing at the gun's report."
Midsummer Night's Dream, Act iii. Sc. 2.

Now the jackdaw, though having a grey head, would more appropriately bear the designation of "russet-pated" than any of his congeners. We may presume, therefore, that this is the species to which Shakespeare intended to refer. The head of the chough, like the rest of its body, is perfectly black.

The Jackdaw (*Corvus monedula*) has not been so frequently noticed by Shakespeare as many other birds, and in the half-dozen instances in which it is mentioned, we find it referred to as the "daw." The word occurs in *Coriolanus*, Act iv. Sc. 5; *Troilus and Cressida*, Act i. Sc. 2; *Much Ado about Nothing*, Act ii. Sc. 3; *Twelfth Night*, Act iii. Sc. 4; and in a song in *Love's Labour's Lost*. Warwick, expressing his ignorance of legal matters, says:—

"But in these nice sharp quillets of the law,
Good faith, I am no wiser than a daw."
Henry VI. Part I. Act ii. Sc. 4.

And the crafty and dissembling Iago remarks that—

> "When my outward action doth demonstrate
> The native act and figure of my heart
> In compliment extern, 'tis not long after
> But I will wear my heart upon my sleeve
> For daws to peck at."
>
> *Othello*, Act i. Sc. 1.

With the ancients, much superstition prevailed in regard to various species of the crow family; and Shakespeare has specially mentioned three of these as birds of omen:—

> "Augurs that understood relations have,
> By magot-pies, and choughs, and rooks, brought forth
> The secret'st man of blood."
>
> *Macbeth*, Act iii. Sc. 4.

Even at the present day, there are many who profess to augur good or evil from the flight of a magpie, or from the number of magpies seen together at one time. An old rhyme on the subject runs thus:—

> "One for sorrow, two for mirth;
> Three for a wedding, four for a birth."

The origin of the word magpie we have not heard explained, but it is possible, from the manner in which the name is spelled above, that "mag" may be an abbreviation of "maggot," pointing to a certain propensity of the bird, which, however, is not peculiar. Those who have spent much time in the country, must have observed not only the magpie, but also the jackdaw and starling, busily engaged in searching for insects on the back of a sheep.

As in the case of the jackdaw, the magpie is sometimes called by the latter half of his name :—

"And chattering pies in dismal discords sung."

Henry VI. Part III. Act v. Sc. 6.

Before taking leave of the crow family, we have yet to notice another bird mentioned by Shakespeare, which is nearly related to the crow. This is the Rook (*Corvus frugilegus*). But, notwithstanding the usefulness of the bird, the poet has not said much in its favour. It is noticed in the song in *Love's Labour's Lost*, and is included amongst the birds of omen in the quotation lately given from *Macbeth*.

In the *Merry Wives of Windsor*, Act i. Sc. 3, we find the expression "bully-rook," and it would seem that this epithet in Shakespeare's time bore much the same signification as "jolly-dog" does now-a-days. But it came subsequently to have a more offensive meaning, and was applied to a cheat and a sharper.

We had well-nigh forgotten the Jay (*Corvus glandarius*), —*Winter's Tale* (Act iv. Sc. 3),—and only allude to it now to show that Shakespeare has not omitted it from his long list of birds. In *Cymbeline*, the name is applied to a gaudily-dressed person :—

"Some jay of Italy hath betray'd him."

Cymbeline, Act iii. Sc. 4.

No doubt on account of the bright plumage of this bird.

"What, is the jay more precious than the lark,
Because his feathers are more beautiful?"

Taming of the Shrew, Act iv. Sc. 3.

Caliban, addressing Trinculo, in *The Tempest* (Act ii. Sc. 2), exclaims:—

"I pr'ythee let me bring thee where crabs grow,
And I with my long nails will dig thee pig-nuts;
Show thee a jay's nest, and instruct thee how
To snare the nimble marmozet; I'll bring thee
To clust'ring filberds, and sometimes I'll get thee
Young sea-mells from the rock. Wilt thou go with me?"

This tempting offer is irresistible, and Stephano interrupts him at once by saying,—

"I pr'ythee now, lead the way, without any more talking."

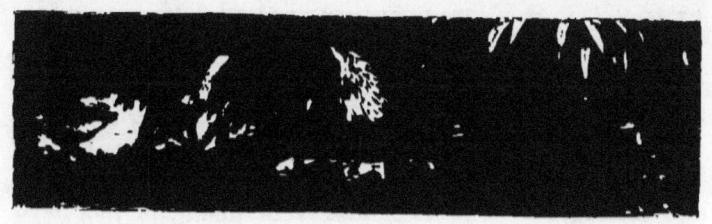

CHAPTER V.

THE BIRDS OF SONG.

IF there is one class of birds more than another to which poets in all ages have been indebted for inspiration, and to which they have directed particular attention, it is that which includes the birds of song. Shakespeare, as a naturalist, could not have overlooked them. Nor has he done so. These "light-wing'd Dryads of the trees" have received at his hands all the praise which they deserve, while oftentimes, for melody and pathos, he may be said to have borrowed from their songs himself.

Of all the singers in the woodland choir the Nightingale (*Luscinia philomela*), by common consent, stands first. For quality of voice, variety of notes, and execution, she is probably unrivalled. Hence, with poets, she has ever been the chief favourite. Izaak Walton has truly said, "The nightingale breathes such sweet loud music out of her little instrumental throat, that it might make mankind to think miracles are not ceased. He that at midnight, when the very labourer sleeps securely, should hear, as I have very often, the clear airs, the sweet descants, the natural rising and falling, the doubling and redoubling, of her voice, might well be lifted above earth and say, Lord, what music hast thou provided for the saints in heaven, when thou affordest bad men such music on earth?" To "sing like a nightingale" has passed into a proverb.

"She sings as sweetly as any nightingale."
Taming of the Shrew, Act ii. Sc. 1.

In Gardiner's "Music of Nature," the following passage is given from the song of the Nightingale:—

Although the male bird only is the songster, yet we talk of *her* singing:—

"It was the nightingale, and not the lark,
That pierc'd the fearful hollow of thine ear;
Nightly *she* sings on yon pomegranate tree;*
Believe me, love, it was the nightingale.
Romeo and Juliet, Act iii. Sc. 5.

The origin of this change of sex is to be found, no

---

* According to Steevens, this is not merely a poetical supposition. "It is observed," he says, "of the nightingale that, if undisturbed, she sits and sings upon the same tree for many weeks together;" and Russell, in his "Account of Aleppo," tells us "the nightingale sings from the pomegranate groves in the day-time."

doubt, in the old fable which tells us of the transformation of Philomela, daughter of Pandion, King of Athens, into a nightingale, when Progne, her sister, was changed to a swallow.*

Hence also the name Philomel, which is often applied by the poets to this bird.

> " Philomel, with melody,
> Sing your sweet lullaby."
> *Song—Midsummer Night's Dream*, Act ii. Sc. 2.

> " By this, lamenting Philomel had ended
> The well-tun'd warble of her nightly sorrow."
> *Lucrece.*

> " His Philomel must lose her tongue to-day."
> *Titus Andronicus*, Act ii. Sc. 3.

The nightingale is again thus designated by Shakespeare in *Cymbeline*, Act ii. Sc. 2, and elsewhere; and "the tragic tale of Philomel" is prettily referred to in *Titus Andronicus*, Act iv. Sc. 1.

In one, if not more, of his poems he has noticed the odd belief which formerly existed to the effect that the mournful notes of the nightingale are caused by the bird's leaning against a thorn to sing!

> " Every thing did banish moan,
> Save the nightingale alone.

* "Ovid. Metamorph." Book vi. Fab. 6.

> She, poor bird, as all forlorn,
> *Lean'd her breast up-till a thorn,*
> And there sung the dolefull'st ditty,
> That to hear it was great pity.
> 'Fie, fie, fie,' now would she cry,
> 'Tereu, tereu!' by and by;
> That, to hear her so complain,
> Scarce I could from tears refrain;
> For her griefs, so lively shown,
> Made me think upon mine own." *
>
> *The Passionate Pilgrim*, xix.

Again, Lucrece, in her distress, invoking Philomel, says:—

> " And whiles against a thorn thou bear'st thy part,
> To keep thy sharp woes waking."—*Lucrece.*

The same idea, too, has been variously expressed by other poets than Shakespeare. Fletcher speaks of—

> " The bird forlorn
> That singeth with her breast against a thorn;"

and Pomfret, writing towards the close of the seventeenth century, says:—

> " The first music of the grove we owe
> To mourning Philomel's harmonious woe;

---

* 'These lines, although included in most editions of Shakespeare's Poems, are said to have been written by Richard Barnefield, and published in 1598 in a volume entitled "Poems in Divers Humors." (*See* Ellis's "Specimens of the Early English Poets," vol. ii. p. 356, and F. T. Palgrave's "Golden Treasury of the Best Songs and Lyrical Poems in the English Language," p. 21.) The "Passionate Pilgrim" was not published until 1599.

> And while her grief in charming notes express'd,
> A thorny bramble pricks her tender breast.
> In warbling melody she spends the night,
> And moves at once compassion and delight."

Thus it was evidently believed by the poets, whether the idea was founded on fact or not, that the nightingale leaned her breast against a thorn when she gave forth her mournful notes. The origin of such a belief it is not easy to ascertain, but we suspect Sir Thomas Browne was not far from the truth when he pointed to the fact that the nightingale frequents thorny copses, and builds her nest amongst brambles on the ground. He inquires "whether it be any more than that she placeth some prickles on the outside of her nest, or roosteth in thorny, prickly places, where serpents may least approach her?"* In an article upon this subject, published in "The Zoologist," for 1862, p. 8,029, the Rev. A. C. Smith has narrated "the discovery, on two occasions, of a strong thorn projecting upwards in the centre of the nightingale's nest." It can hardly be doubted, however, that this was the result of accident rather than design; and Mr. Hewitson, in his "Eggs of British Birds," has adduced two similar instances in the case of the hedge-sparrow. We may accordingly dismiss the idea that there is any real foundation for such belief, and regard it as a poetic license.

* "Sir Thomas Browne's Works" (Wilkin's ed.), Vol. II. p. 537.

There is no doubt that one great charm in the song of the nightingale is, that it is heard oftenest at eve, when nearly every other bird is hushed and gone to roost. We are thus enabled to pay more attention to it, and hear the entire song. This evidently was Milton's idea when he wrote, in " Il Penseroso :"—

> " Sweet bird that shunn'st the noise of folly,
> Most musical, most melancholy!
> Thee, chauntress, oft the woods among,
> I woo, to hear thy evening song."

Portia says, in *The Merchant of Venice*, Act v. Sc. 1,—

> " I think,
> The nightingale, if she should sing by day,
> When every goose is cackling, would be thought
> No better a musician than the wren."

But although she is usually supposed to withhold her notes until sunset, and then to be the only songstress left, she in reality sings in the day often as sweetly and as powerfully as at night, but, amidst the general chorus of other birds, her efforts are less noticed.* Valentine declares that—

> " Except I be by Sylvia in the night,
> There is no music in the nightingale."
>
> *Two Gentlemen of Verona*, Act iii. Sc. 1.

* Not only does the nightingale sing by day, but she is by no means the only bird which sings at night. We have frequently listened with delight to the wood lark, skylark, thrush, sedge-warbler and grasshopper-warbler long after sunset, and we have heard the cuckoo and corncrake at midnight.

And later on—

> " How use doth breed a habit in a man !
> This shadowy desert, unfrequented woods,
> I better brook than flourishing peopled towns :
> Here can I sit alone, unseen of any,
> And to the nightingale's complaining notes
> Tune my distresses and record my woes."
>
> <div align="right"><i>Id.</i> Act v. Sc. 4.</div>

The word "record" here, refers to the singing of birds, and, according to Douce, is derived from the recorder, a sort of flute, by which they were taught to sing.*

The "recording" of young birds is indeed always very different from their song, as is also the warble of old birds after moulting, as Herr Bechstein has justly remarked. " It is," he says, " a very striking circumstance, that birds which continue in song nearly the whole year, such as the redbreast, the siskin, and the goldfinch, are obliged, after their moulting is over, to record, as if they had forgotten their song. I am convinced, however, that this exercise is less a study than an endeavour to bring the organs of voice into proper flexibility, what they utter being properly only a sort of warble, the notes of which have scarcely any resemblance to the perfect song ; and by a little attention we may perceive how the throat is gradually brought to emit the notes of the usual song. This view,

---

* The "recorder" is mentioned in *Midsummer Night's Dream*, Act v. Sc. 1, and in *Hamlet*, Act iii. Sc. 2.

then, leads us to ascribe the circumstance, not to defect of memory, but rather to a roughness in the vocal organs, arising from disuse. It is in this way that the chaffinch makes endeavours during several successive weeks before attaining to its former perfection, and the nightingale tries for a long time to model the strophes of its superb song, before it can produce the full extent of compass and brilliancy." *

The nightingale has not more happily inspired our poets than the Lark (*Alauda arvensis*). Chaucer, Spenser, Milton, Shelley, and Wordsworth have all sung the praises of this famed songster ; while Shakespeare, in undying verse, has paid many a tribute to "the blythesome bird." Let us, then,

" Leave to the nightingale her shady wood,"

and turn our attention to—

" The lark, that tirra-lirra chants."

Winter's Tale, Act iv. Sc. 2.

This "tirra-lirra" with the other notes of the bird is well illustrated in the following lines :—

" La gentille alouette avec son tire-lire,
Tire-lire, à lire, et tirelirau, tire
Vers la voûte du ciel, puis son vol vers ce lieu
Vire, et désire dire adieu Dieu, adieu Dieu."

As the nightingale is called the "bird of eve," so has the

---

* Bechstein "Ornithologisches Taschenbuch."

lark been named the "bird of dawn." Shakespeare has made frequent allusion to the early rising of the lark :—

"I do hear the morning lark."
Midsummer Night's Dream, Act iv. Sc. 1.

"It was the lark, the herald of the morn."
Romeo and Juliet, Act iii. Sc. 5.

"The busy day,
Wak'd by the lark, hath rous'd the ribald crows."
Troilus and Cressida, Act iv. Sc. 2.

"Lo, here the gentle lark, weary of rest,
From his moist cabinet mounts up on high,
And wakes the morning, from whose silver breast
The sun ariseth in his majesty."
Venus and Adonis.

Milton's allusion to the early singing of this bird will be familiar to all :—

"To hear the lark begin his flight,
And, singing, startle the dull night,
From his watch-tower in the skies,
Till the dappled dawn doth rise."
L'Allegro.

While every musician must remember the song in *Cymbeline*, adapted to music since Shakespeare's day by an eminent composer :—

> "Hark! hark! the lark at heaven's gate sings,
>   And Phœbus 'gins arise,
> His steeds to water at those springs
>   On chalic'd flowers that lies;
> And winking Mary-buds begin
>   To ope their golden eyes;
> With everything that pretty is,
>   My lady sweet, arise:
>   Arise, arise.
>   *Cymbeline*, Act ii. Sc. 3

The notion of singing "at heaven's gate" has been again introduced by Shakespeare in one of his Sonnets:—

> "Like to the lark, at break of day arising
> From sullen earth, sings hymns *at heaven's gate.*"

While the same idea, coupled with the mention of Phœbus, has been expressed by earlier poets. Chaucer, in his "Knightes Tale," says:—

> "The busy larke, messager of daye,
> Salueth in hire song the morwe gray:
> And fyry Phebus ryseth up so bright,
> That al the orient laugheth of the light."

So also, Spenser, in his "Epithalamion," 1595:—

> "Hark how the cheerefull birds do chaunt theyr laies,
>   And carroll of loves praise.
> The merry larke hir mattins sings aloft,
> The thrush replyes, the mavis descant playes, .

>   The ouzell shrills, the ruddock warbles soft,
>   So goodly all agree with sweet consent,
>   To this dayes merriment."

And Milton, in the " Paradise Lost," Book v., has—

> " Ye birds
> That, singing, *up to heaven's gate* ascend."

The "rising of the lark" and the "lodging of the lamb" have become synonymous with "morn" and "eve," (*Henry V.* Act iii. Sc. 7); and he that would rise early is counselled to " stir with the lark " (*Richard III.* Act v. Sc. 3).

With the labourer whose avocation takes him across the fields at early dawn, the lark is always an especial favourite; and Shakespeare would have it furnish some indication of the time of day :—

> " When shepherds pipe on oaten straws,
>   And merry larks are ploughmen's clocks."
>   *Song—Love's Labour's Lost.*

Again—

> "O happy fair!
> Your eyes are lode-stars, and your tongue's sweet air
> More tuneable than lark to shepherd's ear,
> When wheat is green, when hawthorn buds appear."
>   *Midsummer Night's Dream*, Act i. Sc. 1.

When Juliet spoke disparagingly of the lark's song, it was because she wished the night prolonged, and knew that his voice betokened the approach of day :—

> "It is the lark that sings so out of tune,
>   Straining harsh discords, and unpleasing sharps.
>
>   .   .   .   .
>
>   Some say the lark and loathed toad change eyes;
>   O, now I would they had changed voices too!
>   Since arm from arm that voice doth us affray."
>
>   *Romeo and Juliet*, Act iii. Sc. 5.

The lark has ugly eyes, and the toad very fine ones; hence arose the saying that the lark and toad changed eyes. Juliet wished they had changed voices too; for then, as Heath has suggested, the croak of the toad would have been no indication of the day's approach, and consequently no signal for Romeo's departure.

To the naturalist who walks abroad at early dawn, there are few sights more pleasing than the soaring of a lark. As the first ray of sunshine dispels the glistening dew-drop and gently falls to earth, the lark, warmed by its soft touch, mounts high in air, and joyfully proclaims to all the advent of a new day. What glee is expressed in the song of that small brown bird, which, as it soars towards heaven and sings, teaches us the first duty of the day—gratitude to our Creator!

> " Higher still and higher
>   From the earth thou springest,
>   Like a cloud of fire ;
>   The blue deep thou wingest,
>   And singing still dost soar, and soaring ever singest.

> What thou art we know not ;
> What is most like thee ?
> From rainbow clouds there flow not
> Drops so bright to see
> As from thy presence showers a rain of melody." *

The bird which could inspire such thoughts as these is indeed noteworthy, and that poets in all ages have singled it out as an especial favourite, can be no matter of surprise.

Who does not remember those beautiful lines of Wordsworth?—

> " Leave to the nightingale her shady wood ;
>   A privacy of glorious light is thine,
> Whence thou dost pour upon the world a flood
>   Of harmony, with instinct more divine ;
> Type of the wise, who soar but never roam—
> True to the kindred points of Heaven and Home!"

But to return to Shakespeare. Perhaps no bird has received more notice at his hands than the one now under consideration. To enumerate all the passages in which it is mentioned, would probably only weary the reader. In addition to those already named, "the shrill-gorg'd lark" is alluded to in *King Lear* (Act iv. Sc. 6); while to sing "as sweetly as the lark" has passed into a proverb (*Merchant of Venice*, Act v. Sc. 1).

* Shelley.

Mention is made of this bird in *Titus Andronicus* (Act ii. Sc. 3, and Act iii. Sc. 1); in *Cymbeline* (Act iii. Sc. 6); and in *Richard II.* (Act iii. Sc. 3).

Formerly, a curious method of taking larks was practised by means of small pieces of looking-glass and red cloth. These were made to move at a little distance from the fowler by means of a string, and when the birds, impelled by curiosity, came within range, they were taken in a net. This practice is referred to by Shakespeare in *Henry VIII.*—

"Let his grace go forward,
And dare us with his cap, like larks."
Henry VIII. Act iii. Sc. 2.

The cap in this case was the scarlet hat of the Cardinal, which it was intended to use as a piece of red cloth. It seems probable, from the context, that the word "dare" should be "draw."

A bird which is often taken with larks, and which, indeed, is not unlike one in appearance, is the Common Bunting (*Emberiza miliaria*). In some parts of the country it is known as the Bunting-Lark, and, from its size and general colouring, a casual observer might easily mistake it for one of the last-named species. No wonder, then, that the old lord Lafeu says:—

"I took this lark for a bunting."
All's Well that Ends Well, Act ii. Sc. 5.

It is somewhat singular that the Thrush (*Turdus musicus*), a bird as much famed for song as either the nightingale or the lark, has been so little noticed by Shakespeare. We have failed to discover more than three passages in the entire works of our great poet in which this well-known bird is mentioned. It is referred to once in *A Winter's Tale* (Act iv. Sc. 2); once in *Midsummer Night's Dream*, Act iii. Sc. 1, where Bottom the weaver, in a doggrel rhyme, sings of—

"The throstle, with his note so true;"

and once again in *The Merchant of Venice* (Act i. Sc. 2), where Portia, speaking of the French Lord Le Bon, and alluding to his national propensity for a dance on every available opportunity, remarks that—

"If a throstle sing, he falls straight a-capering."

Many naturalists, who have paid particular attention to the song of the thrush, have insisted upon its taking equal rank as a songster with the more favoured nightingale. Certain it is, that the notes of this bird, although not so varied, nor so liquid, so to say, as those of Philomel, are yet of a clear, rich tone, and have something indescribably sweet about them. "Listen," says Macgillivray, "to the clear, loud notes of that speckled warbler, that in the softened sunshine pours forth his wild melodies on the gladdened ear. What does it resemble?

> "Dear, dear, dear
>   Is the rocky glen;
> Far away, far away, far away
>   The haunts of men.
> Here shall we dwell in love,
> With the lark and the dove,
> Cuckoo and corn-rail,
> Feast on the banded snail,
>   Worm and gilded fly:
> Drink of the crystal rill
> Winding adown the hill,
>   Never to dry.
>
> With glee, with glee, with glee,
>   Cheer up, cheer up, cheer up, here
> Nothing to harm us, then sing merrily,
>   Sing to the lov'd ones whose nest is near.
>   Qui, qui, qui, kweeu, quip,
>   Tiurru, tiurru, chipiwi.
>   Too-tee, too-tee, chiu choo,
>   Chirri, chirri, chooee,
>   Quiu, qui, qui."

It must be admitted by all who have paid particular attention to the song of the thrush, that this is a wonderful imitation, so far as words can express notes. The first four lines, lines 7, 13, and 14, and the last five lines in particular, approach remarkably close in sound to the original; and this is rendered the more apparent if we endeavour to pronounce the words by whistling.

Intimately associated with the thrush is its congener the Blackbird (*Turdus merula*). Both visitors to our lawns and shrubberies, they remind us of their presence, when we do not see them, by their sweet, clear notes, and when the cold of winter has made them silent, we are still charmed with their sprightly actions, and the beauty of their plumage.

The attractive appearance of the blackbird was not overlooked by Shakespeare, who has mentioned him in one of his songs:—

"The ouzel-cock, so black of hue,
With orange-tawny bill."
Midsummer Night's Dream, Act iii. Sc. 1.

When Justice Shallow inquires of Justice Silence, "And how doth my cousin?" he is answered—

"Alas, a black ouzel, Cousin Shallow."
King Henry IV. Part II. Act iii. Sc. 2;

an expression which was probably equivalent to the modern phrase, a "black sheep."

Amongst the songsters of less note mentioned by Shakespeare, are the Robin-redbreast (*Erythaca rubecula*) and the Wren (*Troglodytes vulgaris*). These two birds have for centuries, from some unexplained cause, been always associated together. The country people, in many parts of England, still regard them as the male and female of one species, and support their assertion with an old couplet—

> "The robin-redbreast and the wren
> Are God Almighty's cock and hen."

In these days, when so much more attention is paid to ornithology than formerly, it will be hardly necessary to observe that the two birds thus associated together are not only of very distinct species, but belong to widely different genera.

An old name for the redbreast is "ruddock"* the meaning of which is illustrated in the word "ruddy;" and the bird is still known by this name in some parts of England.

Shakespeare has thus named it in one of his most beautiful passages :—

> "With fairest flowers
> Whilst summer lasts, and I live here, Fidele,
> I'll sweeten thy sad grave : thou shalt not lack
> The flower that's like thy face, pale primrose, nor
> The azur'd hare-bell, like thy veins ; no, nor
> The leaf of eglantine, whom not to slander,

---

* "The ruddock warbles soft."—SPENSER'S *Epithalamium*, l. 82.

Out-sweeten'd not thy breath: the *ruddock* would,
With charitable bill,—O, bill, sore-shaming
Those rich-left heirs that let their fathers lie
Without a monument!—bring thee all this;
Yea, and furr'd moss besides, when flowers are none,
To winter-ground thy corse."*

Cymbeline, Act iv. Sc. 2.

Bishop Percy asks, " Is this an allusion to the 'Babes in the Wood,' or was the notion of the redbreast covering dead bodies general before the writing of that ballad?" Mr. Knight says, " There is no doubt that it was an old popular belief, and the notion has been found in an earlier book of natural history." John Webster, writing in 1638, says:

" Call for the robin-redbreast and the wren,
   Since o'er shady groves they hover,
   And with leaves and flowers do cover
The friendless bodies of unburied men."

Izaak Walton, in his " Compleat Angler," 1653, speaks of "the honest robin that loves mankind, *both alive and dead.*" Possibly Shakespeare intended only to refer to the ancient and beautiful custom of strewing the grave with flowers.

With all birds it is the habit of the male to sing while

---

* Instead of "winter-ground" in the last line, Mr. Collier's annotator reads "winter-guard;" but "to winter-ground" appears to have been a technical term for protecting a plant from the frost by laying straw or hay over it.

courting the female. So, when Valentine asks Speed, "How know you that I am in love?" he gives, amongst other reasons, that he had learnt "to relish a love-song like a robin-redbreast."—*Two Gentlemen of Verona*, Act ii. Sc. 1.

The meaning of the following dialogue does not seem quite clear :—

"*Hotspur.* Come, sing.

Lady Percy. I will not sing.

Hotspur. 'Tis the next way to turn tailor *or be redbreast teacher.*"

Henry IV. Part I. Act iii. Sc. 1.

Possibly the allusion may be to the " recorder," by which instrument birds were taught to sing.* Hotspur pays a high compliment to the vocal powers of Lady Percy by insinuating that her voice would excel the recorder; and as the bird most frequently taught to pipe is the bullfinch, it is not improbable that this was the bird intended under the title of " redbreast," and not the robin.

Intimately associated with the robin, as we have before remarked, is—

" The wren, with little quill."

Midsummer Night's Dream—Song.

It must often have struck others, as it has us, that for so small a throat, the wren has a wonderfully loud song.

* See *ante*, p. 129.

There is not much variety or tone in it, but the notes at once attract attention, and would lead any one unacquainted with them to inquire the author's name.

Portia evidently had no high opinion of the wren's song, when she said,—

> " The crow doth sing as sweetly as the lark,
> When neither is attended ; and, I think,
> The nightingale, if she should sing by day,
> When every goose is cackling, would be thought
> No better a musician than the wren."
> *Merchant of Venice*, Act v. Sc. 1.

Lady Macduff was reminded of the wren when bewailing the flight of her husband.

> "*Lady M.* His flight was madness.
> *Ross.*   You know not
> Whether it was his wisdom or his fear.
> *Lady M.* Wisdom! to leave his wife, to leave his babes,
> His mansion, and his titles, in a place
> From whence himself does fly? He loves us not ;
> He wants the natural touch : for the poor wren,
> The most diminutive of birds, will fight,
> Her young ones in her nest, against the owl."
> *Macbeth*, Act iv. Sc. 2.

There are three statements here which are likely to be

criticised by the ornithologist. First, that the wren is the smallest of birds, which is evidently an oversight. Secondly, that the wren has sufficient courage to fight against a bird of prey in defence of its young, which is doubtful. Thirdly, that the owl will take young birds from the nest. As to this last point, see *ante*, pp. 91-94.

Imogen has made mention of the wren, as follows :—

> " I tremble still with fear : but if there be
> Yet left in heaven as small a drop of pity
> As a wren's eye, fear'd gods, a part of it."
>
> *Cymbeline*, Act iv. Sc. 2.

And allusions to this little bird will be found in *Twelfth Night*, Act iii. Sc. 2; *Richard III*. Act i. Sc. 3; *King Lear*, Act iv. Sc. 6; *Pericles*, Act iv. Sc. 3; and *Henry VI.* Part II. Act iii. Sc. 2.

"The Finch" is only once mentioned, *i. e.* in a song in *Midsummer Night's Dream*, Act iii. Sc. 1. In *Troilus and Cressida*, however, when Thersites and Patroclus are abusing each other (Act v. Sc. 1), the former calls the latter "finch-egg." But what species of Finch the poet had in view, it is not easy to determine. It may have been the Bullfinch, but it is more likely to have been the Chaffinch, which has always been a favourite cage-bird with the lower classes.

The Hedge-sparrow (*Accentor modularis*), a frequenter of the same haunts, has been more frequently noticed by

Shakespeare than the wren. In many passages throughout the Plays mention is made of "the sparrow" without the prefix "hedge" or "house." Occasionally we are enabled, from the context, to determine the species; but as this is not always the case, we propose to consider under one head all that Shakespeare has said of either species.

The sparrow appears to have been early known by the name of "Philip," perhaps from its note, to which Catullus alludes:—

"Sed circumsiliens, modo huc, modo illuc,
   Ad solam dominum usque *pipilabat.*"

In Lyly's "Mother Bombie,"
"Cry
Phip, phip, the sparrows as they fly."
And Skelton, the Poet Laureate of Henry VIII.'s reign, wrote a long poem entitled "Phylyppe Sparrow," on the death of a pet bird of this species. Shakespeare thus names it in *King John* (Act i. Sc. 1):—

"*Gurney.* Good leave, good Philip.

Bastard. Philip! sparrow!"

We are told of Cressida, when getting ready to meet her lover, that—

"She fetches her breath so short as a new-ta'en sparrow."
Troilus and Cressida, Act iii. Sc. 2.

Lucio, referring to Angelo, the severe Deputy Duke of Vienna, says:—

"This ungenitured agent will unpeople the province with continency; sparrows must not build in his house, because they are lecherous."—*Measure for Measure*, Act iii. Sc. 2.

Iris tells us that Cupid—

"Swears he will shoot no more, but play with sparrows,
And be a boy right out."
Tempest, Act iv. Sc. 1.

In *Troilus and Cressida*, as well as in *Hamlet*, are passages in which it is evident the poet had in his mind the words of Matthew x. 29 :—

"Are not two sparrows sold for a farthing? And one of them shall not fall on the ground without your Father."

"I will buy nine sparrows for a penny, and his pia mater is not worth the ninth part of a penny."—*Troilus and Cressida*, Act ii. Sc. 1.

"There's a special providence in the fall of a sparrow."
Hamlet, Act v. Sc. 2.

Again, in the following lines, there is an evident allusion to Psalm cxlvii. 9 ("He feedeth the young ravens that call upon him") :—

"And He that doth the ravens feed,
Yea, providently caters for the sparrow,
Be comfort to my age!"
As You Like It, Act ii. Sc. 3.

In *Macbeth* (Act i. Sc. 2), and *Midsummer Night's Dream* (Act iii. Sc. 1), the sparrow is mentioned; and the following passage in *Henry IV.* will doubtless be remembered by all readers of Shakespeare's Plays:—

"*Falstaff.* "That sprightly Scot of Scots, Douglas, that runs o' horseback up a hill perpendicular.

P. Henry. He that rides at high speed, and with his pistol kills a sparrow flying.

Falstaff. You have hit it.

P. Henry. So did he never the sparrow."—*Henry IV.* Part I. Act ii. Sc. 4.

The Fool in *King Lear* reminds us that it is in the hedge-sparrow's nest that the Cuckoo (*Cuculus canorus*) frequently deposits her egg:—

"For you know, nuncle, the hedge-sparrow fed the cuckoo so long, that it had its head bit off by its young."—*King Lear*, Act i. Sc. 4.

Mr. Guest, in adopting the reading of the first folio, observes (*Phil. Pro.*, i. 280) that "in the dialects of the North-western counties, formerly *it* was sometimes used for *its*. So in the passage just quoted we have 'For you know,' &c., 'that *its* had *it* head bit off by *it* young;' that is, that it *has had* its head, not that it *had* its head, as the modern editors give the passage, after the second folio."

" So likewise, long before *its* was generally received, we have *it self* commonly printed in two words, evidently under the impression that *it* was a possessive of the same syntactical force with the pronouns in my self, your self, her self."*

So in *Timon of Athens* (Act v. Sc. 1), we have—

"The public body . . .
. . . . . feeling in itself
A lack of Timon's aid, hath sense withal
Of *it* own fall."

Again, in *Winter's Tale* (Act ii. Sc. 3) :—

"to *it* own protection."

And—

"The innocent milk in *it* most innocent mouth."

Winter's Tale, Act iii. Sc. 2.

The popular notion referred to by the poet in *King Lear*, is again mentioned by Worcester in *Henry IV.*—

"And, being fed by us, you us'd us so
As that ungentle gull, the *cuckoo's bird*,†
Useth the sparrow; did oppress our nest,
Grew by our feeding to so great a bulk,
That even our love durst not come near your sight,
For fear of swallowing."

Henry IV. Part I. Act v. Sc. 1.

---

* "The English of Shakespeare," by G. L. Craik.

† That is, the young cuckoo. The expression occurs again in *The Merry Wives of Windsor*, Act ii. Sc. 1 :—

"Take heed, ere summer comes, or cuckoo-birds do sing."

The ingratitude of the young cuckoo, which is said to turn out the young of its foster parent as soon as it is sufficiently strong, has given rise in France to the proverb "Ingrat comme un coucou."

The word "gull" above mentioned is usually applied to the person "gulled," *i.e.* beguiled. Here it must either mean the "guller," or it must have a special application to the voracity of the cuckoo, as the sea-gull is supposed to be so called from *gulo—ōnis*.

We gather from Decker's "English Villanies" that formerly the sharpers termed their gang a *warren*, and their simple victims *rabbit-suckers*, or *conies*. At other times their confederates were called *bird-catchers*, and their prey *gulls;* and hence it was common to say of any person who had been swindled or hoaxed, that he was *coney-catched*. or *gulled*.

"Why, 'tis a *gull*, a fool!"—*Henry V.* Act iii. Sc. 6.

In a subsequent chapter we shall have occasion to refer to various other passages in which the word *gull* is thus employed. But to return to the cuckoo, and its foster parent the hedge-sparrow:—

"Why should the worm intrude the maiden bud,
Or hateful cuckoos hatch in sparrows' nests?"—*Lucrece.*

The solution of this question is the more puzzling from the fact that this parasitical habit is not common to all species of the genus cuckoo. An American species builds a nest for itself, and hatches its own eggs.

The habits of our English bird must always be as much a marvel to us as its remarkable voice.

> " He knows me, as the blind man knows the cuckoo,
> By the bad voice."
> *Merchant of Venice*, Act v. Sc. 1.

> " The plain song cuckoo gray,
> Whose note full many a man doth mark,
> And dares not answer, nay—

for, indeed, who would set his wish to so foolish a bird? who would give a bird the lie, though he cry 'cuckoo' never so?"—*Midsummer Night's Dream*, Act iii. Sc. 1.

This passage always brings to our recollection those beautiful lines which Wordsworth addressed "To the Cuckoo," and which must be so well known to all.

The cuckoo, as long ago remarked by John Heywood,* begins to sing early in the season with the interval of a minor third; the bird then proceeds to a major third, next to a fourth, then a fifth, after which its voice breaks, without attaining a minor sixth. It may, therefore, be said to have done much for musical science, because from this bird has been derived the

---

* " Epigrams (Black Letter), 1587."

minor scale, the origin of which has puzzled so many; the cuckoo's couplet being the minor third sung downwards. Kircher, however,* gives it thus :—

In Gardiner's "Music of Nature" it is rendered as follows :—

A friend of Gilbert White's found upon trial that the note of the cuckoo varies in different individuals. About Selborne Wood he found they were mostly in D. He heard two sing together, the one in D, the other in D sharp, which made a very disagreeable duet. He afterwards heard one in D sharp, and about Wolmer Forest some in C.

Gungl, in his "Cuckoo Galop," gives the note of the cuckoo as B natural and G sharp. Dr. Arne, in his music to the cuckoo's song in *Love's Labour's Lost*, gives it as C natural and G.

And now "will you hear the dialogue that the two learned men have compiled in praise of the owl and the cuckoo? This side is Hiems, Winter; this Ver, the Spring; the one maintained by the owl, the other by the cuckoo.

"Ver, begin :—

* "Musurgia Universalis." 1650. p. 30.

I.

" When daisies pied,* and violets blue,
And lady-smocks† all silver white,
And cuckoo-buds‡ of yellow hue,
Do paint the meadows with delight ;
The cuckoo then, on every tree,
Mocks married men, for thus sings he,
Cuckoo ;
Cuckoo, cuckoo, O word of fear,
Unpleasing to a married ear.

* *Pied*, that is parti-coloured, of different hues. So in *The Merchant of Venice*, Act i. Sc. 3 :—

"That all the yeanlings (*i.e.* young lambs) which were streaked and *pied*."

And in *The Tempest*, Caliban, alluding to the parti-coloured dress which Trinculo, as a jester, wore, says :—

"What a *pied* ninny 's this."

Milton, in "L'allegro," speaks of "meadows trim with daisies *pied*."

† "Lady-smocks" (*Cardamine pratensis*), a common meadow plant appearing early in the spring, and bearing white flowers. Sir J. E. Smith says they cover the meadows as with linen bleaching, whence the name of "ladysmocks" is supposed to come. Some authors say it first flowers about Ladytide, or the Feast of the Annunciation, hence its name.

‡ Botanists are not agreed as to the particular plant intended by "cuckoo-buds." Miller, in his "Gardener's Dictionary," says the flower here alluded to is the *Ranunculus bulbosus*. One commentator on this passage has mistaken the *Lychnis flos cuculi*, or "cuckoo-flower" for "cuckoo-buds." Another writer says, "cuckoo-flower" must be wrong, and believes "cowslip-buds" the true reading, but this is clearly a mistake. Walley, the editor of Ben Jonson's Works, proposes to read "crocus-buds," which is likewise incorrect. Sidney Beisley, the author of "Shakespeare's Garden," thinks that Shakespeare referred to the lesser celandine, or pilewort (*Ranunculus ficaria*), as this flower appears early in Spring, and is in bloom at the same time as the other flowers named in the song.

II.

When shepherds pipe on oaten straws,
  And merry larks are ploughmen's clocks ;
When turtles tread, and rooks, and daws ;
  And maidens bleach their summer smocks ;
The cuckoo then, on every tree,
Mocks married men, for thus sings he,
    Cuckoo ;
Cuckoo, cuckoo, O word of fear,
Unpleasing to a married ear."

In the old copies the four first lines of the first stanza are arranged in couplets thus :—

" When daisies pied, and violets blue,
  And cuckoo-buds of yellow hue,
  And lady-smocks all silver white,
  Do paint the meadows with delight."

But, as in all the other stanzas the rhymes are alternate, this was most probably an error of the compositor. The transposition now generally adopted was first made by Theobald.

The notion which couples the name of the cuckoo with the character of the man whose wife is unfaithful to him, appears to have been derived from the Romans, and is first found in the middle ages in France, and in the countries of which the modern language is derived from the Latin. We are not aware that it existed originally amongst the Teutonic race, and we have doubtless received it from the Normans. The opinion that the cuckoo made no nest of its own, but laid its eggs in that of another bird, which brought up the young cuckoo to the detriment of its own offspring, was well-known to the ancients, and is mentioned by Aristotle and Pliny.

So in *Antony and Cleopatra* (Act ii. Sc. 6):—

> "Thou dost o'ercount me of my father's house;
> But since the cuckoo builds not for himself,
> Remain in't as thou may'st."

But the ancients more correctly gave the name of the bird, not to the husband of the faithless wife, but to her paramour, who might justly be supposed to be acting the part of the cuckoo. They gave the name of the bird in whose nest the cuckoo's eggs were usually deposited —"*curruca*"—to the husband. It is not quite clear how, in the passage from classic to mediæval, the application of the term was transferred to the husband.* In allusion to this are the following lines of Shakespeare:—

> "For I the ballad will repeat,
>   Which men full true will find;
> Your marriage comes by destiny,
>   Your cuckoo sings by kind."
>   *All's Well that Ends Well*, Act i. Sc. 3.

---

* See Chambers's "Book of Days," i. 531.

This would appear to be only a new version of an old proverb, for in "Grange's Garden," 4to, 1577, we have—

"Content yourself as well as I,
Let reason rule your minde,
As cuckoldes come by destinie,
So cuckowes sing by kinde."

If Shakespeare is to be believed, marriage is not the only thing that goes by destiny:—

"The ancient saying is no heresy,
Hanging and wiving goes by destiny."
Merchant of Venice, Act ii. Sc. 9.

King Henry IV., alluding to his predecessor, says:—

"So when he had occasion to be seen,
He was but as the cuckoo is in June,
Heard, not regarded."
Henry IV. Part I. Act iii. Sc. 2.

For in June the cuckoo has been in song for a month, and is therefore less noticed than on its first arrival in April, when listened to as the harbinger of Spring.

Apropos of the cuckoo's song, the following ballad is considered to be the earliest in the English language now extant. Its date is about the latter part of the reign of Henry III., and it affords a curious example of the alterations which our language has undergone since that time;

while the descriptions, which breathe of rural sights and sounds, show that nature has suffered no change :—

" Sumer is icumen in,	Summer is come in,
Lhudè sing cuccu;	Loud sing cuckoo;
Groweth sed and bloweth med,	The seed groweth and the mead bloweth,
And springeth the wdè nu;	And the wood shoots now;
Sing cuccu.	Sing cuckoo.
Awe bleteth after lamb,	The ewe bleats after the lamb,
Lhouth after calvè cu ;	The cow lows after the calf;
Bulluc sterteth, buckè verteth,	The bullock starts, the buck verts,
Murie sing cuccu;	Merrily sing cuckoo;
Cuccu, cuccu ;	Cuckoo, cuckoo ;
Wel singes thu cuccu,	Well singest thou cuckoo,
Ne swik thu naver nu."	Mayest thou never cease.

This song is preserved amongst the Harleian MSS., No. 978, and is remarkable for being accompanied with musical notes, and as being the oldest sample of English secular music.

The Wagtail (*Motacilla Yarrellii*) has no claim to be included amongst the birds of song, but as the latter are chiefly small birds, and as Shakespeare has only alluded to it once, we may be excused for introducing it in the present chapter.

In an opprobrious sense, the word "wagtail" would doubtless denote a pert, flippant fellow. Kent, in *King Lear* (Act ii. Sc. 2), says,—

"Spare my grey beard, you *wagtail!*"

In many parts of the country this bird is called "dishwasher," and the name appears to be of some antiquity. Turbervile, in his "Booke of Falconrie," 1575, speaking of the various kinds of animals and birds whose flesh is proper for hawks to feed on, says (p. 137),—"The flesh of these flesh-crowes (*i.e.* carrion crows), and of the wagtayles (or *dishwasher*, as we tearme them, in Latin called *Motacilla*), and the cormorant, is of euil nourishment and digestion."

While on the subject of small birds in general, and song birds in particular, it will be interesting to glance at the methods which were formerly practised for catching them. These methods were many and various in kind. Springes, gins, bat-fowling, bird-lime, bird-bolts, and birding-pieces are all mentioned by Shakespeare.

The "springe" and the "gin" we shall have occasion to notice later in our remarks upon the Woodcock, for which bird these snares were usually employed. The ancient practice of "bat-fowling," or "bat-folding," is noticed in "*The Tempest*," Act ii. Sc. 1 :—

"He would so, and then go *a bat-fowling.*"

In Markham's "Hunger's Prevention," 1600, are some curious directions on this subject, which afford a very good idea of the way in which this sport was practised formerly :—

"For the manner of bat-fowling, it may be used either with nettes or without nettes.

"If you vse it without nettes (which indeed is the most common of the two), you shall then proceed in this manner.

First, there shall be one to carry the cresset of fire * (as was showed for the *low-bell*), then a certaine number, as two, three, or foure (according to the greatness of your company), and these shall have poales bound with dry round wispes of hay, straw, or such like stuffe, or else bound with pieces of linkes or hurdes dipt in pitch, rosen, grease, or any such like matter that will blaze. Then another company shall be armed with long poales, very rough and bushy at the vpper endes, of which the willow, byrche, or long hazell are best, but indeede according as the country will afford, so you must be content to take.

" Thus being prepared, and comming into the bushy or rough grounde, where the haunts of byrdes are, you shall then first kindle some of your fiers, as halfe or a third part, according as your prouision is, and then with your other bushy and rough poales you shall beat the bushes, trees, and haunts of the birds, to enforce them to rise, which done you shall see the birds which are raysed, to flye and playe about the lights and flames of the fier, for it is their nature through their amazednesse and affright at the strangenes of the light and the extreame darknesse round about it, not to depart from it, but, as it were, almost to scorch their wings in the same : so that those whice haue the rough bushye poales may (at their pleasures) beat

---

* The "cresset-light" was a large lanthorn placed upon a long pole, and carried upon men's shoulders. (*See* Strutt's "Sports and Pastimes," Introduction.)

them down with the same and so take them. Thus you may spend as much of the night as is darke, for longer is not conuenient, and doubtlesse you shall find much pastime, and take great store of birds, and in this you shall obserue all the obseruations formerly treated of in the *Low-bell;* especially that of silence, until your lights be kindled, but then you may use your pleasure, for the noyse and the light when they are heard and seene afarre of, they make the byrdes sit the faster and surer.

"The byrdes which are commonly taken by this labour or exercise are, for the most part, the rookes, ring-doues, blackbirdes, throstles, feldyfares, linnets, bulfinches, and all other byrdes whatsouer that pearch or sit vpon small boughes or bushes."

The term "bat-fowling," however, had another signification in Shakespeare's day, and it may have been in this secondary sense that it is used in the last quotation. It was a slang word for a particular mode of cheating, just as other modes, in the same age, were known as "gull-groping," "sheep-shearing," "lime-twigging " " spoon-dropping," "stone-carrying," &c.

"Bat-fowling" was practised about dusk, when the rogue pretended to have dropped a ring or a jewel at the door of some well-furnished shop, and, going in, asked the apprentice of the house to light his candle to look for it. After some peering about, the bat-fowler would drop the candle, as if by accident.

"Now, I pray you, good young man," he would say, "do so much as light the candle again." While the boy was away the rogue plundered the shop, and having stole everything he could find, stole away himself.*

"Birdlime," which, as most people know, is made from the bark of the holly, has long been in use for taking small birds. Shakespeare makes frequent mention of it:—

" The bird that hath been *limed* in a bush,
With trembling wings misdoubteth every bush;
And I, the hapless mate to one sweet bird,
Have now the fatal object in my eye
Where my poor young was *lim'd*, was caught and kill'd."
Henry VI. Part III. Act v. Sc. 6.

A similar idea will be found in *Lucrece*:—

"Birds never *lim'd*, no secret bushes fear."

Again—

"They are *limed* with the twigs that threaten them."
All's Well that ends Well, Act iii. Sc. 5.

And—

"She's *limed*, I warrant you."
Much Ado, Act iii. Sc. 1.

Suffolk, speaking to Queen Margaret of Duke Humphrey's wife, says:—

* Thornbury, "Shakespeare's England," vol. i. p. 339.

> "Madam, myself have *lim'd* a bush for her,
> And plac'd a quire of such enticing birds,
> That she will light to listen to their lays,
> And never mount to trouble you again."
>
> *Henry VI.* Part II. Act i. Sc. 3.

And the Duchess of Gloucester, addressing her husband, warns him that—

> . . "York and impious Beaufort, that false priest,
> Have all *lim'd* bushes to betray thy wings,
> And, fly thou how thou cans't, they'll tangle thee."
>
> *Henry VI.* Part II. Act ii. Sc. 4.

Further allusions to the use of birdlime will be found in *Othello* (Act ii. Sc. 1), and *Twelfth Night* (Act iii. Sc. 4).

Now-a-days the practice is to set up a stuffed bird of the species required against a tree by means of a wire, and surround it with three or four other wires well smeared with birdlime, placing a live call-bird in a small dark cage at the foot of the tree to attract the attention of the wild birds. These latter, on hearing the notes of the captive, fly towards the spot, and deceived by the appearance of the stuffed specimen, perch close to it upon a limed wire and are caught, the owner of the snare generally coming out of ambush to take them before they have time to free themselves.

A simple and effective bird-trap was made as follows :—

Procure a square frame covered on one side with wire netting, as shown in the woodcut.

Tie each end of a pliant stick to two corners of the frame, to form a hoop. Cut a straight stick, forked at one end, and a shorter pliant stick.

Lift the front of the trap; place the forked stick in an upright position against the *outside* of the front, and also *outside* the hoop. Insert one end of pliant twig between fork and front, and after raising hoop about two inches, insert the other end of the twig, so as to rest against the hoop, and press *outwards*. This will hold the hoop up. A bird, on approaching the trap, hops on the hoop to get at the grain within it, when the hoop will go down with the weight and let go the twig, which being pliant flies out, and the fork (being only *outside* the front) of course falls, and so does the trap.

The "bird bolts" mentioned by Shakespeare in *Twelfth Night* (Act i. Sc. 5), *Love's Labour's Lost* (Act iv. Sc. 3), and *Much Ado about Nothing* (Act i. Sc. 1), were the "bolts," or "quarrels" as they were sometimes called, which were shot from the cross-bow, or "stone-bow," *Twelfth Night* (Act ii. Sc. 5). The latter was simply a cross-bow made for propelling stones or bullets, in contradistinction to a bow that shot arrows. Sir John Bramston, in his Autobiography (p. 108) says:—"Litle more than a yeare after I maried, I and my wife being at Skreenes with my father (the plague being soe in London, and my building not finished), I had exercised myself with a *stone-bow*, and a spar-hawke at the bush."

There were two denominations of cross-bows—latches and prodds. The former were the military weapons, and were bent with one or both feet, by putting them into a kind of stirrup at the extremity, and then drawing the cord upward with the hands; the latter were chiefly used for sporting purposes. They were bent with the hand, by means of a small steel lever, called the goat's-foot, on account of its being forked or cloven on the side that rested on the cross-bow and the cord. The bow itself was usually made of steel, though sometimes of wood or horn.*

The missiles discharged from them were not only arrows, which were shorter and stouter than those of the long-bow, but also bolts (*bolzen*, German; *quarreaux*, or *carricaux*, French; *quadrelli*, Latin, corrupted into

---

* Sir S. D. Scott, "The British Army: its Origin, Progress, and Equipment," vol. ii. pp. 80, 81.

" quarrels," from their pyramidal form), and also stones or leaden balls.

Apropos of "bolts," who does not remember Oberon's poetical story of the wild pansy (*Viola tricolor*) marked by Cupid's " bolt ?"

"Yet mark'd I where the bolt of Cupid fell :
It fell upon a little western flower,—
Before, milk white, now purple with love's wound,—
And maidens call it ' Love-in-idleness.' "
Midsummer Night's Dream, Act ii. Sc. 1.

The " birding-pieces " which Mrs. Ford tells Falstaff are always " discharged " up the chimney, were no doubt the old-fashioned fowling-pieces which were in use in those days.

According to Sir S. D. Scott,* the " birding-piece " was identical with the " snap-hance," the early form of that process of ignition—the flint and steel lock—which has survived nearly 300 years, and specimens of which, although now becoming rare, may occasionally be met with in use, even at the present day. It was a Dutch invention ; and is said to have been brought into use by marauders, whom the Dutch called *snap-haans*, or poultry stealers. The light from the burning match, which necessarily accompanied the match-lock, exposed them to

---

* " The British Army : its Origin, Progress, and Equipment," London, 1868, vol. ii. pp 284-286.

detection; and the wheel-lock was an article too expensive for them to purchase, as well as being liable to get out of order; so this lock was devised, and was suggested, no doubt, by the wheel-lock. It consisted in the substitution of flint for pyrites, and a furrowed plate of steel in lieu of the wheel. When the trigger was pulled, it brought this jagged piece of steel in collision with the flint, which threw down its shower of sparks into the open pan, and lighted the priming. This improvement apparently took place about the close of the sixteenth century.

There is a very early "snap-hance" in the Tower Collection, numbered $\frac{4\,8}{1\,9}$. It is a "birding-piece" of Prince Charles, afterwards King Charles I., date 1614, and furnishes a good illustration of the form of gun in use in Shakespeare's day. It is engraved both on lock and barrel. The butt is remarkably thin; the length of the

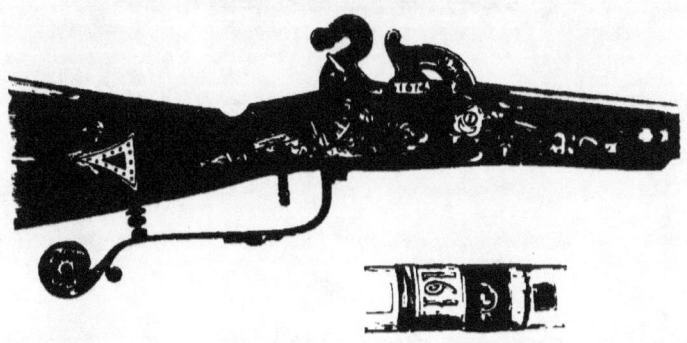

whole arm is four feet two inches, and was consequently

adapted for a youth like the Prince, who, at the date above mentioned, was fourteen years of age.

On looking at the curious specimens which are still treasured up as heirlooms, or in museums, one cannot help thinking that the person who pulled the trigger must have been in far greater danger than the bird at which he aimed.

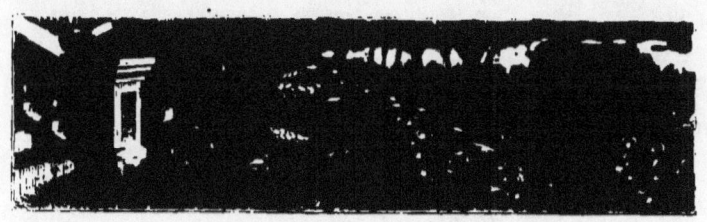

CHAPTER VI.

THE BIRDS UNDER DOMESTICATION.

IT would hardly be supposed that the birds under domestication could inspire much poetical feeling, or indeed that they could furnish the dramatist with much imagery. Those, however, who may entertain this view, on reading the works of Shakespeare, must admit that in his case at least they are mistaken. The Cock, the Peacock, the Turkey, the Pigeon, the Goose, the Duck and the Swan, are all noticed in their turn, and indeed, in the ordinary list of poultry, hardly a species has escaped mention. In the succeeding chapter, when treating of the game-birds, we shall notice the Pheasant, Partridge, and Quail, which are occasionally domesticated. For the present, it will be as well to confine our attention to the birds above mentioned.

"The early village cock" (*Richard III.* Act v. Sc. 3), "the trumpet to the morn" (*Hamlet*, Act i. Sc. 1), is often noticed by Shakespeare. In the prologue to the fourth act of *King Henry V.*—

"The country cocks do crow, the clocks do toll,
And the third hour of drowsy morning name."

Steevens has shown that the popular notion of a phantom disappearing at cock-crow is of very ancient date. The conversation of Bernardo, Horatio, and Marcellus, on the subject of Hamlet's ghost, affords a good illustration of this:—

"*Bern.* It was about to speak, when the cock crew!
Hor. And then it started like a guilty thing
  Upon a fearful summons. I have heard,
  The cock, that is the trumpet to the morn,
  Doth with his lofty and shrill-sounding throat
  Awake the god of day; and, at his warning,
  Whether in sea or fire, in earth or air,
  The extravagant * and erring spirit hies
  To his confine: and of the truth herein,
  This present object made probation.
Mar. It faded on the crowing of the cock.
  Some say that ever 'gainst that season comes
  Wherein our Saviour's birth is celebrated,
  The bird of dawning singeth all night long:
  And then, they say, no spirit dare stir abroad;

---

* Note here the use of the word "extravagant' in its primary signification, implying, of the ghost, its wandering beyond its proper sphere.

The nights are wholesome; then no planets strike,
No fairy takes, nor witch hath power to charm,
So hallow'd and so gracious is the time."
Hamlet, Act i. Sc. 1.

" Hark! hark! I hear the strain of strutting chanticleer cry cockadidle-dowe.—*Tempest*, Act i. Sc. 2.

Just as "cock-crow" denotes the early morning, so is "cock-shut-time" or "cock-close," expressive of the evening; although some consider that the latter phrase owes its origin to the practice of netting woodcocks at twilight, that is, shutting or enclosing them in a net.

The origin of the phrase "cock-a-hoop," which occurs in *Romeo and Juliet*, Act i. Sc. 5, is very doubtful: the passage is—

" You'll make a mutiny among my guests!
You will set *cock-a-hoop!* you'll be the man!"

Some commentators consider that this refers in some way to the boastful crowing of the cock, but we do not think that Shakespeare intended any allusion here to the game-fowl. We take it that the reference is to a cask of ale or wine, and that the phrase "to set cock-a-hoop" means to take the cock, or tap, out of the cask and set it on the hoop, thus letting all the contents escape. The man who would do such a reckless act, would be just the sort of man to whom Shakespeare refers.

The ale-house sign of "The Cock and Hoop" represents a game-fowl standing upon a hoop, but we have little doubt that the original sign was a cask flowing, with the tap laid on the top. The modern version is no doubt a corruption, just as we have "The Swan with Two *Necks*" for "The Swan with Two *Nicks*," *i. e.* marks on the bill to distinguish it; "The Devil and the Bag o' Nails" for "Pan and the Bacchanals;" "The Goat and Compasses" for the ancient motto "God encompasseth us;" &c., &c.*

The popular adjuration, "by cock and pye," which Shakespeare has put in the mouth of Justice Shallow, was once supposed to refer to the sacred name, and to the table of services, called "the pie;" but it is now thought to be what Hotspur termed a mere "protest of pepper gingerbread," as innocent as Slender's, "By these gloves," or, "By this hat." In "Soliman and Perseda" (1599,) it occurs coupled with "mousefoot;"—"By cock and pye and mousefoot." Again, in "The Plaine Man's Pathway to Heaven," by Arthur Dent (1607), we have the following dialogue:—

Asunctus.—"I know a man that will never swear but by *cock* or *py*, or *mousefoot*. I hope you will not say these be

---

* *Apropos* of ale-house signs, Shakespeare gives us the origin of "The Bear and Ragged Staff." It is the crest of the Earls of Warwick.

Warwick. "Now, by my father's badge, old Neville's crest,
The rampant bear chain'd to the ragged staff."
Henry VI. Part II. Act v. Sc. 1.

oaths. For he is as honest a man as ever brake bread. You shall not hear an oath come out of his mouth."

Theologus.—" I do not think he is so honest a man as you make him. For it is no small sin to swear by creatures."

The Cock and Pye (*i. e.* Magpie) was an ordinary ale-house sign, and may thus have become a subject for the vulgar to swear by. Douce, however, ascribes to it a less ignoble origin, and his interpretation is too ingenious to be passed over in silence:—"It will no doubt be recollected that in the days of ancient chivalry it was the practice to make solemn vows or engagements for the performance of some considerable enterprise. This ceremony was usually performed during some grand feast or entertainment, at which a roasted peacock or pheasant being served up by ladies in a dish of gold or silver, was thus presented to each knight, who then made the particular vow which he had chosen with great solemnity. When this custom had fallen into disuse, the peacock nevertheless continued to be a favourite dish, and was introduced on the table in a pie, the head, with gilded beak, being proudly elevated above the crust, and the splendid tail expanded. Other birds of less value were introduced in the same manner, and the recollection of the old peacock vows might occasion the less serious, or even burlesque, imitation of swearing not only by the bird itself, but also by the *pye;* and hence, probably, the oath 'by cock and pye,' for the use of which no very old authority can be found."

Shallow. "By cock and pye, sir, you shall not away to-night."—*Henry IV.* Part II. Act v. Sc. 1.

The pastime of cock-fighting, to which Shakespeare has alluded in *Antony and Cleopatra*, is no doubt of some antiquity. Strutt, in his "Sports and Pastimes of the People of England," does not give any history of its introduction, but quotes from Burton (1660), and Powell (1696), to show that the sport was well known at those dates. It was much in vogue in Shakespeare's day, and the great dramatist is probably not wrong in leading us to suppose that it was first introduced by the Romans:—

" His cocks do win the battle still of mine,
When it is all to nought."

Antony and Cleopatra, Act ii. Sc. 3.

"Cock-fighting took place generally between August and May. Six weeks before a battle, the champions were confined in separate pens, and fed with bread. Their spurs were then wrapped in leather, and they were allowed to spar, and sweated in straw baskets, and fed with sugar-candy, chopped rosemary, and butter, to strengthen them and give them wind. Roots dipped in wine, and oatmeal kneaded with ale and eggs, were also allowed them, as purges and diaphoretics. Every day the feeder had to lick his bird's eye, and lead and encourage him to pursue a dunghill fowl which he held in his arms, and ran with before him. The last fortnight the sparring was discontinued, and four days next allowed before the bird was brought into the pit, and always fasting.

"In matching birds, it was necessary to consider their strength and length—the weak, long bird rising with more ease, and the short, strong bird giving the surer and deadlier blow.

"The game cocks were prepared for battle by cutting off the mane all but a small ruff, and clipping off the feathers from the tail. The wings were cut short, and sharp points left, to endanger the eye of the antagonist. The spurs were scraped and sharpened, but steel spurs were not used at this early period, though the sport was as old as the Athenians. The preparation was completed by removing all the feathers from the crown of the head. The feeder, then licking his pupil all over, turned him into the pit, to win his gold and move his fortune.

"The birds were generally brought into the arena in linen bags, in which they came from Norwich or Wisbeach.

"They began the combat by whetting their beaks upon the ground, and continued the fight till they were both blind, or faint from loss of blood. The feeder had to suck the wounds of the living bird, and powder them with dust of the herb Robert. If the eye were hurt, the cocker chewed ground ivy, and applied the juice to the wound."*

Whether the various breeds of domestic fowls have diverged by independent and different roads from a single type, which is most probable, or whether they have descended from several distinct wild species, as some naturalists maintain, is a question which can scarcely be answered in the present treatise. A separate volume might be written on the subject. Nevertheless, the general opinion is that all the various breeds have descended from a common wild ancestor—the *Gallus bankiva* of India. This species has a wide geographical range. It inhabits Northern India as far west as Scinde, and ascends the Himalaya to a height of 4,000 feet. It is found in Burmah, the Malay Peninsula, the Indo-Chinese countries, the Philippine Islands, and the Malayan Archipelago, as far eastward as Timor. Mr. Darwin has shown † that it varies considerably in the wild state, and observes ‡ that "from the extremely close resemblance in colour, general structure, and especially in voice, between *Gallus bankiva* and the game-fowl; from their fertility, as far as this has been ascertained, when crossed; from the possibility of the wild species being tamed, and from its varying in the wild state, we may confidently look at it as the parent of the

---

* "The Compleat Gamester," 1709.
† "The Variation of Animals and Plants under Domestication," i. 235.
‡ Id. i. 236, 237.

most typical of all the domestic breeds, namely, the gamefowl. It is a significant fact that almost all the naturalists in India, namely, Sir W. Elliot, Mr. S. N. Ward, Mr. Layard, Mr. T. C. Jerdon, and Mr. Blyth, who are familiar with *Gallus bankiva*, believe that it is the parent of most or all of our domestic breeds."

Another species of Eastern origin noticed by Shakespeare is the Peacock (*Pavo cristatus*):—

" Let frantic Talbot triumph for awhile,
And, like a peacock, sweep along his tail;
We'll pull his plumes and take away his train."

Henry VI. Part I. Act iii. Sc. 3.

And elsewhere—

" Why, he stalks up and down like a peacock,—a stride and a stand."—*Troilus and Cressida*, Act iii Sc. 3.*

Ælian says peacocks were brought into Greece from some barbarous country, and were held in such estimation that a pair was valued at Athens at 1,000 drachmæ, or £32 5s. 10d. Peacocks' crests in ancient times were among the ornaments of the Kings of England.

Ernald de Aclent paid a fine to King John in 150 palfreys, with sackbuts, lorains, gilt spurs, and peacocks' crests, such as would be for his credit.

* See also *Taming of the Shrew*, Act iv. Sc. 1, and *Tempest*, Act iv. Sc. 1.

Whether our birds are descended from those introduced into Europe in the time of Alexander, or have been subsequently imported, is doubtful. They vary but little under domestication, except in sometimes being white or piebald.*

A curious fact with respect to the peacock may here be noticed, namely, the occasional appearance in England of the "japanned" or "black-shouldered" kind. This form has been regarded by Mr. Sclater as a distinct species, under the name of *Pavo nigripennis*, and he believes it will hereafter be found wild in some country, but not in India, where it is certainly unknown.† These japanned birds differ conspicuously from the common peacock, and can be propagated perfectly true. Nevertheless, Mr. Darwin gives it as his opinion that "the evidence seems to preponderate strongly in favour of the black-shouldered breed being a variation, induced either by the climate of England, or by some unknown cause, such as reversion to a primordial and extinct condition of the species." ‡

Formerly the peacock was in much request for the table, but now-a-days the species appears to be preserved for ornament rather than use. According to the "Nor-

---

* Darwin, "Variation of Animals and Plants under Domestication," i. 290.
† Pro. Zool. Soc. April 24th, 1860.
‡ Darwin, op. cit.

thumberland Houschold Book," the price of a peacock for the table in 1512 was twelvepence; but we must recollect that this was a much larger sum in those days than it is now considered to be.

Shakespeare has committed a curious anachronism in introducing the domestic Turkey in the play of *Henry IV.*, the species being unknown in England until the later reign of Henry VIII. The passage referred to runs thus :—

First Carrier. "'Odsbody! the turkeys in my pannier are quite starved. What, ostler!"—*Henry IV.* Part I. Act ii. Sc. 1.

The turkey was imported into Spain by the Spanish discoverers in the New World, early in the sixteenth century, its wild prototype being the *Gallipavo Mexicana* of Gould, and from Spain it was introduced into England in 1524. In 1525 a rhyme was composed, celebrating the introduction of this bird, as well as other good things, into this country :—

"Turkies, carps, hoppes, piccarell, and beere,
Came into England all in one yeare." *

A writer in the "Encyclopædia Britannica" says :—
"This fowl was first seen in France in the reign of Francis I., and in England in that of Henry VIII. By

* Baker's "Chronicle."

the date of the reigns of these monarchs, the first turkies must have been brought from Mexico, the conquest of which was completed A.D. 1521." *

"These facts," observes Mr. Blyth,† "are generally known, but not the fact for which there is abundant evidence, that the *domestic* turkey was introduced *from Europe* into the North American colonies, where a kindred wild species abounded in the forest."

The origin of the English name turkey, as applied to a bird indigenous to America, has provoked much discussion. The best explanation is that given by Mr. Blyth, in the work last quoted ‡ :—

"It is certain," he says, "that the *Guinea-fowl* was commonly termed the *Turkey-hen* in former days, and hence a difficulty sometimes in knowing which bird is meant by sundry old authors. As the Portuguese discoveries along the west coast of Africa preceded those of the Spaniards in America, there is reason to infer that our British ancestors became acquainted with the guinea-fowl prior to their knowledge of the turkey; and the English trade being then chiefly with the Levantine countries, our ancestors may well have fancied that it came from thence. Referring to a curious old dictionary in my possession (published in 1678) for the word

---

* It is observable, however, that in "The Privy Purse Expenses of King Henry VIII." turkies are not once mentioned amongst the fowls to be provided for the table.

† "Journal Asiatic Society, Bengal," vol. xxix. p. 38.   ‡ Pp. 390, 391.

Meleagris, I find it translated 'a Guinny or Turkey Hen:' *Gallinæ Africanæ seu Numidicæ*, Var. 'sine quæ vulgo Indicæ' (*Coq d'Inde* of the French, corrupted into *Dinde* and *Dindon!*). Again, *Numidica guttata* of Martial is rendered 'a Ginny or Turkey Hen.' Looking also into an English and Spanish Dictionary of so late a date as 1740, I find *Gallipavo* rendered 'a Turkey or Guinea Cock or Hen.' Well, it is known that our British forefathers originally derived the domestic turkey from Spain, and meanwhile they are likely to have obtained a knowledge of the true *habitat* of the guinea-fowl, and therefore may very probably have supposed the former to be the real *turkey*-fowl, as distinguished from the *guinea*-fowl; and if the word 'fowl' be dropped in the one instance and not in the other, be it remembered that there was another special meaning for the word *Guinea*, having reference to the Gold Coast, otherwise the bird might have come to be known as the 'guinea,' as the bantam-fowl is now currently designated the 'bantam,' and the canary-bird as the 'canary,' or the turkey-fowl the 'turkey.' The Latin-sounding name *Gallipavo* seems to be of Spanish origin, and obtains among the Spaniards to this day; but their earliest name for it was '*Pavon de las Indias*,' 'c'est-à-dire,' as Buffon remarks, '*Paon des Indes Occidentales*;' which explains the reference to India perpetuated in '*Dindon*.'"

The turkey is again mentioned by Shakespeare in

Twelfth Night, where Fabian, speaking of Malvolio to Andrew Aguecheek, says:—

"Contemplation makes a rare turkey-cock of him : how he jets under his advanc'd plumes!"—*Twelfth Night*, Act ii. Sc. 5.

The Pigeon and the Dove are repeatedly mentioned in the works of Shakespeare, although on different grounds. The former bird is noticed as a letter-carrier (*Titus Andronicus*, Act iv. Sc. 3), as an article of food (*Henry IV.* Part II. Act v. Sc. 1), and as an example of conjugal fidelity and attachment to offspring (*As You Like It*, Act i. Sc. 2, and Act iii. Sc. 3). The latter is alluded to as the emblem of peace (*Henry IV.* Part I. Act iv. Sc. 1.; *Henry VIII.* Act iv. Sc. 1), modesty (*Taming of the Shrew*, Act iii. Sc. 2), patience (*Hamlet*, Act v. Sc. 1), innocence (*Henry VI.* Part II. Act iii. Sc. 1), fidelity (*Troilus and Cressida*, Act iii. Sc. 2 ; *Winter's Tale*, Act iv. Sc. 3), and love (*Venus and Adonis;* *Henry VI.* Part I. Act ii. Sc. 2 ; *Romeo and Juliet*, Act ii. Sc. 5).

In one passage only is the word "dove" used synonymously for "pigeon." In *Romeo and Juliet* we are told of the nurse "sitting in the sun under the *dove*-house wall" (Act i. Sc. 3).

The practice, here alluded to, of keeping pigeons in a domesticated state is of very ancient date. Mr. Darwin has been at considerable pains to collect information upon this point, and in his admirable work "On the Variation of Animals and Plants under Domestication," he gives the following results :—

"The earliest record, as has been pointed out to me by Professor Lepsius, of pigeons in a domesticated condition, occurs in the fifth Egyptian dynasty, about 3000 B.C.; but Mr. Birch, of the British Museum, informs me that the pigeon appears in a bill of fare in the previous dynasty.* Domestic pigeons are mentioned in Genesis, Leviticus, and Isaiah. In the time of the Romans, as we hear from Pliny, immense prices were given for pigeons; 'nay, they are come to this pass, that they can reckon up their pedigree and race.' In India, about the year 1600, pigeons were much valued by Akber Khan: 20,000 birds were carried about with the court, and the merchants brought valuable collections. 'The monarchs of Iran and Turan sent him some very rare breeds. His Majesty,' says the courtly historian, 'by crossing the breeds, which method was never practised before, has improved them astonishingly. Akber Khan possessed seventeen distinct kinds, eight of which were valuable for beauty alone. At

---

* In the ruined temple of Medineet Haboo is a representation of the coronation of the famous warrior, King Rameses III. (B.C. 1297). "The conquering hero, among the clamours of the populace, and shouts of his victorious army, is depicted proceeding to the temple to offer his grateful thanks to the gods; and whilst certain priests in their gorgeous robes are casting incense about, and offering up sacrifices at many a smoking altar, others are employed in letting off carrier-pigeons to announce the glad tidings to every quarter of the globe."—LEITH ADAMS, *Notes of a Naturalist in the Nile Valley and Malta*, p. 27.

about this same period of 1600, the Dutch, according to Aldrovandus, were as eager about pigeons as the Romans had formerly been. The breeds which were kept during the fifteenth century in Europe and in India, apparently differed from each other. Tavernier, in his 'Travels,' in 1677, speaks as does Chardin, in 1735, of the vast numbers of pigeon-houses in Persia; and the former remarks, that as Christians were not permitted to keep pigeons, some of the vulgar actually turned Mahometans for this sole purpose. The Emperor of Morocco had his favourite keeper of pigeons, as is mentioned in Moore's treatise, published 1737. In England, from the time of 1678 to the present day, as well as in Germany and in France, numerous treatises have been published on the pigeon. In India, about a hundred years ago, a Persian treatise was written; and the writer thought it no light affair, for he begins with a solemn invocation, 'In the name of God, the gracious and merciful.' Many large towns in Europe and the United States now have their societies of devoted pigeon-fanciers: at present there are three such societies in London. In India, as I hear from Mr. Blyth, the inhabitants of Delhi and of some other great cities are eager fanciers. Mr. Layard informs me that most of the known breeds are kept in Ceylon. In China, according to Mr. Swinhoe of Amoy, and Dr. Lockhart of Shangai, carriers, fantails, tumblers, and other varieties are reared with care, especially by the bonzes, or priests.

"The Chinese fasten a kind of whistle to the tail-feathers of their pigeons, and as the flock wheels through the air, they produce a sweet sound.* In Egypt, the late Abbas Pacha was a great fancier of fantails. Many pigeons are kept at Cairo and Constantinople, and these have lately been imported by native merchants, as I hear from Sir W. Elliot, into Southern India, and sold at high prices.

"The foregoing statements show in how many countries, and during how long a period, many men have been passionately devoted to the breeding of pigeons."†

In *Titus Andronicus* (Act iv. Sc. 3), upon the entry of a clown with two pigeons Titus exclaims:—

"News, news from heaven! Marcus, *the post is come*.
Sirrah, what tidings? have you any letters?"

The practice of using pigeons as letter-carriers, here alluded to by Shakespeare, is doubtless of very ancient origin. The old historian Diodorus Siculus, informs us that above two thousand years ago they were employed for this purpose; and five hundred years since relays of carrier-pigeons formed part of a telegraphic system adopted by the Turks. "Regular chains of posts were established, consisting of high towers between thirty and

---

* A good description of these whistles, by Mr. Tegetmeier, with illustrations, will be found in the *Field* of the 12th March, 1870.
† Darwin, "Variation of Animals and Plants under Domestication," i. pp. 204, 205.

forty miles asunder, provided with pigeons, and sentinels stood there constantly on the watch, to secure the intelligence communicated by the birds as they arrived, and to pass it on by means of others. The note was written on a thin slip of paper, enclosed in a very small gold box, almost as thin as the paper itself, suspended to the neck of the bird; the hour of arrival and departure were marked at each successive tower, and for greater security a duplicate was always despatched two hours after the first. The despatches were, however, not always enclosed in gold, but merely in paper, in which case, to prevent the letters being defaced by damp, the legs of the pigeon were first bathed in vinegar, with a view to keep them cool, so that they might not settle to drink, or wash themselves on the way, which in that hot climate they were often doing."

The modern mode of transmitting messages by pigeon-post is much more ingenious, and less irksome to the bird. The slip of paper is rolled up very tightly, and inserted in a small quill, which is stitched to one of the tail-feathers.

Formerly it was not an uncommon thing to send a pair of doves or pigeons as a present—

"I have brought you a letter and a couple of pigeons here."—*Titus Andronicus*, Act iv. Sc. 4.

The constancy evinced by pigeons towards each other,

when paired, has been already referred to. (*As You Like It*, Act iii. Sc. 3 ; *Winter's Tale*, Act iv. Sc. 3, &c.)

It has been stated that the absence of a gall-bladder in pigeons is compensated for by the extraordinary development of the crop, by the aid of which the food becomes so thoroughly digested, that the gall is rendered unnecessary. This, however, is not strictly correct, as the food is only macerated in the crop; and the gall, as it is secreted, passes, by two ducts, from the liver into the duodenum, instead of into a gall-bladder. Shakespeare has alluded to this peculiarity in the digestive organs of pigeons in *Hamlet*, where the Prince says :—

" I am pigeon-liver'd, and lack gall
To make oppression bitter."

Hamlet, Act ii. Sc. 2.

The manner in which they feed their young, to which allusion is made in *As You Like It* (Act i. Sc. 2), is very remarkable.

Most birds *collect* for their young, but in the case of pigeons and some others, there exists a provision very similar to that of milk in quadrupeds. "I have discovered," says John Hunter,* "in my enquiries concerning the various modes in which young animals are nourished, that all the dove kind are endowed with a similar power.

"The young pigeon, like the young quadruped, till it is capable of digesting the common food of its kind, is fed

* Hunter "On the Animal Economy," p. 194.

with a substance secreted for that purpose by the parent animal; not, as in the mammalia, by the female alone, but also by the male, which perhaps furnishes this nutriment in a degree still more abundant.

"It is a common property of birds, that both male and female are equally employed in hatching and in feeding their young in the second stage, but this particular mode of nourishment, by means of a substance secreted in their own bodies, is peculiar to certain kinds, and is carried on in the crop.

"Besides the dove kind, I have some reason to suppose parrots to be endowed with the same faculty, as they have the power of throwing up the contents of the crop, and feeding one another.

"I have seen the cock parrakeet regularly feed the hen, by first filling his own crop, and then supplying her from his beak. Parrots, macaws, cockatoos, &c., when they are very fond of the person who feeds them, may likewise be observed to have the action of throwing up the food, and often do it. The cock pigeon, when he caresses the hen, performs the same kind of action as when he feeds his young, but I do not know if at this time he throws up anything from the crop.

"During incubation, the coats of the crop in the pigeon are gradually enlarged and thickened, like what happens to the udder of females of the class mammalia, in the term of uterine gestation. On comparing the state of the crop when the bird is not sitting, with its appearance during incubation, the difference is very remarkable. In the first case it is thin and membranous, but by the time the young are about to be hatched, the whole, except what lies on the trachea or windpipe, becomes thickened, and takes on a glandular appearance, having its internal surface very irregular. It is likewise evidently more vascular than in its former state, that it may convey a quantity of blood, sufficient for the secretion of this substance, which is to nourish the young brood for some days after they are hatched. Whatever may be the consistence of this substance when just secreted, it most probably soon coagulates into a granulated white curd, for in such a form I have always found it in the crop; and if an old pigeon is killed just as the young ones are hatching, the crop will be found as above described, and in its cavity pieces of white curd, mixed with some of the common food of the pigeon, such as barley, beans, &c.

"If we allow either of the parents to feed the young, its crop, when examined, will be discovered to contain the same curdled substance, which passes thence into the stomach, where it is to be digested. The young pigeon is fed for some time with this substance only, and about the third day some of the common food is found mingled with it; and as the pigeon grows older, the proportion of common food is increased, so that by the time it is seven, eight, or nine days old, the secretion of the curd ceases in the old ones, and of course will no more be found in the crop of the young.

"It is a curious fact that the parent pigeon has at first the power to throw up this curd without any mixture of common food, although afterwards both are thrown up according to the proportion required for the young ones. I have called this substance curd, not as being literally so, but as resembling that more than anything I know; it may, however, have a greater resemblance to curd than we are perhaps aware of; for neither this secretion, nor curd from which the whey has been pressed, seem to contain any sugar, and do not run into the acetous fermentation. The property of coagulating is confined to the substance itself, as it produces no such effect when mixed with milk. This secretion in the pigeon, like all other animal substances, becomes putrid by standing, though not so readily as either blood or meat, it resisting putrefaction for a considerable time; neither will curd much pressed become so putrid as soon as either blood or meat."

Selby says,* "The young remain in the nest till they are able to fly, and are fed by the parent birds, who disgorge into their mouths the food that has undergone a maceration, or semi-digestive process, in that part of the œsophagus usually called the crop or craw."

Colonel Montagu appears to be one of the few original

* "Illustrations of British Ornithology."

observers who has confirmed the account given by Hunter. "The rook," he says, "has a small pouch under the tongue, in which it carries food to its young. It is probable the use of the craw may be extended further than is generally imagined, for, besides the common preparation of the food to assist its digestion in the stomach, there are some species that actually secrete a lacteal substance in the breeding season, which, mixing with the half-digested food, is ejected to feed and nourish the young. The mammæ from which this milky liquor is produced, are situated on each side of the upper part of the breast, immediately under the craw. In the female turtle-dove we have met with these glands tumid with milky secretion, and we believe it common to both sexes of the dove genus."*

It is not surprising that so great an authority on the subject as Mr. Tegetmeier should have adverted to Shakespeare's knowledge of these birds. At p. 133 of his work upon Pigeons,† he says:—" The Barb, or Barbary Pigeon, is one of those varieties whose history can be traced back for a considerable period: it was certainly well known in England during the sixteenth century, for Shakespeare, in *As You Like It*, which was entered at Stationers' Hall in 1600, makes Rosalind, when disguised as a youth, say, 'I will be more jealous of thee than a Barbary cock-pigeon over his hen.'—Act iv. Sc. 1. Our intercourse with

---

* "Ornithological Dictionary," Preface, 1st edition.

† "Pigeons: their Structure, Varieties, Habits, and Management." By W. B. Tegetmeier, F.Z.S. London, 1868.

the north of Africa was at that period not unfrequent, and many of the domestic animals of the district had been imported into this country. Shakespeare frequently alludes to Barbary horses; and in the Second Part of *King Henry IV.* Act ii. Sc. 4, makes Falstaff say, 'He's no swaggerer, hostess . . . . he'll not swagger with a Barbary hen, if her feathers turn back with any show of resistance.' This allusion was most probably to a frizzled fowl. In this singular variety the feathers upon the head and neck are reversed or curled, which gives the hen at all times the appearance of a cock in fighting attitude. Hence Shakespeare's apt allusion."

There seems to be no doubt that all the various races of the domestic pigeon are descended from a single stock, namely, the wild rock-pigeon (*Columba livia*). A mass of interesting evidence on this subject will be found in Darwin's "Variation of Animals and Plants under Domestication," vol. i. chap. 5.

Frequent allusion has been made by Shakespeare to the "Doves of Venus" (*Lucrece, Venus and Adonis*, and *Midsummer Night's Dream*, Act i. Sc. 1), and "Venus' Pigeons" (*Merchant of Venice*, Act ii. Sc. 6).

Some explanation of this is to be found in the following passage from *Venus and Adonis :*—

"Thus weary of the world, away she (Venus) hies,
  And yokes her silver doves; by whose swift aid

> Their mistress, mounted, through the empty skies
> In her light chariot quickly is convey'd ;
> Holding their course to Paphos, where their queen
> Means to immure herself and not be seen."

This will also explain the reference to

> " The dove of Paphos."
>
> Pericles, Act iv. Introd.

The towns of Old and New Paphos are situate on the S.W. extremity of the coast of Cyprus. Old Paphos is the one generally referred to by the poets, being the peculiar seat of the worship of Venus, who was fabled to have been wafted thither after her birth amid the waves. The "dove of Paphos" therefore, may be considered as synonymous with the "dove of Venus." Sometimes by Paphos is understood the city of Cyprus, which is said to have been founded by Paphos, son of Pygmalion, and was known by his name :—

> " Illa Paphon genuit : de quo tenet insula nomen."
>
> Ovid Metam. Bk. 10, Fab. 8.

The Turtle-dove (*Columba turtur*) has been noticed by poets in all ages as an emblem of love and constancy.

Shakespeare has—

> " When arm in arm they both came swiftly running,
> Like to a pair of loving turtle-doves."
>
> Henry VI. Part I. Act ii. Sc. 2.

And elsewhere—

"So turtles pair that never mean to part."
Winter's Tale, Act iv. Sc. 3.

Again—

"As true as steel, as plantage to the moon,
As sun to day, as turtle to her mate."
Troilus and Cressida, Act iii. Sc. 2.

An inquiry into the meaning of the word *plantage* leads to some curious information. Archdeacon Nares observes* that "plantage" is probably for anything that is planted. Plants were supposed to improve as the moon increased, and from an old book entitled "The Profitable Art of Gardening," by Thos. Hill, the third edition of which was printed in 1579, we learn that neither sowing, planting, nor grafting was ever undertaken without a scrupulous attention to the increase or waning of the moon. Dryden does not appear to have understood the above passage, and has accordingly altered it to "As true as *flowing tides* are to the moon." But the meaning of the original words seem sufficiently clear, and may be fully illustrated by the following quotation from Scott's "Discoverie of Witchcraft":—"The poore husband man perceiveth that the increase of the moone maketh plants frutiful, so as in the full moone they are in the best strength; decaieing in

* "Glossary," 4to. Lond. 1822.

the wane, and in the conjunction do utterlie wither and vade."

The following lines from *Pericles* are somewhat to the point :—

> "How dare the plants look up to heaven, from whence
> They have their nourishment?"
>
> *Pericles*, Act i. Sc. 2.

It is possible that particular reference may be had to the plant "Honesty," or "Lunary" (*Lunaria*), which was so named from the circular shape of its pod, which was thought to resemble the moon (*Luna*), not only in its form, but in its silvery brightness. The title of "Honesty" appears to have been given it from the transparent nature of the pod, which discovers those seed-vessels that contain seed from such as are barren or have shed their seed. We learn from Chaucer that "Honesty" (*Lunaria*), was one of the plants used in incantations. Drayton calls it "Lunary" :—

> "Then sprinkles she the juice of rue,
> With nine drops of the midnight dew
> From *Lunary* distilling."
>
> *Nymphid.*

But to return to our doves. It is related that Mahomed had a dove which he used to feed with wheat out of his ear, which dove, when it was hungry, lighted on Mahomed's shoulder and thrust its bill in to find its breakfast,

Mahomed persuading the rude and simple Arabians that it was the Holy Ghost that gave him advice.* Hence Shakespeare's query—

"Was Mahomed inspired with a dove?"
Henry VI. Part I. Act i. Sc. 2.

As the crow has been held the type of blackness, so has the dove been considered the emblem of the opposite colour:—

"So shows a snowy dove trooping with crows,
As yonder lady o'er her fellows shows."
Romeo and Juliet, Act i. Sc. 5.

"As soft as dove's down, and as white as it."
Winter's Tale, Act iv. Sc. 4.

In the very humorous Interlude which is introduced by the clowns in *Midsummer Night's Dream*, we have the gentle voice of the dove contrasted with the mighty roar of the lion:—

"*Bottom.* Let me play the lion too: I will roar, that I will do any man's heart good to hear me; I will roar, that I will make the Duke say, 'Let him roar again, let him roar again.'

Quince. An you should do it too terribly, you would fright the Duchess and the ladies, that they would shriek; and that were enough to hang us all.

---

* Sir W. Raleigh, "History of the World," Book I. Part i. c. 6.

All. That would hang us, every mother's son.

Bottom. I grant you, friends, if that you should fright the ladies out of their wits, they would have no more discretion but to hang us; but I will aggravate my voice so, that I will roar you as gently as any sucking dove; I will roar you an't were any nightingale."—*Midsummer Night's Dream*, Act i. Sc. 2.

We have before drawn attention to the fact that birds which are by nature weak and timid, flying at the approach of man, will nevertheless show fight in defence of their young. Shakespeare has noticed this in the case of the wren,* and the dove:—

"And doves will peck in safeguard of their brood."

Henry VI. Part III. Act ii. Sc. 2.

And in the same play—

"So doves do peck the falcon's piercing talons."

Henry VI. Part III. Act i. Sc. 4.

Again—

"To be furious,
Is to be frighted out of fear; and in that mood
The dove will peck the ostrich."

Antony and Cleopatra, Act iii. Sc. 13.

And yet there can scarcely be a more timid bird than the dove, as Falstaff well knew, when he said ironically:—

* See *ante*, p. 143.

"Thou wilt be as valiant as the wrathful dove, or most magnanimous mouse."—*Henry IV.* Part II. Act iii. Sc. 2.

The custom of bestowing a pair of doves as a present or peace-offering has been before alluded to (*Titus Andronicus*, Act iv. Sc. 4).

Izaak Walton tells us that "for the sacrifice of the Law a pair of turtle-doves or young pigeons were as well accepted as costly bulls and rams." When Gobbo wished to curry favour with Bassanio he began by saying :—

"I have here a dish of doves, that I would bestow on your worship."—*Merchant of Venice*, Act ii. Sc. 2.

These were no doubt intended to be eaten. Paris, speaking to Helen of Pandarus, says,—

"He eats nothing but doves, love."—*Troilus and Cressida*, Act iii. Sc. 1.

A weakness which he deprecates as being heating to the blood. Justice Shallow, when ordering dinner, showed his appreciation of pigeons as well as of other good cheer. He says :—

"Some pigeons, Davy; a couple of short-legged hens; a joint of mutton, and any pretty little tiny kickshaws, tell William cook."—*Henry IV.* Part II. Act v. Sc. 1.

The price of a pigeon at this time, as we learn from

"The Northumberland Household Book," was "iij for a penny," while hens could be bought "at ijd. a pece."

"Item, it is thoughte goode to by PIDGIONS for my Lords Meas, Maister Chambreleyne, ande the Stewardes Meas, so they be boughte after iij for a penny.

"Item, it is thoughte goode HENNES be boughte from Cristynmas to Shroftide, so they be good and at ijd. a pece. Ande my Lorde Maister Chambreleyne and the Stewardes Meas to be syrved with theym and noon outher."

A much more notable bird for the table is the Goose.

"Item, it is thoughte goode to by GEYSSE so that they be good and for iijd. or iiijd. at the moste seynge that iij or iiij Meas may be served thereof."

This bird is mentioned in *As You Like It*, Act iii. Sc. 4 ; *Love's Labour's Lost*, Act iii. Sc. 1, and Act iv. Sc. 3 ; *Midsummer Night's Dream*, Act v. Sc. 1 ; *Tempest*, Act ii. Sc. 2 ; *Merry Wives of Windsor*, Act v. Sc. 1 ; *Romeo and Juliet*, Act ii. Sc. 4 ; *Coriolanus*, Act i. Sc. 4 ; and *Merchant of Venice*, Act v. Sc. 1.

Shakespeare draws a distinction between a grass-fed and a stubble-fed goose :—

"The spring is near, when *green geese* are a-breeding."
Love's Labour's Lost, Act i. Sc. 1.

May is the time for a green or grass-fed goose, while the

stubble-goose comes in at Michaelmas. King, in his "Art of Cookery," has—

"So stubble-geese at Michaelmas are seen
Upon the spit; next May produces green."

In the old "Household Books," it is not unusual to find such entries as the following :—

"Itm̃, the xxvij daye to a s'vñt of maister Becks in rewarde for bringing a present of Grene Gees .   .   iiijs. viijd.

A "green goose" is mentioned again in *Love's Labour's Lost*, Act iv. Sc. 3.

Launce, enumerating the various occasions on which he had befriended his dog, says,—

"I have stood on the pillory for geese he hath killed, otherwise he had suffered for 't."—*Two Gentlemen of Verona*, Act iv. Sc. 4.

"Goose, if I had you upon Sarum plain,
I'd drive you cackling home to Camelot."
King Lear, Act ii. Sc. 2.

There appears to be some difference of opinion as to what place is meant by the ancient name *Camelot*. Selden, in his notes to Drayton's "Polyolbion," says :— "By *South Cadbury* is that Camelot; a hill of a mile compass at the top; four trenches encircling it, and betwixt every of them an earthen wall; the contents of it within about twenty acres full of ruins and relics of old buildings."

In the " History of King Arthur " (Chap. 26), Camelot is located in the west of England, *Somersetshire ;* while in Chapter 44, it is related that Sir Balen's sword "swam down the stream to the citie of Camelot, that is, in English, *Winchester.*" When Caxton finished the printing of the "Mort d'Arthur,"* he says of the hero :— " He is more spoken of beyond the sea, ... and yet of record remain witness of him in *Wales*, in the town of Camelot, the great stones and marvelous works," &c. Tennyson, in his " Mort d'Arthur," twice mentions Camelot, and in his " Lady of Shalott " frequently alludes to "many-tower'd Camelot," but in neither poem is any clue to its precise situation given.

"*Mercutio.* Nay, if our wits run the *wild-goose chase*, I am done ; for thou hast more of the wild-goose in one of thy wits, than, I am sure, I have in my whole five. Was I with you there for the goose ?

Romeo. Thou wast never with me for anything, when thou wast not there for the goose.

Mer. I will bite thee by the ear for that jest.

Rom. Nay, good goose, bite not.

---

* Translated from the French by Sir Thos. Mallory, Knt., and first printed by Caxton, A.D. 1481.

Mer. Thy wit is very bitter sweeting; it is a most sharp sauce.

Rom. And is it not well served in to a sweet goose?

Mer. O, here's a wit of cheverel, that stretches from an inch narrow to an ell broad!

Rom. I stretch it out for that word—broad: which, added to the goose, proves thee far and wide a broad goose."

Romeo and Juliet, Act ii. Sc. 4.

The "wild-goose chase" above alluded to was a reckless sort of horserace, in which two horses were started together, and the rider who first got the lead, compelled the other to follow him over whatever ground he chose.*

Burton, in his "Anatomy of Melancholy," 1660, gives us a general view of the sports most prevalent in the seventeenth century, and after naming the "common recreations of country folks," he alludes to "riding of great horses, running at rings, tilts and tournaments, and *wild-goose chases*, which are disports of greater men and good in themselves, though many gentlemen by such means gallop quite out of their fortunes."

Shakespeare has many observations relating to Ducks, but as his remarks illustrate more appropriately what we shall have to say under the head of "wild-fowl," we reserve them accordingly for a future chapter.

---

* See "Chambers's Dictionary," last ed., article "Chase;" also Holt White's note to this passage in the "Variorum Shakespeare."

The Swan (*Cygnus olor*), being identified with Orpheus, and called also the bird of Apollo, the god of music, powers of song have been often attributed to it, and as often denied :—

"I will play the swan, and die in music."
Othello, Act v. Sc. 2.

"A swan-like end, fading in music."
Merchant of Venice, Act iii. Sc. 2.

Prince Henry, at his father's death-bed, exclaims,—

" 'Tis strange that death should sing!
I am the cygnet to this pale, faint swan,
Who chants a doleful hymn to his own death;
And, from the organ-pipe of frailty, sings
His soul and body to their lasting rest."
King John, Act v. Sc. 7.

Again, in *Lucrece*, we read—

"And now this pale swan in her watery nest,
Begins the sad dirge of her certain ending."

But although the swan has no "song," properly so called, it has a soft and rather plaintive note, monotonous, but not disagreeable. I have often heard it in the spring, when swimming about with its young.

Colonel Hawker, in his "Instructions to Young Sportsmen" (11th ed. p. 269), says :—"The only note which I ever heard the wild swan, in winter, utter, is his well-known 'whoop.' But one summer evening I was amused with watching and listening to a domesticated one, as he swam up and down the water in the Regent's Park. He turned up a sort of melody, made with two notes, C and the minor third, E flat, and kept working his head as if delighted with his own performance.

"The melody, taken down on the spot by a first-rate musician, Auguste Bertini, was as follows:—

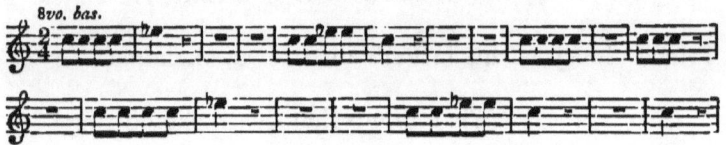

The Abbé Arnaud has written some interesting remarks upon the voice of the swan.* He says:—

"The swan, with his wings expanded, his neck outstretched, and his head erect, places himself opposite his mate, uttering a cry to which the female replies by another half a note lower. The voice of the male rises from A (*la*), to B flat (*si bemol*); that of the female from G sharp (*sol dièse*), to A.† The first note is short and transient, and has the effect which our musicians term *sensible;* so that it is not separated from the second, but seems to glide into it. Observe that, fortunately for the ear, they do not both sing at once; in fact, if, while the male sounded B flat, the female gave A, or if the male

* Wood's "Buffon," xix. p. 511, note.
† This, it will be observed, differs materially from Col. Hawker's observation.

uttered A while the female gave G sharp, there would result the harshest and most insupportable of discords. We may add that this dialogue is subjected to a constant and regular rhythm, with the measure of two times (?). The keeper assured me that during their amours, these birds have a cry still sharper, but much more agreeable."

The late Charles Waterton once had an opportunity, which rarely occurs, of seeing a swan die from natural causes. "Although I gave no credence," he says,[*] "to the extravagant notion which antiquity had entertained of melody from the mouth of the dying swan, still I felt anxious to hear some plaintive sound or other, some soft inflection of the voice, which might tend to justify that notion in a small degree. But I was disappointed. He nodded, and then tried to recover himself, and then nodded again, and again held up his head; till, at last, quite enfeebled and worn out, his head fell gently on the grass, his wings became expanded a trifle or so, and he died whilst I was looking on. He never even uttered his wonted cry, nor so much as a sound to indicate what he felt within.

"The silence which this bird maintained to the last tends to show that the dying song of the swan is nothing but a fable, the origin of which is lost in the shades of antiquity. Its repetition can be of no manner of use, save as a warning to ornithologists not to indulge in the

[*] "Essays on Natural History," second series, p. 128.

extravagancies of romance—a propensity not altogether unknown in these our latter times."

Yarrell has remarked, in his "History of British Birds," that "the young, when hatched, which is generally about the end of May, are conducted to the water by the parent bird, and are even said to be carried there: it is certain that the cygnets are frequently carried on the back of the female when she is sailing about in the water. This I have witnessed on the Thames, and have seen the female, by raising her leg, assist the cygnets in getting upon her back." Mr. Jesse, also, in his "Gleanings in Natural History," correctly observes: "Where the stream is strong the old swan will sink herself sufficiently low to bring her back on a level with the water, when the cygnets will get upon it, and in this manner are conveyed to the other side of the river, or into stiller water."

From a passage in *King Henry VI.* we may presume that this habit had been noticed by Shakespeare:—

"So doth the swan her downy cygnets save,
Keeping them prisoner underneath her wings."
Henry VI. Part I. Act v. Sc. 3.

By the expression "underneath her wings" we may understand under shelter of her wings, which she arches over her back whereon the young are seated.

This habit of carrying the young has been observed in the case of many other water birds. Mr. W. Proctor, of

Durham, speaking of the habits of the horned grebe (*Podiceps cornutus*), as observed by him in Iceland, says:—
"One day, having seen one of these birds dive from its nest, I placed myself with my gun at my shoulder, waiting its reappearance. As soon as it emerged I fired and killed it, and was surprised to see two young ones, which it seems had been concealed beneath the wings of the parent bird, drop upon the water. I afterwards shot several other birds of this species, all of which dived with their young under their wings. The young were placed with their heads towards the tail, and their bills resting on the back of the parent bird."

But to return to the swan:—

"For all the water in the ocean
Can never turn a swan's black legs to white,
Although she lave them hourly in the flood."
Titus Andronicus, Act iv. Sc. 2.

"I have seen a swan
With bootless labour swim against the tide,
And spend her strength with overmatching waves."
Henry VI. Part III. Act i. Sc. 4.

Those who are familiar with the late Mr. Wolley's sketch of the wild swan's nest, published by Professor Newton in the "Ootheca Wolleyana" (Part I. Plate 9), will recognize in it an excellent illustration to the following passage :—

> "I' the world's volume
> Our Britain seems as of it, but not in 't;
> In a great pool, a swan's nest."
>
> *Cymbeline*, Act iii. Sc. 4.

For the purpose of comparison, Shakespeare has found the swan very useful in metaphor.

Benvolio, referring to Rosaline, says,—

> "Compare her face with some that I shall show,
> And I will make thee think thy swan a crow."
>
> *Romeo and Juliet*, Act i. Sc. 2.

Troilus, descanting on the charms of Cressida, speaks of—

> "Her hand
> .   .   .   .   .
> .   .   .   to whose soft seizure
> The cygnet's down is harsh." .   .   .
>
> *Troilus and Cressida*, Act i. Sc. 1.

Amongst the numerous classical allusions to be found throughout the Plays, we are reminded in the present chapter of Juno's chariot drawn by swans:—

> "And wheresoe'er we went, like Juno's swans,
> Still we went coupled and inseparable."
>
> *As You Like It*, Act i. Sc. 3.

Falstaff, too, with some humour, thus alludes to the loves of Leda :—

"O powerful love! that, in some respects, makes a beast a man; in some other, a man a beast. You were also, Jupiter, a swan, for the love of Leda; O, omnipotent love! how near the god drew to the complexion of a goose!"
—*Merry Wives of Windsor*, Act v. Sc. 5.

The swan, in Shakespeare's day, was in much request for the table, and, for those who could afford it, was served up at all the principal feasts. In "The Northumberland Household Book," such items as the following constantly occur:—

"ITEM. It is thoughte goode that my Lordis SWANNES be taken and fedde to serve my Lordis house and to be paide fore as they may be boughte in the countrey, seeing that my Lorde hath Swannes enoughe of his owne.

"ITEM a Warraunte to be servide oute yerely at Michaelmas for xx SWANNES for th' expencez of my Lordis house as too say for Cristynmas Day v—Saynt Stephyns Day ij —Saynt John Day ij—Childremas Day ij—Saint Thomas Day ij—New Yere Day iij—ande for the xijth Day of Cristynmas iiij Swannys."

These were not to be old birds, however. The "Warraunt" referred to expressly provides that they should be "signetts."

In the case of the swan, as with many other species, were we to call attention to every passage throughout the works of Shakespeare wherein it is mentioned or referred to, we fear the reader's patience might become exhausted. Where such allusions, therefore, are trifling, we have thought it well to pass them by.

In the present chapter, enough has probably been said to show that while more attractive species have claimed a larger share of the poet's attention, the birds under domestication have been by no means neglected.

CHAPTER VII.

THE GAME-BIRDS AND "QUARRY" FLOWN AT BY FALCONERS.

GAME-PRESERVING, as we now understand the term, was probably unknown in Shakespeare's days, for sportsmen at that time had not the means of making such large bags, and consequently the necessity for breeding and rearing game artificially did not exist. Nature's liberal supply sufficed to satisfy the moderate demand, and the sportsman always returned home well pleased. We take it, however, that this satisfaction resulted more from an appreciation of sport than from the possession of a heavy bag. What more enjoyable than the pursuit of partridges, "with grey gos-hawk in hand," as Chaucer hath it, or a flight at heron with a falcon?

The skill, too, which was required to kill a bird or rabbit with a single bolt from a cross-bow was far greater than that which is needed to achieve the same result with an ounce of shot from a breech-loader. Not that

F. F.

guns were unknown in Shakespeare's day, for the old-fashioned "birding-piece" was then in use, as we have already noticed.* But, partly in consequence of its inferiority and cost, and partly because its use was so little understood, the majority of folks preferred to carry a weapon with which they were more skilled, and on which they could consequently place more reliance. Gradually, as the fowling-piece became more and more perfect, the long-bow and cross-bow were laid aside, and hawking became almost forgotten.

Notwithstanding that the Pheasant (*Phasianus colchicus*) must have been well-known in Shakespeare's day, the poet has only once made mention of this bird. The passage occurs in *The Winter's Tale*, Act iv. Sc. 3, and runs thus :—

"*Shepherd.* My business, sir, is to the king.

Autolycus. What advocate hast thou to him?

Shepherd. I know not, an 't like you.

Clown (*jokingly aside to Shepherd*). Advocate's the court-word for a *pheasant:* say you have none.

Shepherd. None, sir ; I have no *pheasant*, cock nor hen.

Autolycus. How blessed are we that are not simple men!"

The precise date of the introduction of the pheasant into Great Britain is uncertain, but there is evidence to show that it was prior to the invasion of the Normans,

* See end of Chapter V.

and that we are probably indebted for this game-bird to the enterprise of the Romans. The earliest record, we believe, of the occurrence of the pheasant in this country will be found in the tract " De inventione Sanctæ Crucis nostræ in Monte Acuto et de ductione ejusdem apud Waltham," edited by Prof. Stubbs from manuscripts in the British Museum, and published in 1861.* In one of these manuscripts, dated about 1177, is the following bill of fare prescribed by Harold for the Canons' Households, in 1059:—

"Erant autem tales pitantiæ unicuique canonico: a festo Sancti Michaelis usque ad caput jejunii, aut xii. merulæ, aut ii. agauseæ, aut ii. perdices, *aut unus phasianus,* reliquis temporibus aut ancæ, aut gallinæ."

Yarrell, in his " History of British Birds," gives an extract from Dugdale's " Monasticon Anglicanum" to the effect that the Abbot of Amesbury obtained a licence from the king to kill pheasants, in the first year of Henry I. (1100).

Leland, in his account of the feast given at the inthronisation of George Nevell, Archbishop of York, in the reign of Edward IV., tells us that, amongst other good things, two hundred "fesauntes" were provided for the guests.

In the " Privy Purse Expenses of Elizabeth of York,"

* *See* " The Ibis," 1869. p. 358.

under date "the xiiijth day of Novembre," the following entry occurs:—

"Itm. The same day to Richard Mylner of Byndfeld for bringing a present of fesauntes cokkes to the Queene to Westminster . . . vs."

In the "Household Book" of Henry Percy, fifth Earl of Northumberland, which was commenced in 1512, the pheasant is thus referred to:—

"Item, FESAUNTES to be hade for my Lordes own Mees at Principall Feestes and to be at xijd. a pece."

"Item, FESSAUNTIS for my Lordes owne Meas to be hadde at Principalle Feistis ande to be at xijd. a pece."*

* As a copy of the "Northumberland Household Book" is not readily accessible, we give the following interesting extract, showing the price, at that date, of various birds for the table:—

Capons at iid. a pece leyn (lean).
Chickeyns at ½d. a pece.
Hennys at iid. a pece.
Swannys (no price stated).
Geysse iiid. or iiiid. at the moste.
Pluvers id. or i½d. at moste.
Cranys xvid. a pece.
Hearonsewys (*i.e.* Heronshaws or Herons) xiid. a pece.
Mallardes iid. a pece.
Teylles id. a pece.
Woodcokes id. or i½d. at the moste.
Wypes (*i.e.* Lapwings) id. a pece.
Seegulles id. or i½d. at the moste.
Styntes after vi. a id.
Quaylles iid. a pece at moste.
Snypes after iii. a id.

Perttryges at iid. a pece.
Redeshankes i½d.
Bytters (*i.e.* Bitterns) xiid.
Fesauntes xiid
Reys (*i.e.* Ruffs and Reeves) iid. a pece.
Sholardes vid. a pece.
Kyrlewes xiid. a pece.
Pacokes xiid. a pece
See-Pyes (no price).
Wegions at i½d. the pece.
Knottes id. a pece.
Dottrells id. a pece.
Bustardes (no price).
Ternes after iiii. a id.
Great byrdes after iiii. a id.
Small byrdes after xii. for iid.
Larkys after xii. for iid.

In the year 1536, Henry VIII. issued a proclamation in order to preserve the partridges, pheasants, and herons "from his palace at Westminster to St. Giles-in-the-Fields, and from thence to Islington, Hampstead, Highgate, and Hornsey Park." Any person, of whatever rank, who should presume to kill, or in any wise molest these birds, was to be thrown into prison, and visited by such other punishments as to the King should seem meet.

Some interesting particulars in regard to pheasants are furnished by the " Privy Purse Expenses of King Henry VIII." For example, under date xvjth Nov. 1532, we have :—

"Itm̄ the same daye paied to the
 fesaunt breder in rewarde   ixs̄.   iiijd.

" Itm̄ the xxv daye paied to the preste
 the fesaunt breder at Elthm in
 rewarde ij corons .   ixs̄.   iiijd.

And in December of the same year :—

" Itm̄ the xxijd. daye paied to the french
 Preste the fesaunt breder for to bye
 him a gowne and other necesarys .   xls̄."

From these entries it would appear that even at this date some trouble and expense was incurred in rearing pheasants. No allusion, however, is made to their being shot. They must have been taken in a net or snare, or killed with a hawk. The last-named mode is indicated from another source *:—

"Item, a Fesant kylled with the Goshawke.

"A notice, two Fesants and two Partridges killed with the hawks."

As a rule, they are only referred to as being "brought in," the bearer receiving a gratuity for his trouble.

"Jany. 1536-7. Itm̃. geuen to Hunte yeoman of the pultry, bringing to hir g̃ce two qwicke (*i.e.* live) phesants . . vijs̃. vjd.

"Ap^{l.} 1537. Itm̃. geuen to Grene the ptrich taker bringing a cowple of Phesaunts to my lady's grace . . iijs̃. ixd.

"Jan. 1537-8. Itm̃. geuen to my lady Carow's s'uñt bringing a qwicke Phesaunt . ijs̃.

"Jan. 1543-4. Itm̃. geuen to Hawkyn, s'uñte of Hertford bringing a phesant and ptriches† . . iijs̃. iiijd."

In a survey of the possessions of the Abbey of Glastonbury made in 1539, mention is made of *a "game" of sixteen pheasants* in the woods at Meare, a manor near Glastonbury belonging to the Abbey.

* "Extracts from the Household and Privy Purse Accounts of the L'estranges of Hunstanton, 1519—1578." (Trans. Roy. Soc. Antiq. 1833.)

† "The Privy Purse Expenses of the Princess Mary, 1536—1544." (Edited by Sir F. Madden, 1831.)

According to Fynes Morrison ("Itinerary," 1617), there was in Ireland "such plenty of *pheasants* as I have known readie served at one feast."

The value set upon pheasants and partridges at various periods, as shown by the laws fixing penalties for their destruction, seems to have fluctuated considerably.

By a statute passed in the eleventh year of the reign of Henry VII. it was forbidden "to take pheasants or partridges with engines in another's ground without license in pain of ten pound, to be divided between the owner of the ground and the prosecutor." By 23 Eliz. c. 10, "None should kill or take pheasants or partridges by night in pain of 20s. a pheasant, and 10s. a partridge, or one month's imprisonment, and bound with sureties not to offend again in the like kind." By 1 Jac. I. c. 27, "No person should kill or take any pheasant, partridge, (&c.), or take or destroy the eggs of pheasants, partridges, (&c.), in pain of 20s., or imprisonment for every fowl or egg, and to find sureties in £20 not to offend in the like kind." Under the same statute, no person was permitted "to buy or sell any pheasant or partridge, upon pain to forfeit 20s. for every pheasant, and 10s. for every partridge." By 7 Jac. I. c. 11, "every person having hawked at or destroyed any pheasant or partridge between the 1st of July and last of August, forfeited 40s. for every time so hawking, and 20s. for every pheasant or partridge so destroyed or taken." Lords of manors and their servants might take pheasants or partridges in their own grounds or precincts in the day-time between Michaelmas and Christmas. But every person of a mean condition having killed or taken any pheasant or partridge, forfeited 20s. for each one so killed, and had to find surety in £20 not to offend so again.

In some of these old statutes, however, it was expressly stated that although pheasants and partridges could not be killed by any one with impunity, no penalty should attach for killing such birds as crows, kites, and buzzards, as these were well known to be destructive to the game which the statutes were framed to protect.

In the second part of *Henry VI.* Act iii. Sc. 2, we find the Partridge (*Perdix cinerea*) appropriately placed by Shakespeare in the nest of the kite :—

"Who finds the partridge in the puttock's nest,
But may imagine how the bird was dead,
Although the kite soar with unbloodied beak."

Henry VI. Part II. Act iii. Sc. 2.

Such was the beautiful metaphor uttered by the Earl of Warwick upon the occasion of the Duke of Gloucester's death. The unfortunate Duke was discovered dead in his bed, with marks of violence upon his features, and grave suspicion fell upon the Duke of Suffolk, who "had him in protection." This circumstance, coupled with the fact that Suffolk was a sworn enemy of Duke Humphrey, placed a heavy weight in the balance against him.

The provincial name of "puttock," which occurs in the above quotation, is sometimes applied to the kite, sometimes to the common buzzard. In this case, as shown by the context, the kite is the bird referred to. A greater enemy to the partridge than either of these birds is the peregrine, whose skill in taking this game was early turned to advantage by falconers. Partridge-hawking was formerly a favourite pastime, and is still, to a certain extent, with those few who still maintain the practice of falconry. For this sport either the peregrine or the goshawk may be used. Aubrey has recorded a curious event which happened when he was a freshman at Oxford in 1642. He frequently supped with Charles I., who then resided at the University; and on one of these occasions he heard the King say that—"As he was hawking in Scotland, he rode into the quarry, and found the covey of partridges falling upon the hawk." He adds that the King said—"I will swear upon the book that it is true." Mr. F. H. Salvin has been very successful in taking pheasants with the male goshawk, which he found required no "entering," but flew and killed even old cocks, threading his way through the trees in a wonderfully rapid manner.*

Those who made their living by fowling, and could not afford to hawk, took their birds by springe and net; and

---

* Some interesting remarks on pheasant and partridge-hawking will be found in Freeman and Salvin's " Falconry ; its Claims, History, and Practice," pp. 233, 235.

partridge-netting was, perhaps, as much in vogue in Shakespeare's day as now.

In *Much Ado about Nothing*, allusion is again made to the partridge by Beatrice, who, referring to the ill-humour of Benedick, says,—

"He'll but break a comparison or two on me; which, peradventure, not marked or not laughed at, strikes him into melancholy; and then there's a partridge wing saved, for the fool will eat no supper that night."—*Much Ado about Nothing*, Act ii. Sc. 1.

As we speak of a "covey" of partridges, so we say a "bevy" of quails:—

"And many more of the same bevy."
Hamlet, Act v. Sc. 2.

It was formerly the practice to keep Quails, and make them fight like game-cocks. Solon directed that quails should be made to fight in the presence of the Athenian youths, in order to inflame their courage, and the Romans held quail-fighting in still higher estimation. Augustus punished a prefect of Egypt with death for buying and bringing to table a quail which had acquired celebrity by its victories.*

Shakespeare was doubtless alluding to this sport when he wrote:—

* *Vide* Julius Pollux, "De ludis," lib. ix.

"Here's Agamemnon, an honest fellow enough, and one that loves quails."—*Troilus and Cressida*, Act v. Sc. 1.

Even at the present day this sort of amusement is common in some parts of Italy, and still more so in China. In Italy, the practice is to feed up two quails very highly, and then place them opposite to each other at the end of a long table, throwing between them a few grains of millet-seed to make them quarrel. At first they merely threaten, lowering the head and ruffling all the neck feathers, but at length they rush on furiously, striking with their bills, erecting their heads, and rising upon their spurs, until one is forced to yield.

In *Antony and Cleopatra* (Act ii. Sc. 3), Antonius says of Cæsar:—

"His cocks do win the battle still of mine,
When it is all to nought; and his quails ever
Beat mine inhoop'd at odds."

That there was some foundation for this assertion, we may gather from the following extract from North's "Plutarch":—

"With Antonius there was a soothsayer or astronomer in Egypt that coulde cast a figure and judge of men's nativities, to tell them what should happen to them. He told Antonius plainly that his fortune (which of itself was excellent good and very great) was altogether blemished and obscured by Cæsar's fortune ; and therefore he counselled him utterly to leave his company, and get him as farre from him as he coulde. Howsoever it was, the event ensuing proved the Egyptian's words true ; for it is said that as often as they drew lots for pastime, who should have anything, or whether they played at dice, Antonius always lost. *Oftentimes when they were disposed to see cock-fights, or quails that were taught to fight one with another, Cæsar's cocks or quails did ever overcome.* The which spited Antonius in his mind, although he made no outward show of it, and therefore he believed the Egyptian the better."

In Kircher's " Musurgia " the note of this bird is thus faithfully rendered* :—

Bi - ko - bik, Bi - ko - bik, Bi - ko - bik.

Quails have always been considered a delicacy for the table, and those who may have the curiosity to visit the London markets in the spring of the year, will see large boxes full of live quails, which have been taken in nets and imported to this country for food.

In the same way immense numbers of Lapwings (*Vanellus cristatus*), or Green Plovers, as they are called, find their way into the London markets. This bird has been noticed by Shakespeare chiefly on account of a peculiar trait in its character, with which most naturalists

* " Musurgia Universalis," 1650, p. 30.

are very familiar. Like the partridge and some other birds, it has a curious habit of trying to draw intruders away from its nest or young by fluttering along the ground in an opposite direction, or by feigning lameness, or uttering melancholy cries at a distance :—

"Far from her nest the lapwing cries away."
Comedy of Errors, Act iv. Sc. 2.

Allusions to this habit are not unfrequent in our older poets. Lily, in his "Campaspe," 1584, says :—

"You resemble the lapwing, who crieth most where her nest is not."

So also Greene, in the second part of his "Coney Catching," 1592 :—

"But again to our priggers, who, as before
I said, cry with the lapwing farthest from her nest."

And in Ben Jonson's *Underwoods* we are told,—

"Where he that knows will like a lapwing flie,
Farre from the nest, and so himselfe belie."

Hence the phrase "to seem the lapwing," which occurs in *Measure for Measure*, Act i. Sc. 4. So also in *Much Ado about Nothing*,—

"For look where Beatrice, like a lapwing, runs,
Close by the ground, to hear our conference."
Act iii. Sc. 1.

It is rather curious that Shakespeare has not alluded to this bird under its popular name of "Peewit,"—a name which, derived from its cry, we believe to be of some antiquity. Nor has he referred to it by another name, which must have been commonly applied to it in his day, *i.e.*, "Wype." In the old "Household Books" and "Privy Purse Expenses," we frequently meet with such entries as the following :—

"Item, it is thought goode that wypes* be hade for my Lordes own mees onely and to be at jd. a pece."

The young of this, and many other, species run almost as soon as hatched, and Shakespeare has not overlooked this peculiarity :—

"This lapwing runs away with the shell on his head."
Hamlet, Act v. Sc. 2.

We have before had occasion to make a passing allusion to the Heron, and in the present chapter this bird deserves more particular attention, from the fact of its being so frequently flown at by falconers.

Hawking at herons was thought to be "a marvellous and delectable pastime," and in all the published treatises upon falconry, many pages are dedicated to this particular branch of the sport.

Not only were herons protected by Act of Parliament,

---

* In Sweden the bird is known as *wipa* to this day.

but penalties were incurred for taking the eggs,* and no one was permitted to shoot within 600 paces of a heronry, under a penalty of £20 (7 Jac. I. c. 27).

We should scarcely have thought it possible to find a man who would not know a hawk from a heron when he saw it, and Hamlet evidently considered that such an one would not be in his right mind, for he says of himself:—

"I am but mad north-north-west: when the wind is southerly, I know a hawk from a *handsaw.*"—*Hamlet,* Act ii. Sc. 2.

He referred here to an old proverbial saying, originally "he does not know a hawk from a hernshaw," that is, a heron; but the word was thus corrupted before Shakespeare's day. (See *ante*, p. 75.)

John Shaw (M.A., of Cambridge), who published a curious book in 1635, entitled "Speculum Mundi," tells us therein that "the heron or *hernsaw* is a large fowle that liveth about waters," and that "hath a marvellous hatred to the hawk, which hatred is duly returned. When they fight above in the air, they labour both especially for this one thing—that one may ascend and be above the other. Now, if the hawk getteth the upper place, he overthroweth and vanquisheth the heron with a marvellous earnest flight." This old passage contrasts quaintly with the animated description of heron-hawking in Freeman and

* The fine was 8*d.* for every egg. *See* 3 & 4 Ed. VI. c. 7, and 25 Hen. VIII. c. 11.

Salvin's modern treatise.* Those who have taken part in the sport cannot fail to be interested in a truthful narrative of what they must so often have witnessed; while those who have never seen a trained falcon on the wing will learn a good deal from the following excellent description :—

"'Well, then, here goes,' says the falconer; and having let the heron get a little past, off go the hoods. For a moment one hawk looks up, and is cast off; the other a moment or two afterwards. They both see him ; now for a flight. The heron was about 250 yards high, and perhaps a quarter of a mile wide. The hawks had gone up about a quarter of the way before the heron saw them in hot pursuit. 'Now he sees them!' is exclaimed ; and the riders rattle their horses as hard as they can, over deep sand-hills, down wind. The heron, in the meanwhile, vomits up his fish to lighten himself, and begins ringing-up down wind. It is a curious thing to see the different manœuvres of the birds. With his large wings, the heron can mount very fair, and has a far better chance of beating off the hawks than if he flew straight forward. This he knows full well by instinct, and puts on accordingly all sail for the upper regions, generally in short rings. Hawks make larger rings as a general rule, if, like these, they are good ones. Those have but a bad chance with a

---

* " Falconry; its History, Claims, and Practice," by G. E. Freeman and F. H. Salvin. London, 1859.

good heron if they adopt the same tactics that he does in mounting. This the two old hawks know full well. So far they have been pretty near together, but, seeing the prey beginning to mount, they separate, each their own way, now taking a long turn down wind, and then breasting the wind again. 'De Ruyter' makes the best rings, and after having gone a mile, there is a shout— 'Now "De Ruyter" is above him!' and the hawk is seen poising herself for a stoop; down she comes, with closed wings, like a bullet, and hits the heron; it is too high to see *where*, but the scream the quarry gives is tremendous. Hurrah! there's a stoop for you! Both hawk and heron have descended some yards; the former, from the impetus of her stoop, much beneath the heron, but she shoots up again to a level. In fact, it was a perfect stoop. Though so near the heron, she does not attempt a *little* stoop, but again heads the wind so that the heron appears to be flying the hawk. 'Sultan' is now above both, and makes her stoop, but not so good as her partner's. However, she makes two quickly, and is within an ace of catching; but the good heron will not give an inch, and 'Sultan' will have to give another ring for another stoop. But where is 'De Ruyter' all this time? She has made a long ring, and is now a long way above them. She makes another full stoop, and this time there is no mistake about it, for she hits the heron so hard that he is nearly stupefied. 'Sultan' joins in the fray and catches. Whoo-whoo-o-p! down they come. Down they all three go together, till, just before reaching the ground, the two old hawks let go of their prey, which falls bump. Before he has had time to recover himself, in a moment the hawks are on him, 'De Ruyter' on the neck, and 'Sultan' on his body. Hurrah for the gallant hawks! and loud whoops proclaim his capture. 'Wouldn't take £100 for them,' says their owner, who has ridden well, judiciously as well as hard, and has got up in time to save the heron's life. He gives the hawks a pigeon, and puts the heron between his knees in a position so that he can neither spike him nor the hawks with his bill. He has two beautiful long black feathers, which are duly presented to Prince Alexander—alas! now no more—who is well up at the take. These feathers are the badge of honour in heron-hawking in Holland, as the fox's brush is in hunting in England. The hawks are fed up as speedily as possible, the heron has a ring put round his leg, and is let loose, evidently not knowing what to make of it.

"We hasten back as fast as we can, but the weather being now hot, the herons move more by night than by day. Many anxious eyes search the horizon for another.

"The two sets of falconers, with their hawks, place themselves about half a mile apart, to intercept the herons on their passage back from their fishing-grounds.

"There is no lack of herons. The little wind there was has fallen to a calm, and they come home higher. All the better, for we have some good casts to fly. One is soon 'hooded off' at, and, after a capital flight, is taken high in the air. The pet hawks are now taken in hand—'De Ruyter' and 'Sultan;' and, as there is no wind, the owner says he will fly at the first '*light one*,' that comes at all fair. All is excitement when one is seen coming *from* the *heronry*, and therefore unweighted. They are 'hooded off' in his face; he sees them directly, and proceeds to mount. 'Now, good hawks, you will have some work to do before you overtake him!' The knowing riders are down wind as hard as they can go. Ring after ring is made, and yet the hawks seem to gain but little on him. Still they are flying like swallows: 'De Ruyter' makes a tremendous ring, but still fails to get above him. Again and again they ring, and have attained a great height. A scream of delight is heard: they are above him; 'De Ruyter' is at him! A fine stoop, but the heron dodges out of the way. Now for. 'Sultan;' but she misses too; the heron is up like a shot, and three or four rings have to be made before there is another stoop. Another and another stoop, with loud cheers from below. 'Sultan' *just* catches him once, but can't hold; it seems still a doubtful victory, when 'De Ruyter' hits him *hard;* and, after two or three more stoops, 'Sultan' catches him, amidst the excitement of hurrahs and whoops; a really good flight; *can't be better*,—two and a half miles from where they were 'hooded off.'

"Thus ended as good a day's sport as any one could wish to see."

The heron, besides affording great sport with hawks, was considered, when killed, a delicacy for the table. At the ancient City feasts and entertainments to royalty, the heron always appeared amongst the other good things;* and from the old "Household Books" it appears that the price usually paid for this bird was xijd. Of late years the heron has dropped out of the bill of fare, and no longer forms a fashionable dish. One of the last records of its appearance at table which we have met with, is in connection with the feast which was given by the Executors of Thomas Sutton, the founder of the London Charter House, on the 18th May, 1812, in the Hall of the Stationers' Company. "For this repast were provided 32 neats' tongues, 40 stone of beef, 24 marrow-bones, 1 lamb, 46 capons, 32 geese, 4 pheasants, 12 pheasants' pullets, 12 godwits, 24 rabbits, 6 *hearnshaws*," &c., &c.

Amongst the other "lang-nebbit things" which interest both sportsman and gourmand, the Woodcock and Snipe received almost as much attention in Shakespeare's day as they do at the present time—with this difference, however, that where the gun is now employed, the gin or springe was formerly the instrument of their death.

* Leland states, that at the feast given on the inthronisation of George Neville, Archbishop of York, in the reign of Edward IV., no less than "400 Heronshawes" were served up!

"Four woodcocks in a dish."
Love's Labour's Lost, Act iv. Sc. 3.

The woodcock, for some unaccountable reason, was supposed to have no brains, and the name of this bird became a synonym for a fool. It is to this that Claudio alludes when he says :—

"Shall I not find a woodcock too?"
Much Ado about Nothing, Act v. Sc. 1.

Again—

"O this woodcock! what an ass it is!"
Taming of the Shrew, Act i. Sc. 2.

Shakespeare has many allusions to the capture of this bird by springe and gin—

"Aye, springes to catch woodcocks."
Hamlet, Act i. Sc. 3.

In his "Natural History and Sport in Moray," Mr. St. John describes a springe with which he used to take both snipe and woodcocks very successfully. It was made as follows :—

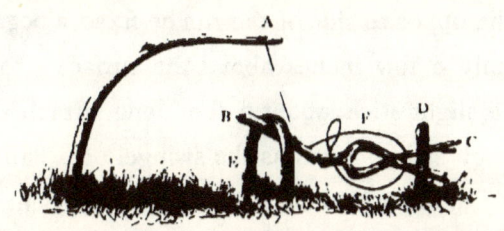

A. Rod like a mole-trap stick. B. Short piece of stick. C. Forked stick with one end passed through the other. D. Straight stick. E. Bent stick. F. Hair-snare.

A, by pulling on B, presses it against the forked stick C, which in turn is pressed against the upright stick D, and this keeps it all in place. But on a bird stepping on the forked stick C, the weight of the bird loosens its hold, and the long stick A flies up, catching the victim in the snare, which is laid flat on the forked stick C.

Then, as Shakespeare hath it,—

"If the springe hold, the *cock's* mine."

Winter's Tale, Act iv. Sc. 2.

Mr. A. E. Knox, in his "Game-Birds and Wild-Fowl," has described a very similar trap, and his description is so animated, while at the same time so instructive, that we are tempted to overlook the similarity and quote his words:—

"We soon found many tracks of the woodcock on the black mud; and on one spot these, as well as the borings of his beak, were very numerous. Here my companion halted, and pulling out his knife, cut down a tall willow rod, which he stuck firmly into the ground in nearly an upright position, or perhaps rather inclining backwards.

"On the opposite side of the run he fixed a peg, so as to project only a few inches above the surface; to this he fastened a slight stick about a foot long, attached loosely with a tough string, much as the swingel of a flail is to its handstaff: another branch of a willow was bent into an arch, and both ends driven into the soft ground to a considerable depth on the opposite side of the track, and nearer to the tall upright wand. To the top of the latter a string was now fastened, the end of which was formed into a large running noose ; while, about half way down, another piece of stick, about six inches long, was tied by its middle. The flexible wand was then bent forcibly downwards, one end of the little stick overhead was passed under the arch, while it was retained in this position, and at the same time the bow prevented from springing upwards, by the other extremity being placed against a notch at the end of the stick which had been fastened to the peg on the other side of the run, across which it now lay, two or three inches from the ground, and supported the noose. This, in fact, constituted the trigger, which was to be released when struck by the breast of the woodcock. The old man constructed his trap in much less time than I have taken to describe it. His last care was to weave the sedges on either side of the run into a kind of screen, so as to *weir* the woodcock into the snare, and this he accomplished with much skill and expedition."

"We have caught the woodcock."
All's Well, Act iv. Sc. 1.

Another method of taking this bird was with a steel trap called "a gin :"

"Now is the woodcock near the gin."
Twelfth Night, Act ii. Sc. 5.

This trap, being commonly used now-a-days for rats, is probably too well known to need a description here.

"So strives the woodcock with the gin."
Henry VI. Part III. Act i. Sc. 4.

Under the head of "Wild-Fowl" we shall have occasion, in a subsequent chapter, to allude to the opinion of Pythagoras on the transmigration of souls, and to the discussion on this subject in *Twelfth Night*, when the clown portentously observes to Malvolio,—

"Fear to kill a woodcock, lest thou dispossess the soul of thy grandam. Fare thee well."—*Twelfth Night*, Act iv. Sc. 2.

The "woodcock's head" in Shakespeare's day, on account of its shape, was a fashionable term for a tobacco-pipe.* "Those who loved smoking sat on the stage-stools, with their three sorts of tobacco, and their lights by them, handing matches on the point of their swords, or sending out their pages for real Trinidado. They actually practised smoking under professors who taught them tricks; and the intelligence offices were not more frequented, no, nor the pretty seamstresses' shops at the Exchange, than the new tobacco office."†

It is somewhat remarkable that while Shakespeare's contemporary, Ben Jonson, has founded whole scenes upon

* *Every Man Out of his Humour*, Act iii. Sc. 3.
† Thornbury, "Shakespeare's England," vol. i. pp. 169, 170.

the practice of smoking, he himself has made no mention of it. Some commentators have brought this forward as a proof of the comparative earliness of many of his dramas, but smoking was in general use long before Shakespeare left London, and he drew his manners almost entirely from his own age, making mention of masks, false hair, pomanders, and fardingales, all of which were introduced about the same time. But *apropos* of "the woodcock's head," we are wandering away from Shakespeare's birds.

The Snipe (*Scolopax gallinago*) has been less frequently noticed by him than the woodcock. Indeed we have been unable to find more than one passage in which it is mentioned.

Iago, alluding to Roderigo, says:—

"For I mine own gain'd knowledge should profane,
If I would time expend with such a snipe,
But for my sport and profit."

Othello, Act i. Sc. 3.

The speaker being evidently of opinion that a snipe was too insignificant a bird to the sportsman to warrant his taking much trouble to kill it, except for mere sport.

That there was a good deal more "sport" than "profit" is extremely likely; for it is difficult to believe that the sportsmen of Shakespeare's day, with guns such as we have described, fired with either fuze or flint, could have successfully stopped the erratic flight of a snipe. That large numbers of snipe were brought to market, and appeared at table, in Shakespeare's time, is clear from the numerous entries in the old "Household Book," where their value is stated to have been "after iii a j d." There can be little doubt, however, that these were not "shot birds," but were taken in snares and nets, as our modern fowlers take plovers and other fen birds.

CHAPTER VIII.

WILD-FOWL AND SEA-FOWL.

TO the general reader these terms may appear synonymous, but to the sportsman and naturalist they have a very different signification. Under the head of "wild-fowl" may be placed the various species of wild geese, swans, and ducks, which, though often found at sea, evince a partiality for fresh water, rear their young in the neighbourhood of fresh water, and, as an article of food, are especially sought after by the amateur for sport, and by the professional gunner for profit; while the group of "sea-fowl" may be said to include the gulls, terns, guillemots, auks, cormorants, and various other birds, which, making the sea their home, rear their young upon its shelving beach or frowning cliffs, and, except on an emergency, are seldom cooked and eaten.

Shakespeare has given us a peep at both. At one time we see—

"Strange fowl light upon neighbouring ponds."
Cymbeline, Act i. Sc. 4;

at another—

"A flight of fowl
Scatter'd by winds and high tempestuous gusts."

Titus Andronicus, Act v. Sc. 3.

Anon the scene changes, and leaving the green fields of which Falstaff "babbled," and the "great pool" with its "swan's nest" (*Cymbeline*, Act iii. Sc. 4), we are led to—

"That pale, that whitefaced shore,
Whose foot spurns back the ocean's roaring tides."

King John, Act ii. Sc. 1;

there to contemplate "the sea-mells" on the rock (*Tempest*, Act ii. Sc. 2), or watch the movements of the "insatiate cormorant" (*Richard II.* Act ii. Sc. 1).

Nor are we left entirely to our own reflections in these situations. Some trait or other is noticed in the habits of the bird alluded to, some curious instinct pointed out. We pause insensibly to admire the appropriate haunts in which the poet has discovered the fowl, and carry out with him, in thought, the crafty device of the fowler to which a passing allusion is made.

Naturalists have frequently observed that when any of the diving-ducks are winged or injured, they generally make for the open water, and endeavour to escape by diving or swimming away, while those which do not excel in diving, usually make for the shore when wounded, and, as Shakespeare tells us, "creep into sedges."

"Alas! poor hurt fowl, now will he creep into sedges."
Much Ado about Nothing, Act ii. Sc. 1.

"Duck-hunting," *i.e.*, hunting a tame duck in the water with spaniels, was a favourite amusement in Shakespeare's day. "Besides the clear streams that ran into the Thames, old London boasted of innumerable wells, now lost, sullied, or bricked up. There was Holy-well, Clement's-well, Clerken-well, Skinners-well, Fay-well, Fede-well, Leden-well, and Shad-well. West Smithfield had its horse-pond, its pool of Dame Annis le Cleare, and the Perilous Pond. The duck-hunting in these pools, and at Islington, was a favourite amusement with the citizens." *

"And 'hold-fast' is the only dog, my duck."
Henry V. Act ii. Sc. 3.

The sense of smell and hearing is possessed by most wild-fowl in an extraordinary degree, and, except under favourable circumstances—favourable that is to the shooter—they display what Falstaff would call "a want of valour," and, as soon as they become aware of the approach of the enemy, ignominiously take to flight:—

"*Falstaff.* There is no more valour in that Poins than in a wild duck."—*Henry IV.* Part I. Act ii. Sc. 2.

But, if the better part of valour be discretion, Poins, like the wild duck, displays the better part:—

* Thornbury, "Shakespeare's England," i. p. 21; see also p. 33.

"Claps on his sea wing, and like a doting mallard,
Leaving the fight in height, flies after it."

Antony and Cleopatra, Act iii. Sc. 10.

To swim like a duck is proverbial—

"*Stephano.* Here; swear then how thou escapest.

Trinculo. Swam ashore, man, like a duck; I can swim like a duck, I'll be sworn."—*Tempest*, Act ii. Sc. 2.

An ancient device for getting within shot of wild-fowl was "the stalking-horse." Hence the allusion—

"Stalk on, stalk on, the fowl sits."

Much Ado about Nothing, Act ii. Sc. 3.

And again—

"He uses his folly like a stalking-horse, and under the presentation of that he shoots his wit."—*As You Like It*, Act v. Sc. 4.

Gervase Markham tells us[*] that "sometime it so happeneth that the fowl are so shie there is no getting a shoot at them without 'a stalking-horse,' which must be some old jade trained up for that purpose, who will gently, and as you will have him, walk up and down in the water which way you please, plodding and eating on the grass that grows therein. You must shelter yourself and gun behind his fore-shoulder, bending your body down low by his side, and keeping his body still full

[*] "The Gentleman's Recreation." 1595.

between you and the fowl. Being within shot, take your level from before the fore part of the horse, shooting as it were between the horse's neck and the water. . .
Now to supply the want of a stalking-horse, which will take up a great deal of time to instruct and make fit for this exercise, you may make one of any piece of old canvass, which you must shape into the form of an horse, with the head bending downwards, as if he grazed. You may stuff it with any light matter; and do not forget to paint it of the color of an horse, of which the brown is the best. . . . It must be made so portable that you may bear it with ease in one hand, moving it so as it may seem to graze as you go."

Sometimes the stalking-horse was made in shape of an ox; sometimes in the form of a stag; and sometimes to represent a tree, shrub, or bush. In every case it had a spike at the bottom, to stick into the ground while the fowler took his aim.

In the "Privy Purse Expenses of King Henry VIII." are various entries referring to stalking-horses, all of which appear to refer to the live animal; and there is one entry relating to a stalking-ox.

The gun used on these occasions was either the "birding-piece" already described,* or the "caliver." Shakespeare has appropriately mentioned the latter in connection with wild ducks, in the first part of his

* See pp. 164, 165.

Henry IV., where Falstaff speaks of cowards "such as fear the report of a 'caliver' worse than a struck fowl or a hurt wild-duck."—*Henry IV.* Part I. Act iv. Sc. 2.

The derivation of the word "caliver" is not quite clear, unless it be the same weapon as the "culverin," in which case it may be derived from the French *couleuvrin*, adder-like. In Cotgrave's French and English Dictionary, 1660, the word is spelled "calœver," and translated "harquebuse." In Bailey's "Dictionarium Britannicum," 1736, the caliver is described as "a small gun used at sea." In Worcester's "Dictionary of the English Language," 1859, "caliver" is said to be corrupted from *caliber*, and described as—1. a hand-gun or large pistol, an arquebuse; 2. a kind of light matchlock. In Scheler's "Dictionnaire d'Etymologie Française," 1862, we find—"couleuvre du L. *colubra*; It. *colubro*; Prov. *colobre*; du L. masc. *coluber*, bri; D. *couleuvreau*, *couleuvrine*, ou *coulevrine*, pièce d'artillerie; cp. les termes *serpentin*, et All. *feldschlange*."

From these various explanations, as well as from that given by Archdeacon Nares in his "Glossary," it would seem to have been a military rather than a sporting weapon. The best description which we have met with is that given by Sir S. D. Scott.* He says :—

"The Caliver was a kind of short musket or harquebus, fired by a matchlock, and from its lightness did not require a rest."

* "The British Army: its Origin, Progress, and Equipment," vol. ii. p. 286.

"'Put me a caliver in Wart's hands,' says Falstaff, reviewing his recruits, meaning thereby that Wart, who was a weak, undersized fellow, was not capable of managing a heavier weapon. It was sometimes called *arquebuse de calibre*, and was in fact an arquebus of specified bore, having derived its name from the corruption of calibre into caliver. 'I remember,' writes Edmund York, an officer who had served in the Netherlands, and was appointed by the Privy Council to report on the best mode of organizing the militia of London, in expectation of the Spanish invasion, 'when I was first brought up in Piemount, in the Countie of Brisack's Regiment of the old Bandes, we had our particular calibre of Harquebuze to our Regiment, both that for one bullett should serve all the harquebuses of our Regiment, as for that our Collonell would not be deceaved of his armes; of which worde Calibre, came first that unapt term we used to call a harquebuze a calliver, which is the height of the bullett, and not of the piece. Before the battell of Mountgunter (*Moncontour*, A.D. 1569) the Prynces of the Religion caused seven thousand harquebuzes to be made, all of one calibre, which were called *Harquebuze du calibre de Monsieur le Prince*. So as, I think, some man not understanding French brought hither the name of the height of the bullet of the piece; which worde calibre is yet contynued with our good cannoniers.'"*

* *See* the Report in Maitland s "Hist. of London," p. 594.

A contemporary military writer, Sir John Smythe, gives his opinion that the term was derived from "the height of the bullet"—*i.e.* the bore. He says, "The caliver is only a harquebuse; savinge, that it is of greater circuite, or bullet, than the other is of; wherefore the Frenchman doth call it a *piece de calibre*, which is as much as to saie, a piece of bigger circuite.* I would that all harquebuses throughout the field should be of one caliver and height, to the intent that every soldier on the lack of bullets might use his fellows' bullets."

There are two specimens in the Tower Collection, of a caliver and a musket of the sixteenth century, from Penshurst Place, Kent. The length of the former (here figured) is 4 ft. 10 in., the latter 5 ft. 5¼ in.†

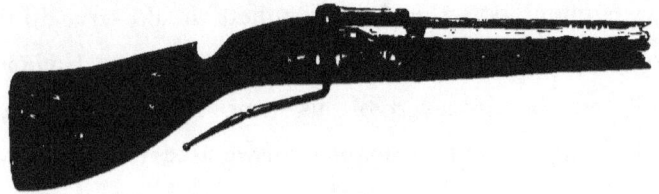

Notwithstanding the "bigger circuite," the musket was considered twice as efficient in its effects, and Sir Roger Williams corroborates the fact, admitting the advantage possessed by the caliver of being more rapidly discharged. "The calivers may say they will discharge two shot for one, but cannot denie that one musket-shot doth more hurt than two calivers' shot." ‡

* "An Answer to the Opinion of Captain Barwicke." (Harl. MSS., No. 4,685.)
† Their numbers, in Mr. Hewitt's official *Tower Catalogue*, are 18 and 19.
‡ "Brief Discourse of War, 1590."

THE CALIVER.

In the *Lancashire Lieutenancy* is preserved the price of the caliver and its appendages, and the equipment of the bearer, in 1574:—"Everie caliũ his peece, flaxe & touche-box xiiij^s; his morion vij^s viij^d, sworde & dagger vij^s, his hose viij^s, his showes ij^s, his shirtt iiij^s, his dublett iiij^s, his coate xij^s iiij^d, money in his purse xxvj^s viij^d."

For some unexplained reason, the price of a caliver, which, with flask and touch-box, was charged only 14s. in 1574, in 1576 cost 24s.:—

"Itm̃ a calliũ . . . xxiiij^s."

In 1581, we find the charges for "A Shoot:—Caliu, flaxe, tuche box & scorier xvj;" and in a "Schedule of such rates of money as armor may be provided for at the Cyttie of Chester, for such souldiors as shall repaire thither out of the county of Lancaster," the caliver furnished with flask, and touch-box, laces and moulds, xiij^s vj^d.*

In 1620, a caliver, with bandoleers,† is valued at 14s. 10d.‡ According to a passage in Brantôme,§ it would appear that the Spaniards originated this improvement in fire-arms, "la façon et l'usage des belles harquebuzes de calibre;" and that it was introduced by Phillippe Strozzi into the French infantry, under Charles IX., but it was

---

* Peck's "Desid. Cur."
† Bandoleers consisted of a belt of leather worn over the left shoulder, on which were suspended little metal, wooden, leather, or horn cylinders, each containing one charge. Examples are preserved in the Tower of London.
‡ Harl. MSS., No. 5,109.
§ Brantôme, "Œuvres," tom. vii. pp. 425-429.

evidently not adopted by the English troops till several years afterwards.

It will readily be understood by all sportsmen, that with such a weapon as the "caliver," much practice and patience must have been requisite to bring it within range of the fowl, and use it with effect. The successful use of a modern punt-gun necessitates an amount of skill and judgment which those only who have tried it can really appreciate. How much greater must have been the difficulties of the wild-fowler of the sixteenth century, whose rude gun and inferior powder necessitated a much nearer approach to the birds! We can sympathize with Cardinal Beaufort, when he exclaimed—

"Believe me, cousin Gloster,
Had not your man put up the fowl so suddenly,
We had had more sport."

Henry VI. Part II. Act ii. Sc. 1.

The wild-fowler who could not succeed in "stalking" and shooting the birds in the way we have described, often employed another method of securing them, namely, by means of "a stale," as it was termed. This was a stuffed bird of the species the fowler wished to decoy, and which was set up in as natural a position as possible, either before a net or in the midst of several "springes." By imitating the call of the passing birds, the fowler would draw their attention to the "stale," and as soon as they alighted near it either the net was pulled over them, or they were caught in the snares.

Beaumont and Fletcher speak of "stales to catch kites" (*Hum. Lieut.* iii. 2). Sometimes a live bird was pegged down instead of a stuffed one, and was doubtless much more effective, since "one bird caught, served *as a stale* to bring in more."*

Shakespeare has employed the word "stale" in this its primary sense, in his *Comedy of Errors* (Act ii. Sc. 1), in *The Tempest* (Act iv. Sc. 1), and in the *Taming of the Shrew* (Act iii. Sc. 1). But commentators do not seem to be agreed on its meaning. In Act i. Sc. 1, of the last-mentioned play, where it occurs again, it certainly admits of a different interpretation.

Instructions for making a "stale" will be found in "The Experienced Fowler" (London, 1704). At page 18 of this curious little volume, the author says:—"You may shoot a lark or some other bird, take out the entrails, stuff him with tow, and dry him in an oven, his wings set in a flying posture; and so you may be furnished at all times." This device was chiefly resorted to for taking the ruff and reeve, and other fen birds, which fetched good prices for the table. Now-a-days, the bird-catchers who take linnets, goldfinches, and other small songsters, almost invariably peg down live decoy birds with a foot or so of string to the legs, in the centre of a pair of clap-nets.

But to return to wild-fowl. Puck compares the fright-

---

* Sidney, "Arcadia," ii. p. 169.

ened varlets who fled at the sight of Bottom with the ass's head to "wild-geese that the creeping fowler eye."—*Midsummer Night's Dream*, Act iii. Sc. 2.

"They flock together in consent, like so many wild-geese."—*Henry IV.* Part II. Act v. Sc. 1.

And Marcius, addressing the retreating Romans before Corioli, reproaches them as having no more courage than geese:—

"You souls of geese,
That bear the shapes of men, how have you run
From slaves that apes would beat!"

Coriolanus, Act i. Sc. 4.

The Fool in *King Lear* reminds us of the old proverb—

"Winter's not gone yet, if the wild-geese fly that way."

King Lear, Act ii. Sc. 4.

It is not surprising that, to so common a bird, numerous allusions should be made in the Plays of Shakespeare, and, in addition to the passages quoted in Chapter VII.,* many others might here be mentioned, were it not that the repetition might prove tedious.

It was anciently believed that the Bernacle Goose (*Anser bernicla*) was generated from the Bernacle or Barnacle (*Lepas anatifera*). Shakespeare has alluded to the metamorphosis in the following line:—

"And all be turned to barnacles."

Tempest, Act iv. Sc. 1.

* See *ante*, p. 197.

It is strange that in matters concerning the marvellous, even men of education will take pains to deceive themselves, and, instead of investigating nature with a "learned spirit," give a license to ill-directed imagination, and credit absurdities. When such men are so credulous, how can we wonder at the superstitions of the illiterate?

The first phase of the story in question is, that certain trees, resembling willows, more particularly in one of the Orkneys, Pomona, produced at the ends of their branches small swelled balls, containing the embryo of a goose suspended by the bill, which, when ripe, fell off into the sea and took wing.

So long ago as the twelfth century, the story was pro-

THE BARNACLE GOOSE.

mulgated by Giraldus Cambrensis, in his "Topographia Hiberniæ," and Munster, Saxo Grammaticus, Scaliger, Fulgosus, Bishop Leslie, and Olaus Magnus, all attested to the truth of this monstrous absurdity. Gesner, too, and Aldrovandus * may be also cited.

THE BARNACLE GOOSE TREE. *From Aldrovandus.*

A second phase or modification of the story is that given by Boëce, the oldest Scottish historian: he denies that the geese (Scotticè, Claiks) grow on trees by their bills, as some believe, but that, as his own researches and personal experience prove, they are first produced in the form of worms, in the substance of old trees or timber floating in the sea; for such a tree, cast on shore in 1480, was brought to the laird, who ordered it to be sawn asunder, when there appeared a multitude of worms, "throwing themselves out of sundry holes and bores of

* Aldrovandi Opera Omina: Ornithologia. 3 vols. Bononiæ. 1599.

the tree; some of them were rude, as they were new-shapen; some had both head, feet, and wings, but they had no feathers; some of them were perfect-shapen fowls. At last the people, having this tree each day in more admiration, brought it to the kirk of St. Andrew's, beside the town of Tyre, where it yet remains to our days." Other instances he adduces by way of proof, and at length he comes to the conclusion, that the production of these geese from fruits is the erroneous opinion of the ignorant; it being ascertained that "they are produced only by the nature of the ocean sea, which is the cause and production of many wonderful things."

In this view he was supported by Turner and others: "When," says Turner, "at a certain time an old ship, or a plank, or a pine-mast rots in the sea, something like a little fungus at first makes its appearance, which at length puts on the manifest form of birds; afterwards these are clothed with feathers, and at last become living and flying fowl." ("Avium Præcip. Hist.," *Art.* "ANSER.") Turner, however, does not give up the goose-tree, but informs Gesner that it is a different bird from the brent or bernicle goose, which takes its origin from it. (Gesner, "De Avibus," iii. p. 107.) Passing a host of other authorities, with their accumulated proofs, and the depositions of unimpeachable witnesses, we may come to Gerard, who, in 1597, published the following account in his "Herball, or Generall Historie of Plantes":—

"There is a small island in Lancashire, called the Pile of Foulders, wherein are found the broken pieces of old and bruised ships, some whereof have been cast thither by shipwracke, and also the trunks or bodies, with the branches, of old and rotten trees, cast up there likewise; whereon is found a certaine spume, or froth, that in time breedeth unto certaine shels, in shape like those of the muskle, but sharper pointed, and of a whitish colour, wherein is contained a thing in forme like a lace of silke,

THE BARNACLE GOOSE TREE. *From Gerard.*

finely woven as it were together, of a whitish colour; one ende whereof is fastened unto the inside of the shell, even as the fish of oisters and muskles are; the other ende is made fast unto the belly of a rude masse or lumpe, which in time cometh to the shape and forme of a bird: when it is perfectly formed the shell gapeth open, and the first thing that appeareth is the foresaid lace or string; next come the legs of the bird hanging out, and as it groweth greater, it openeth the shell by degrees, till at length it is all come forth, and hangeth only by the bill: in short space after, it cometh to full maturitie, and falleth into the sea, where it gathereth feathers, and groweth to a fowle bigger than a mallard and lesser than a goose, having blacke legs and bill or beake, and feathers blacke and white, spotted in such manner as is our magge-pie, called in some places a pie-annet, which the people of Lancashire call by no other name than a tree-goose; which place aforesaide, and all those parts adjoining, do so much abound therewith, that one of the best is bought for three-pence. For the truth hereof, if any doubt, may it please them to repaire unto me, and I shall satisfie them by the testimonie of good witnesses."

Meyer, who wrote a treatise on this "bird without father or mother," states that he opened a hundred of the goose-bearing shells, and in all of them found the rudiments of the bird completely formed.

Sir Robert Murray, in an account of the barnacle published in the "Philosophical Transactions," says that "these shells are hung at the tree by a neck, longer than the shell, of a filmy substance, round and hollow, and creased not unlike the windpipe of a chicken, spreading out broadest where it is fastened to the tree, from which it seems to draw and convey the matter which serves for the growth and vegetation of the shell, and the little bird within it.

"In every shell that I opened," he continues, "I found a perfect sea-fowl; the little bill like that of a goose; the eyes marked; the head, neck, breast, wing, tail, and feet formed; the feathers everywhere perfectly shaped, and blackish coloured; and the feet like those of other water-fowl, to my best remembrance."

It is not to be supposed, however, that there were none who doubted this marvellous story, or who took steps to refute it. Belon, so long ago as 1551, and others after him, treated it with ridicule, and a refutation may be found in Willughby's "Ornithology," which was edited by Ray in 1678. An excellent account of the Barnacle was published by Mr. Thompson in the "Philosophical Transactions" for 1835, while the latest and most complete treatise on the subject is Mr. Darwin's "Monograph of the Cirrhipedia," published by the Ray Society.

What, then, is the marine production from which the Barnacle Goose was thought to be engendered? Merely certain shell-covered cirrhipedous creatures, called Barnacles (*Lepas anatifera*—Linn.), which are to be found adhering in clusters to floating logs of wood, the timbers of wrecked vessels, the sides of rocks, and other objects which afford a secure attachment.

Each individual consists of a body enclosed in a shell, not unlike that of a mussel in figure, and of a fleshy worm-like stem or peduncle, the extremity of which is fixed to the object upon which the animal is stationed. This stem is tubular, tolerably firm, and has a fleshy feel;

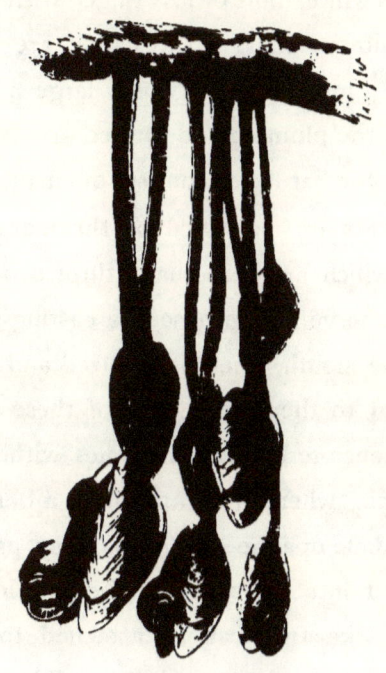

BARNACLES. *From nature.*

it is composed exteriorly of a fine coriaceous outer membrane, bedewed with a watery fluid, and beneath this, of an inner membrane of considerable density, apparently consisting of muscular fibres, running for the most part in parallel longitudinal lines. That these fibres are muscular we may conclude from the animal having the power of contracting the stem, or of twisting it in various directions. Within the tube there is a fluid secretion.

The shell is composed of five pieces, four of which are lateral, two on each side; while between the valves down the back is interposed a single narrow slip uniting them together. Their colour is white, more or less tinged with purplish blue. Along the anterior margin the valves are but partially connected by a membrane, leaving a large fissure, through which emerge the plumose and jointed arms or cirrhi.

The food of the Barnacles consists of small crustacea and mollusca. These are entangled by the many-jointed plumose cirrhi, which are perpetually thrown out and folded again, so as to serve the purpose of a casting-net, and drag the prey to the mouth, where it is seized and crushed.

With regard to the reproduction of these creatures, the eggs are seen enclosed at certain times within the hollow of the peduncle, where they appear of a blue colour, and render the pedicle opaque; from this they pass through a minute conduit into the cavity of the mantle, where they are arranged like two leaflets, attached to the septum between the body and the peduncle. They are enclosed in a film, out of which they fall when ready to hatch.

It is a remarkable fact, as we learn from Mr. Thompson[*], that the young barnacles and other cirrhi-

---

[*] "Philosophical Transactions," l.c.

peda on emerging from the egg are quite free, and very different from their parents. "They possess locomotive organs, consisting of a large anterior pair of limbs, provided with a sucker, and hooks for the purpose of mooring themselves at pleasure to various objects—and also of six pairs of swimming-limbs, acting in concert like oars. Besides these, they have a tail bent under the body, consisting of two joints and terminating in four bristles: this is an additional locomotive organ. Thus endowed, they swim along in a series of bounds, the oars and tail giving in measured time successive impulses. They have, moreover, large lateral eyes set on peduncles, and the body is covered with a sort of shell, as in certain crustacea (*e.g. Cyclops*), which they closely resemble," and for which Mr. Thompson at first mistook them.

In due time a metamorphosis takes place; the shell is thrown off, the eyes disappear, the limbs become transformed to cirrhi, the regular valves develop themselves, the peduncle shoots forth, and the animal becomes permanently fixed.

Believing these little creatures to be the larvæ of some crustaceous animal, some of them, says Mr. Thompson, were collected in the spring, and in order to see what changes they might undergo, were kept in a glass vessel, covered by such a depth of sea-water, that they could be examined at any time by means of a common magnifying-glass. They were taken May 1st, and on the night of the 8th the author had the satisfaction to find that two of them had thrown off their exuviæ, and, wonderful to say, were firmly adhering to the bottom of the vessel, and changed to young barnacles. In this stage the sutures between the valves of the shell and of the operculum were visible, and the movements of the arms of the animal within, although these last were not completely developed: the eyes also were still perceptible, although the principal part of the colouring-matter appeared to have been thrown off with the exuviæ. On the 10th another individual was seen in the act of throwing off its shell, and attaching itself as the others to the bottom of the glass. It only remains to add, that as the secretion of the calcareous matter goes on in the compartments destined for the valves of the shelly covering, the eyes gradually disappear, from the increasing opacity thence produced, and the visual ray is extinguished for the remainder of the animal's life; the arms at the same time acquire their usual ciliated appearance. Thus, then, an animal originally natatory and locomotive, and provided with a distinct organ of sight, becomes permanently and immovably fixed, and its optic apparatus obliterated; and furnishes not only a new and important physiological fact, but is the only instance in nature of so extraordinary a metamorphosis.

We have been thus led to dilate upon barnacles in connection with Shakespeare's allusion to them, at somewhat greater length than we should otherwise have done, on account of the interest which attaches to the old story, handed down through so many centuries, and because we have looked into many books in vain for a plain account of its origin, and a modern description of the cirrhiped devoid of scientific technicalities.

With this apology, then, to the reader, we return to the birds.

The following dialogue between Malvolio and the Clown, in *Twelfth Night*, concerning wild-fowl, has reference to the theory of Pythagoras on the subject of the transmigration of souls, and is quite as applicable to birds in general as to wild-fowl in particular:—

"*Clo.* What is the opinion of Pythagoras concerning wild-fowl?

Mal. That the soul of our grandam might haply inhabit a bird.

Clo. What thinkest thou of his opinion?

Mal. I think nobly of the soul, and no way approve his opinion.

Clo. Fare thee well: remain thou still in darkness: thou shalt hold the opinion of Pythagoras ere I will allow of thy wits; and fear to kill a woodcock, lest thou dispossess the soul of thy grandam. Fare thee well."—*Twelfth Night*, Act iv. Sc. 2.*

* The doctrine of Pythagoras is again alluded to by Gratiano, who says:—
"Thou almost mak'st me waver in my faith,
To hold opinion with Pythagoras,
That souls of animals infuse themselves
Into the trunks of men."
Merchant of Venice, Act iv. Sc. 1.

Amongst the wild-fowl may be classed the various species of divers and grebes which frequent our shores and harbours, especially in winter, and which afford good sport to the gunner, by their wonderful power of diving long distances in their efforts to escape.

The provincial name of "loon" (*Macbeth*, Act v. Sc. 3) is applied both to a diver and to a grebe. On many parts of the coast the red-throated diver (*Colymbus septentrionalis*) is known as the "loon," "speckled loon," and "sprat loon." In Norfolk, the name is applied to the great-crested grebe (*Podiceps cristatus*).

Shakespeare employs the term "loon" as synonymous with "coward;" and if we call to mind the habits of the two birds to which the same name has been applied, it is certainly not ill bestowed upon one who lacks courage to face an enemy.

Another species of grebe is referred to by Shakespeare in his *Venus and Adonis*:—

> "Like a *dive-dapper* peering through a wave,
> Who, being look'd on, ducks as quickly in."

This is the little grebe, or dabchick (*Podiceps minor*). In some parts of the country we have heard it called "di' dapper," but it was not until we had met with the passage above quoted that the meaning of the word became apparent.

On the subject of "loons," the Rev. H. Jones has some

appropriate remarks in a volume of essays entitled "Holiday Papers" (p. 65). "The great-crested grebe, or loon," he says, "is a giant compared to our little friend the dabchick, and altogether makes a more respectable appearance, both in picture and pond. The habits and figure of the two birds, though, are much the same. There are numbers of loons on the 'broads' of Norfolk. Indeed it is in East Anglia that I have most especially watched the dabchick. These loons, like the lesser grebes, incubate and leave their eggs in the wet, and meet with the same ridiculous failure when they attempt to walk. Like them, they are capital divers, and begin from the egg."

Close to the divers in the natural system of birds come the cormorants, whose powers of swimming are in no way inferior to those of the species we have just named. They swim so low in the water that nothing but the head, neck, and top of the back appear above the surface. The tail, composed of stiff elastic feathers, is submerged and used as a rudder, and the wings as oars. The address with which they dive, and the rapidity of their movements, are wonderful; no less so than the pertinacity with which they pursue their prey. Voracious in the extreme,—

"Insatiate cormorant."
Richard II. Act ii. Sc. 1;

they are unwearied and active fishers, following their prey

under water like the otter, only coming to the surface occasionally for breath.

Indeed the voracity of this bird, which, doubtless, suggested the name *cormoranus*, has become so proverbial, that a man of large appetite is often likened to a cormorant.

In this sense Shakespeare has frequently employed the word as an adjective, and we find such expressions as—

"The cormorant belly."
Coriolanus, Act i. Sc. 1.

"This cormorant war."
Troilus and Cressida, Act ii. Sc. 2.

And—

"Cormorant devouring time."
Love's Labour's Lost, Act i. Sc. 1.

Ravenous as the cormorant is, it is easily tamed, and becomes very attached and familiar. The use of trained cormorants for fishing is very ancient, and is believed to have originated with the Chinese.* The practice has been known in England, however, for many centuries. Ogleby, who went on an embassy to China in the time of James I., and who published an account of his travels on his return, describes the way in which the Chinese take

---

* In China, at the present day, an allied species, *Ph. sinensis*, is reared and trained to fish.

fish with cormorants. James himself, who was a great sportsman, kept trained cormorants for many years, and was accustomed to travel about the country with them, fishing as he went.

We have seen a curious MS. diary * in the British Museum, written in old French, by Hans Jacob Wurmser v. Vendenheym, who accompanied Lewis Frederick, Duke of Wurtemberg, in his diplomatic mission to England in 1610, from which it appears that the Duke, proceeding by Ware, Royston, Cambridge, and Newmarket, arrived at Thetford on the 7th of May,† where King James the First was then amusing himself with hunting, hawking, and fishing with cormorants.

The entry with reference to the cormorants is as follows:—

_{Lundy} Thetford.
_{7.}

S. E. soupa derechef avecq sa Ma^{tc}. Lesquel en sortans de table, entrerent en carrosse pour aller à la rivière, ou ils virent des Cormorants, oyseau qui par signe que maistre qui les addressez leur donne, se plongent sous l'eaux et prennent des Anguilles et autre poisson; lequel aussy par signe l'on le faict rendir et vomir tous vifs,

---

* This diary is amongst the additional MSS. in the British Museum. It is bound in soft parchment, and entered in the catalogue as "Wurmser, H. J.: Travels with Louis, Count (?) of Wurtemberg, 20,001."

† The presence of the King at Thetford at this date, as on other occasions, is recorded in the "Progresses, Processions, and Magnificent Festivities of King James the First," as published in four volumes by John Nichols, F.S.A., in 1828.

chose bien meruielleuse a voir. Sur toute chose estoit les sages discours de sa Ma^{te} *tres admirable."*

The King had a regular establishment for his cormorants on the river at Westminster, and created a new office, "Master of the Royal Cormorants," which office was first held by John Wood, as appears from various documents in the Record Office. Amongst other entries, for a knowledge of which I am indebted to Mr. F. H. Salvin, the distinguished falconer, are the following:—

"No. 1, James I., 1611, April 11.—To John Wood, the sum of £30, in respect he hath been at extraordinary charge in bringing up and training of certain fowls called cormorants, and making of them fit for the use of fishing, to be taken to him of His Majesty's free gift and reward. By writ, dated the 5th day of April, 1611.

"No. 2, May 27th, 1612.—Payment to the said John Wood for getting cormorants from the north.

"No. 3, August 31st, 1618.—James I. to Robert Wood. Advance of £66 13s. 4d., in part payment of the sum of £286 due in respect of the cormorant houses, and making nine ponds, &c., at Westminster, the ground called the Vine-garden having been taken upon lease of the Lord Danvers.

["In this document," says Mr. Salvin, "this Wood is described as keeper of His Majesty's cormorants, ospreys, and otters. It is therefore clear that the fishing-hawk was tried, and as we hear so little about it afterwards, there can be no doubt but that it proved a failure, which, indeed, might have been expected, as the bird is what falconers would call an habitual 'carrier.' Neither do the otters seem to have answered. Vines were grown in Surrey for wine in ancient times, and I wonder if this vine-garden was for that purpose."]

"No. 4, February 28th, 1619.—To John Wood, whom His Majesty heretofore appointed to attend the French ambassadors, with the cormorants sent by His Majesty's good brother, the French King, the sum of £215, for so much by him disbursed and laid out for his charges incident to the performance of the said service, over and above the sum of £50, impressed unto him, for and towards the said charges, appearing by his bill, of the particulars thereof, delivered in upon oath, and allowed by us and the rest of the Commissioners of the Treasury. By writ dated the 18th July, 1609, and by confirmation dated the last of July, 1618.

"14th October, 1619.—To Robert Wood, whom His Majesty intendeth to send, with divers cormorants, to his good cousin, the Duke of Lorraine, the sum of £60, by way of an imprest towards defraying the expenses in that journey. By writ, dated 7th October, 1619.

"28th August, 1624.—To Robert Wood, the sum of £98 8s. 6d., in full satisfaction of the charge and loss sustained by Luke Wood, in his late travels, with three cormorants, to Venice, having been stayed in his passage thither, and his cormorants taken away from him by the Duke of Savoy."

["From these two documents," says Mr. Salvin, "it would appear that cormorant fishing was likely to have become fashionable upon the continent, if poor Wood and his birds had not come to grief.

"The civil wars in the next reign extinguished the office of The Master of the Royal Cormorants, and his assistants, and in the Record Office we find this petition from poor old Mr. Wood, who appears to have been rather hard-up and neglected in his old age.

"'A prayer of Richard Wood, of Walton-on-Thames, Surrey, to Charles II., for restoration to his place as cormorant keeper, which he held, he says, from King James's first coming to England, to the late wars, in which he served as a soldier, but being now ninety-five years old, has been forced to retire to a dwelling at Walton.'"*]

"A document in the State Paper Office, sealed with the royal signet, and addressed to the 'Treasurer of the Chamber' for the time being, authorizes him to pay unto John Harris, gentleman, His Majesty's cormorant keeper, for his repairing yearly unto the north parts of England

---

* The above extracts were communicated by Mr. Salvin to Mr. Frank Buckland's journal, *Land and Water*, in 1867, in a series of articles on "Cormorant Fishing."

Some interesting chapters on the subject will be found at the end of Freeman and Salvin's "Falconry ; its Claims, History, and Practice.' 8vo, 1859.

to take haggard cormorants for His Majesty's disport in fishing, the yearly allowance of eighty-four pounds, to be paid on the four usual feasts of the year, during His Majesty's pleasure, in such manner as John Wood and Robert Wood, or George Hutchinson, gentlemen, formerly received."*

Although Shakespeare has mentioned the cormorant in many of his Plays, he has nowhere alluded to the sport with trained birds; and this is somewhat singular, inasmuch as he has made frequent mention of the then popular pastime of hawking, and he did not die until some years after James I. had made fishing with cormorants a fashionable amusement.† The sport has long since ceased to amuse royalty, and by English sportsmen is now almost abandoned.‡

To return to the sea, the true home of the cormorant; that sea

"Whose rocky shore beats back the envious siege
    Of watery Neptune."
                            Richard II. Act ii. Sc. 1.

"Those who have never observed our boldest coasts," says Oliver Goldsmith, " have no idea of their tremendous

---

* Sidney Bere, in *Land and Water*, April 20, 1867.

† In "Chambers's Journal" for 1859, will be found an interesting article upon the subject, entitled "The King and his Cormorants."

‡ Mr. Salvin, to whom we have before referred, and Mr. E. C. Newcome, of Feltwell Hall, Norfolk, still keep and use trained cormorants; as, through the kindness of the former, we have had pleasant opportunities of attesting.

sublimity. The boasted works of art, the highest towers, and the noblest domes, are but ant hills when put in comparison. . . . . . .

"To walk along the shore when the tide is departed, or to sit in the hollow of a rock when it is come in, attentive to the various sounds that gather on every side, above and below, may raise the mind to its highest and noblest exertions.

"The solemn roar of the waves, swelling into and subsiding from the vast caverns beneath, the piercing note of the gull, the frequent chatter of the guillemot, the loud note of the auk, the screams of the heron, and the hoarse, deep periodical croaking of the cormorant, all unite to furnish out the grandeur of the scene, and turn the mind to Him who is the essence of all sublimity."

It is amid such scenes as these that we naturally look for and find the next of Shakespeare's birds, the Gull, or, as he sometimes calls it, the "Sea-mell" (*The Tempest*, Act ii. Sc. 2).

In no passage, however, do we find a reference to any particular species of gull; the word is used in its generic sense only, and is most frequently applied metaphorically to a dupe or a fool :—

"Why, 'tis a gull, a fool!"

Henry V. Act iii. Sc. 6.

The gull is said to have derived its name from its voracious habits, *i.e.*, from "*gulo—ōnis*," a gormandizer. Tooke holds that gull, guile, wile, and guilt, are all from the Anglo-Saxon "*wiglian, gewiglian*," that by which any one is deceived. Archdeacon Nares suggests that gull is from the old French *guiller*.

Malvolio asks :—

"Why have you suffer'd me to be imprison'd,
Kept in a dark house, visited by the priest,
And made the most notorious geck* and gull,
That e'er invention play'd on? tell me why."
Twelfth Night, Act v. Sc. 1.

In the same play we find the word "gull" occurring several times in a similar sense, as in Act ii. Sc. 3, and Act iii. Sc. 2;† and Fabian, on the entry of Maria (Act ii. Sc. 5), exclaims,—

"Here comes my noble *gull-catcher!*"

When sharpers were considered as bird-catchers, a gull was their proper prey.‡ "Gull-catchers," or "gull-gropers," therefore, were the names by which, in Shakespeare's day, these sharpers were known.

"The *gull-groper* was generally an old gambling miser,

---

* *Geck*—a laughing-stock. According to Capel, from the Italian *ghezzo*. Dr. Jamieson, however, derives it from the Teutonic *geck, jocus*.
† See also *Othello*, Act v. Sc. 2, and *Timon of Athens*, Act ii. Sc. 1.
‡ See D'Israeli's "Curiosities of Literature," iii. p. 84.

who frequented the ordinary to save the charge of housekeeping, under the pretext of meeting with travellers and seeking company, and carried in his pouch some hundred or two hundred pounds in twenty-shilling pieces. By long experience he knew to an ace how much the losing player was worth, and as he scratched his head and paced uneasily up and down the room, as if he wanted the ostler, he takes him to a side window and tells him that he was, forsooth, sorry to see so honest a gentleman in bad luck, but that 'dice were made of women's bones and would cozen the wisest,' and that for his father's sake, Sir Luke Littlebrain (he had learned the name from the drawer), if it pleased him he need not leave off play for a hundred pound or two. The youth, eager to redeem his losses, accepted the money ordinarily with grateful thanks. The gold was poured upon the table, and a hard bond was hastily drawn up for the repayment at the next quarter-day, deducting so much for the scrivener's expense at changing the pieces. If he lost, the usurer hugged his bond, and laughed in his sleeve. If Sir Andrew won, the gull-groper would then steal silently out of the noisy room to avoid repayment. The day that the bond became due, Hunks was sure not to be within, and if seen, in some way contrived to make the debtor break the bond, and then transformed himself into two sergeants, who clapped the youth in prison. From thence he usually escaped shorn of a goodly manor or fair lordship, worth three times the money, and which was to be entered upon by Hunks three months after his young friend came of age—an unpleasant thought, when the ox was roasting whole, the bells ringing, and the tenants shouting." *

Not only was the person duped called "a gull," but the trick itself was also known as "a gull," just as we now-a-days term it "a sell."

"*Benedick.* I should think this 'a gull,' but that the white-bearded fellow speaks it: knavery cannot, sure, hide himself in such reverence."—*Much Ado about Nothing,* Act ii. Sc. 3.

But it is not always synonymously with "fool" that Shakespeare employs the word "gull." Caliban, addressing Trinculo, says,—

"Sometimes I'll get thee
Young *sea-mells* from the rock."

Tempest, Act ii. Sc. 2.

Here it is evident that the sea-mall, sea-mew, or sea-gull, is intended, the young birds being taken before they could fly. Young sea-gulls were formerly considered great delicacies, and in the old "Household Books" we often find such entries as the following:—

"Item, it is thought goode that See-gulles be hade for

---

* Thornbury, "Shakespeare's England," vol. i. pp. 311, 312. Doubtless compiled from Greene's "Art of Coney Catching," 1591, and Decker's "English Villanies," 1631.

my Lordes own mees and non other, so they be goode and in season, and at jd. apece or jd. ob. at the moste."

The description of their haunts which the poet gives us in the fourth act of *King Lear* cannot be easily forgotten. We seem to stand when reading it upon the very edge of the cliff!—

> " How fearful
> And dizzy 't is to cast one's eyes so low!
> .   .   .   the murmuring surge,
> That on the unnumber'd idle pebbles chafes,
> Cannot be heard so high.—I 'll look no more,
> Lest my brain turn, and the deficient sight
> Topple down headlong."
>
> *King Lear*, Act iv. Sc. 6.

CHAPTER IX.

VARIOUS BIRDS NOT INCLUDED IN THE FOREGOING CHAPTERS.

NOTWITHSTANDING the comprehensive titles of the preceding chapters, there are several birds mentioned by Shakespeare which cannot, with propriety, be included in any of them. We have, therefore, deemed it advisable to notice them separately under the above heading.

Naturalists have frequently remarked upon the propensity which some birds have to become restless and noisy before rain. Familiar examples are, the Peacock; the Green Woodpecker, which, on this account, in some parts of the country, is called "rain-bird;" the Golden Plover, whose Latin and French name, *Pluvialis* and *Pluvier*, have reference to the same peculiarity; and the Woodcock, which, as Gilbert White says, has been observed "to be remarkably listless against snowy, foul weather." Shakespeare has noticed this peculiarity in the Parrot :—

"More clamorous than a parrot against rain."—*As You Like It*, Act iv. Sc. 1.

It is not quite clear when parrots were first introduced as cage birds, but their attractive colours, and aptitude for learning tricks and words, no doubt brought them into notice at an early period. Shakespeare knew that to ensure success in teaching a parrot, the bird must be rewarded:—

"The parrot will not do more for an almond."—*Troilus and Cressida*, Act v. Sc. 2.

To talk "like a parrot," that is, without reason, is proverbial. Lieutenant Cassio thus upbraids himself after a drunken squabble:—

"I will rather sue to be despised than to deceive so good a commander with so slight, so drunken, and so discreet an officer. Drunk? and *speak parrot?* and squabble? swagger? swear and discourse fustian with one's own shadow? Oh, thou invisible spirit of wine, if thou hast no name to be known by, let us call thee devil!"—*Othello*, Act ii. Sc. 3.

In a witty scene between Beatrice and Benedick, in *Much Ado about Nothing*, the former is likened by the latter to "*a parrot-teacher,*" from her great talkative powers:—

"*Bened.* But it is certain I am loved of all ladies, only you excepted: and I would I could find in my heart that I had not a hard heart, for truly I love now.

Beat. A dear happiness to women; they would else have been troubled with a pernicious suitor. I thank God, and my cold blood, I am of your humour for that; I had rather hear my dog bark at a crow than a man swear he loves me.

Bened. God keep your ladyship still in that mind! so some gentleman or other shall 'scape a predestinate scratched face.

Beat. Scratching could not make it worse, an 'twere such a face as yours were.

Bened. Well, you are a rare *parrot-teacher.**

Beat. A bird of my tongue is better than a beast of yours.

Bened. I would my horse had the speed of your tongue, and so good a continuer: but keep your way, o' God's name! I have done.

Beat. You always end with a jade's trick: I know you of old."

[Whereupon Don Pedro steps in and puts an end to this bantering.]

Much Ado about Nothing, Act i. Sc. 1.

The "Popinjay" (*Henry IV.* Part I. Act i. Sc. 3) apparently is only another name for parrot.

In the Glossary to Chaucer's Works we find the word

---

* Compare "Redbreast-teacher," *Henry IV.* Part I. Act iii. Sc. 1.

thus explained:—"*Popingay*, a parrot; *Papegaut*, Fr.; *Papegaey*, Belg.; *Papagallo*, Ital."

In the Privy Purse expenses of King Henry VIII. the following entry occurs under date November, 1532:—

"Itm.—The laste daye paied in rewarde to a
  woman that wolde have gyven a popingay to the King's grace .   . x s̃.

The practice of turning to advantage the capability which certain birds possess for learning to utter words must be of some antiquity, for Pliny alludes to the starlings which were trained for the amusement of the young Cæsars, as being capable of uttering both Latin and Greek.

Shakespeare thus refers to the starling's talking powers:—

"*Hotspur.* He said, he would not ransom Mortimer;
  Forbade my tongue to speak of Mortimer;
  But I will find him when he lies asleep,
  And in his ear I'll holloa, '*Mortimer!*'
  Nay, I'll have a *starling* shall be taught to speak
  Nothing but 'Mortimer,' and give it him,
  To keep his anger still in motion."
                    Henry IV. Part I. Act i. Sc. 3.

It is stated that when M. Girardin visited his friend M. Thirel in Paris, he was agreeably astonished at hearing a starling articulate a dozen consecutive sentences with the same precision as if they had been spoken by some person in the next room; and when the bell rang for mass, the same bird called to its mistress, by name, "Mademoiselle, entendez-vous la messe que l'on sonne? Prenez votre livre et revenez vite, donner à manger à votre poisson." If this statement can be depended upon, M. Girardin might well have been astonished.

It was formerly believed that during the time the Halcyon or Kingfisher was engaged in hatching her eggs, the water, in kindness to her, remained so smooth and calm, that the mariner might venture on the sea with the happy certainty of not being exposed to storms or tempests; this period was therefore called, by Pliny and Aristotle, "the halcyon days."

"Expect Saint Martin's* summer, *halcyon* days."
Henry VI. Part I. Act i. Sc. 2.

It was also supposed that the dead bird, carefully balanced and suspended by a single thread, would always turn its beak towards that point of the compass from which the wind blew.

Kent, in *King Lear* (Act II. Sc. 2), speaks of rogues who—
"Turn their *halcyon* beaks
With every gale and vary of their masters."

And, after Shakespeare, Marlowe, in his *Jew of Malta*, says,—

---

* To this day the bird is still called "Martin-pêcheur" by the French.

"But how now stands the wind?
Into what corner peers my *halcyon's* bill?"

For brightness and beauty of plumage, the kingfisher has no equal amongst our British birds, and so straight and rapid withal is its line of flight, that when the sunlight falls upon its bright blue back, it seems as if an azure bolt from a crossbow had been suddenly shot across our path.

It is difficult to calculate or limit the speed which can be produced by the effort of a wing's vibration. We may, nevertheless, ascertain with tolerable accuracy the rate of a bird's flight, as follows:—If we note the number of seconds which are occupied by a bird in passing between two fixed points in its line of flight, and measure the distance between these points, we resolve the question to a simple "rule-of-three" sum; inasmuch as, knowing the number of yards flown in a certain number of seconds, we can ascertain the distance traversed in 3,600 seconds, or an hour, and thus obtain the rate of speed per hour; supposing, of course, the speed to be uniform. In this way the flight of the common Swallow (*Hirundo rustica*) has been computed at ninety miles,—

"As swift as swallow flies."

Titus Andronicus, Act iv. Sc. 2;

while that of the swift has been conjectured to be nearly one hundred and eighty miles per hour.

"True hope is swift, and flies with swallow's wings."
Richard III. Act v. Sc. 2.

Those who have watched the swallows upon a dull day, skimming low along the ground, and seeming almost to touch it, although flying with speed as undiminished as if high in air, will readily see the aptness of the simile:—

"And I have horse will follow where the game
Makes way, and run like swallows on the plain."
Titus Andronicus, Act ii. Sc. 2.

"The swallow follows not summer more willingly than we your lordship, nor more willingly leaves winter; such summer-birds are men."—*Timon of Athens*, Act iii. Sc. 6.

The swallow, although one of the earliest, is not always the first of our spring ornaments to appear. There are—

"Daffodils,
That come before the swallow dares, and take
The winds of March with beauty."
Winter's Tale, Act iv. Sc. 3.

A near relative of this bird is the Martin, or, as it is called in the language of heraldry, the "Martlet" (*Hirundo urbica*).

"This guest of summer,
The temple-haunting martlet, doth approve,
By his lov'd mansionry, that the heaven's breath

> Smells wooingly here ; no jutty, frieze,
> Buttress, nor coigne of vantage, but this bird
> Hath made his pendant bed and procreant cradle.
> Where they most breed and haunt, I have observ'd,
> The air is delicate."
>
> <div align="right"><i>Macbeth</i>, Act i. Sc. 6.</div>

Sir Joshua Reynolds was struck with the beauty of this brief colloquy before the castle of Macbeth, and he observes on it :—" This short dialogue between Duncan and Banquo, while they are approaching the gates of Macbeth's castle, has always appeared to me a striking instance of what, in painting, is termed 'repose.' Their conversation very naturally turns upon the beauties of its situation, and the pleasantness of the air; and Banquo, observing the martlets' nests in every recess of the cornice, remarks that where these birds most breed and haunt, the air is delicate. The subject of this quiet and easy conversation gives that repose so necessary to the mind after the tumultuous bustle of the preceding scenes, and perfectly contrasts the scene of horror that immediately succeeds."

The bird is mentioned again in the *Merchant of Venice*, where we are reminded that—

> "The martlet
> Builds in the weather on the outward wall,
> Even in the force and road of casualty."
>
> <div align="right"><i>Merchant of Venice</i>, Act ii. Sc. 9.</div>

Old authors tell us that when the young swallows are hatched, they are blind for some time, and that the parent birds bring to the nest a plant called *Chelidonium*, or Swallow's herb, which has the property of restoring sight. This popular fallacy appears to be widely disseminated. The plant is the well-known Celandine (*Chelidonium majus*). It belongs to the *Papaveraceæ*, or poppies, and may be found growing in waste places to the height of two feet or more. It is brittle, slightly hairy, and full of a yellow, fœtid juice, and bears small yellow flowers in long-stalked umbels.

The name *Chelidonium* is derived no doubt from the Greek χελιδων, a swallow; but the reason for its being thus named is not so obvious. Some authors assert that it was so called on account of its flowering about the time of the arrival of the swallow, while others maintain that it derived its appellation from being the plant medicinally made use of by that bird.

The belief that animals and birds possess a knowledge of certain plants which will cure a disease, or benefit them in some way, is very ancient, and this particular plant is alluded to by old authors as being especially selected for the purpose. Pliny observes (Hist. Nat. fol. 1530, p. 461, xv.): "Animalia quoque invenire herbas, *inprimisque chelidoniam*. Hac enim hirundines oculis pullorum in nido restituunt visum, ut quidam volunt, etiam erutis oculis." (!) And the same author further remarks: "Chelidoniam visui saluberrimam hirundines monstravere vexatis pullorum oculis illa medentes."

Gerard, referring to this plant, in his "Herball, or Generall Historie of Plantes" (1597), observes :—" It is called celandine, not because it then first springeth at the comming in of the swallowes, or dieth when they goe away; for as we haue saide, it may be founde all the yeere; but because some hold opinion that with this herbe the dams restore sight to their yoong ones when their eies be out, the which things are vaine and false : for Cornelius Celsus in his sixt booke doth witnesse that when the sight of the eies of diuers yoong birdes be put foorth by some outward meanes, it will after a time be restored of itselfe, and soonest of all the sight of the swallow, whereupon, (as the same saith) that the tale or fable grew, how, thorow an herbe the dams restore that thing, which healeth of itselfe : the very same doth Aristotle alleadge in the sixt booke of the historie of liuing creatures : the eies of young swallowes, saith he, that are not fledge, if a man do pricke them out, do grow againe, and afterwards do perfectly recouer their sight." Subsequently, when speaking of the "virtues" of the plant, the sage Gerard continues :—" The iuice of the herbe is good to sharpen the sight, for it clenseth and consumeth awaie slimie things that cleaue about the ball of the eie, and hinder the sight." The root was considered good for yellow-jaundice, and also (being chewed) for toothache. Gerard adds, " The roote cut in small peeces is good to be giuen vnto hawkes against sundrie diseases;" and Turbervile, in his "Booke of Falconrie" (1611), treats of a cure for "a blow giuen to the eye, or of some other mischance," as follows:—" Sometimes the eyes of hawkes are hurt by some mishappe, some stripe, or otherwise, as I said afore. Against such unlooked-for mischances, Master Malopin, in his boke of the Prince, willeth to take the juice of *Celondine*, otherwise *Arondell*, or *Swallowes hearbe*, and to convey it into the eye. And if it bee not to be had greene, to take it drie, and to beat it into powder, and to blow it into her eye with a quill, and this shall recure the hawke."

A marginal note to this paragraph informs us that "Arondell" in French is "Hirundo," a swallow, otherwise called "Chelidon."

Parkinson, in his "Theatrum Botanicum" (1640), alludes to two species of Celandine, *C. major* and *minor*, and says:—" Some call them *Chelidonia major* and *minor*, and tooke the name, as Dioscorides saith, because it springeth when swallowes come in; and withered at their going away (which is true in neither, the greater, whereof Dioscorides chiefely speaketh, being greene both winter and sommer; and the lesser springeth before swallowes come in, and is gone and withered long before their departure). Dioscorides likewise, and Pliny also, say it tooke that name from swallowes that cured their young ones' eyes, that were hurt,

* "Arondell," no doubt the old French, or a corruption of "Hirondelle."

with bringing this herbe and putting it to them : but Aristotle, and Celsus from him, doe shew that the young ones of partridges, doves, swallowes, &c., will recover their sight (being hurt) of themselves in time, without anything applyed unto them, and therefore Celsus accounteth this saying but a fable."

It is curious to observe how universally this plant appears to be associated with the swallow. *Chelidonium majus* is *Calidonia maggiore* of the Italians; *Yerva de las gelondrinhas* of the Spaniards; *Chelidoine Felongue* and *Esclaire* of the French; and *Schwalbenkraut* of the Germans; while we, in English, call it *Celandine*, *Swallow's-herb*, and *Swallow-wort*.

Besides the Swallow-herb there is the Swallow-stone, to which wonderful properties have been likewise attributed in connection with diseases of the eye.

Dr. Lebour, in a communication to *The Zoologist*, for 1866, says (p. 523) :—"I met last summer, in Brittany, with a curious fact relating to the habits of the common house-swallow. In Brittany there exists a wide-spread belief among the peasantry that certain stones found in swallows' nests are sovereign cures for certain diseases of the eye. I think the same notion holds in many other parts of France, and also in some of our English counties. These stones are held in high estimation, and the happy possessor usually lets them on hire at a sous or so a day. Now, I had the good fortune to see some of these 'swallow-stones,' and to examine them. I found them to be the hard polished calcareous opercula of some species of *Turbo*, and although their worn state precludes the idea of identifying the species, yet I am confident that they belong to no European *Turbo*. The largest I have seen was three-eighths of an inch long, and one-fourth of an inch broad; one side is flat, or nearly so, and the other is convex, more or less so in different specimens. Their peculiar shape enables one to push them under the eyelid across the eyeball, and thus they remove any eyelash or other foreign substance which may have got in one's eye;* further than this, they have no curing power: the peasants, however, believe they are omnipotent. The presence of these opercula in swallows' nests is very curious,† and leads one to suppose that they must have been brought there from some distant shore in the swallow's stomach. If so, they must have inhabited the poor bird for a considerable time, and proved a great nuisance to it."

The tradition on this subject, current amongst the peasants in Brittany, is no doubt of some antiquity,‡ since

---

* One would suppose that such a foreign substance as a "swallow-stone" in the eye would be much more inconvenient than the eyelash which it was destined to remove.

† Curious, if true. Dr. Lebour does not say that he ever found such stones himself, nor does he vouch for their having been found by others in the nests. We have examined a great number of swallows' nests without being able to discover anything of the kind.

‡ Pliny makes mention of a "swallow-stone," but says nothing about its being found in the nest. On the contrary, he says it is found in the stomach of the

the allusion which Longfellow has made to it in his poem of "Evangeline" would seem to confirm this impression, inasmuch as we may assume that the tradition found its way into Acadia through the French colonists who were the first to settle there.

Longfellow, in his " Evangeline," says,—

"Oft in the barns they climbed to the populous nests in the rafters,
Seeking with eager eyes that wondrous stone which the swallow
Brings from the shore of the sea to restore the sight of its fledglings;
Lucky was he who found that stone in the nest of the swallow!"

The connection between the stone and the herb is, that both were said to be brought to the nest by the swallow, and both were deemed remedies for defective sight. There is this difference, however, between the current opinion in Brittany and the popular notion in Acadia, that in the former case it is the finder of the stone who is thereby benefited, in the latter it is the sight of the fledglings which is thereby restored.

A friend has suggested that the tradition may have originated with the Chinese, to whom the edible swallows'

bird! "In ventre hirundinum pullus *lapilli* candido aut rubenti colore, qui ' chelidonii ' vocantur, magicis narrati artibus reperiuntur."

nests have been so long known, and to whom credit is now given for having been acquainted centuries ago with inventions which until recently were believed to be modern. Not being conversant, however, with Chinese, we are unable to say whether there is in that language any equivalent for "swallow-stone," or "swallow's-herb," or whether ancient Chinese authors in any way throw light upon the subject.*

Pliny's mention of the stone found in the stomach of the swallow brings to mind the stones found in the stomach of the ostrich, and so leads to the consideration of another bird noticed by Shakespeare. The food of the ostrich is said to consist of the tops of shrubby plants, seeds, and grain; strange to say, however, it will swallow, with indiscriminating voracity, stones, sticks, pieces of metal, cord, leather, and other substances, which often occasion its destruction. The extraordinary digestion of the bird is thus alluded to in the threat of the rebel Cade, when confronted by Alexander Iden :—

"Ah! villain, thou wilt betray me, and get a thousand crowns of the king by carrying my head to him! *but I'll make thee eat iron like an ostrich*, and swallow my sword like a great pin, ere thou and I part."—*Henry VI*. Part II. Act iv. Sc. 10.

This curious habit is not peculiar to the ostriches. The same thing has been observed in the bustards. Dr.

---

* The substance of the above remarks was contributed by the author in an article published in *The Zoologist* for 1867, p. 744.

Jerdon, speaking of the Indian Bustard (*Eupodotis Edwardsii*), says, "they will often swallow pebbles or any glittering object that attracts them. I took several portions of a brass ornament, the size of a No. 16 bullet, out of the stomach of one bustard."*

In reply to Hotspur's inquiries for "The madcap Prince of Wales," and his comrades, at the rebel camp near Shrewsbury, he is told that they are

> "All furnish'd, all in arms;
> All plum'd like *estridges* that with the wind
> Bated; like eagles having lately bath'd."†
>
> *Henry IV.* Part I. Act iv. Sc. 1.

Looking to the antiquity of the fable of the Pelican's feeding her young with her own blood, it is not surprising that Shakespeare has alluded to it when mentioning this bird. Laertes says :—

> "To his good friends thus wide I'll ope my arms;
> And, like the kind life-rendering pelican,
> Repast them with my blood."
>
> *Hamlet*, Act iv. Sc. 5.

* "The Birds of India," iii. p. 610.
† Some editions read—

> "All plum'd like estridges that wing the wind;
> Bated like eagles having lately bath'd."

But we have adopted the above reading in preference for three reasons : 1. Considering the rudimentary nature of the ostrich's wing, Shakespeare would not have been so incorrect as to describe them as "winging the wind;" 2. The word "bated," if intended to refer to eagles, and not to ostriches, would have been more correctly "bating;" 3. The expression, "to bate with the wind," is well understood in the language of falconry, with which Shakespeare was familiar.

King Lear, too, likens himself to a pelican when speaking of his ungrateful children :—

" Is it the fashion, that discarded fathers
Should have thus little mercy on their flesh ?
Judicious punishment ! 'T was this flesh begot
Those pelican daughters."
King Lear, Act iii. Sc. 4.

Again—

" *K. Richard.* . . . . .
    Dar'st with thy frozen admonition
    Make pale our cheek ; chasing the royal blood
    With fury from his native residence.
Gaunt. . . . .
    That blood already, like the pelican,
    Hast thou tapp'd out, and drunkenly carous'd.
Richard II. Act ii. Sc. 1.

It is generally supposed that the fable alluded to is a classical one. But this is not the case. Many and various explanations have been offered as regards its origin, but none is more ingenious, and at the same time more plausible, than the explanation suggested by Mr. Bartlett, the energetic Superintendent of the Zoological Society's Gardens. In a letter addressed to the editor of *Land and Water*, dated the 3rd April, 1869, Mr. Bartlett says :—

" Having devoted much attention to investigations upon

the subject of the supply of food provided by several species of birds for their young, I have collected many interesting facts showing that in some instances the parents prepare by partial digestion, and in others by the addition of a secreted nutritive substance, the food intended for the support of their offspring. The one which I am about to relate I was certainly not prepared to expect; nevertheless, such facts as I now lay before you have caused me no little astonishment, as they appear to me to afford a solution to the well-known and ancient story of the Pelican in the Wilderness. I have heard that the so-called fable originated, or is to be found, on some of the early Egyptian monuments (I do not know where), but that the representations are more like flamingoes than pelicans. I have published elsewhere, in the 'Proceedings of the Zoological Society,' for March 1869, what I consider to be the facts of the case, and take this opportunity of referring to the matter. The flamingoes here in the gardens have frequently shown signs of breeding, and have been supplied with heaps of sand to form their nests, but without result; nevertheless they appear to take considerable notice of a pair of Cariamas in the same aviary. These birds have a habit of bending back their heads, and with open gaping mouths utter loud and somewhat distressing sounds. This habit at once attracts the flamingoes, and very frequently one or more of them advance towards the cariamas, and standing erect over the bird, by a slight up-and-down movement of the head, raise up into its mouth a considerable quantity of red coloured fluid. As soon as the upper part of the throat and mouth becomes filled, it will drop or run down from the corners of the flamingo's mouth ; the flamingo then bends its long neck over the gaping cariama and pours this fluid into the mouth, and as frequently on the back of the cariama. Having seen this repeatedly, I took an opportunity of obtaining a portion of this fluid and submitted it to the examination of Dr. Murie. We placed it under the microscope, and find it composed of little else than blood ; in fact, the red blood-corpuscles are wonderfully abundant in the otherwise clear and almost transparent glutinous fluid. That this does not proceed from any disease or injury done to the flamingo, nor arise or is produced by any portion or part of the food taken by them, I am perfectly certain, for the birds are in the most vigorous health and condition ; but I believe that it is an attempt to supply food to the cariamas, just as the hedge-sparrow and other birds supply food to the young cuckoo, and I have no doubt, if a careful observer had the opportunity of watching the flamingoes on their breeding-ground, he would find that this is the mode of feeding their young : no doubt other food is also provided, but most likely mixed with this secretion. I think it highly probable that this habit was noticed in ancient Egypt, and, by the confusion of names in translation, the pelican was supposed to be the bird intended; in fact, I have heard that the representation (which I am very anxious to see) is much more like a flamingo than a pelican. Again, a flamingo is much more a bird of the wilderness than the pelican, seeing that the pelican requires a good supply of fish, while the flamingo can live and does well upon very small insects, seeds, and little fry, and is found in places in which the pelican would starve."

This communication naturally drew forth some comments. Mr. Houghton, in a long letter to the editor of the same journal, dated 24th April, 1869, says:—"That this is the origin of the old story of the pelican feeding its young with its blood seems very plausible. I purpose to examine this ingenious idea, and to offer a few remarks on the old fable. It is commonly supposed—and you will often find it so expressed in works on natural history—that this fable is a classical one. This is an error: I have searched in vain amongst classical authors for any allusion to the pelican feeding its young with its blood. To the Greeks this bird was known by the name of πελεκάν, or πελέκας, or πελεκινος, though it would appear that some species of woodpecker was also intended by the word πελέκας (see Aristoph. *Aves*, 1155). Aristotle mentions pelicans two or three times in his 'History of Animals;' he speaks of their migratory habits and flying in crowds. He says they take large shell-fish into their pouches (ἐν τῷ πρὸ τῆς κοιλίας τόπῳ), wherein the molluscs are softened. They then throw them up and pick out the flesh from the opened valves. Ælian merely repeats this story, only he says the shell-fish are received into the stomach. In another place he says there is mutual hostility between the pelican and the quail. The pelican was known to the Romans under the name of *onocrotalus*. Pliny says this bird is like the swan, except that under the throat there is a sort of second crop of astonishing capacity. There is, of course, no doubt that the pelican is here intended. Cicero says there is a bird called *platalea* which pursues other birds and causes them to drop the fish they have caught, which it devours itself. He then gives the same story as Ælian, viz., that this bird softens shell-fish in its stomach, &c. The first part of this account is true of the parasitic gulls (*Lestris*). It is uncertain what bird Cicero alludes to by the name *platalea*. Pliny gives the same story as Cicero, and calls the bird *platea*. The fable, then, is no classical one. Whence did it originate? Does any pictorial representation occur on the Egyptian monuments, as Mr. Bartlett has been informed? I am inclined to think—but I speak under correction—that such a representation does not occur. Horapollo (i. 54) tells us that when the ancient Egyptians want to represent a fool they depict the pelican, because this bird, instead of laying its eggs on lofty and secure places, merely scratches up the ground and there lays. The people surround the place with dried cow's dung, and set fire to it. The pelican sees the smoke, and endeavours to extinguish the fire with her wings, the motion of which only fans the flame. Thus she burns her wings, and falls an easy prey to the fowlers. Some Egyptian priests, considering this behaviour evinces great love of its young, do not eat the bird; others, again, thinking it is a mark of folly, eat it. The Egyptians, however, did believe in a bird feeding its young with its blood, and this bird is none other than a vulture. Horapollo says (i. 11) that a vulture symbolises a compassionate person (ἐλεήμονα), because during the 120 days of its nurture of its offspring, if food cannot be had, 'it opens its own thigh and permits the young to partake of the blood, so that they may not perish from want.' This is alluded to in the following lines by Georgius Pisidas:—

$$\text{Τὸν μηρὸν ἐκτέμοντες, ἡματωμένοις}$$
$$\text{Γάλακτος ὁλκοῖς ζωπυροῦσι τὰ βρέφη.}$$

Amongst classical authors, the love of the vulture for its young was proverbial. But when do we first hear of the fable of the pelican feeding its young with its blood? In Patristic annotations on the Scriptures. I believe this is the answer. The ecclesiastical fathers transferred the Egyptian story from the vulture to the pelican, but magnified the already sufficiently marvellous fable a hundredfold, for the blood of the parent was not only supposed to serve as food for the young, but was also able to reanimate the dead offspring! Augustine, commenting on Psalm cii. 5—'I am like a pelican in the wilderness'—says: 'These birds [male pelicans] are said to kill their young offspring by blows of their beaks, and then to bewail their death for the space of three days. At length, however, it is said the mother bird inflicts a severe wound on herself, pouring the flowing blood over the dead young ones, which instantly brings them to life." To the same effect write Eustathius, Isidorus, Epiphanius, and a host of other writers, except that sometimes it was the female who killed the young ones, while the male reanimated them with its blood. This fable was supposed to be a symbol of Christ's love to men. I think, then, that the very interesting fact of the flamingo feeding the cariama with the red fluid and other contents of its stomach can hardly be, as Mr. Bartlett conjectures, the origin of the old fable of the pelican feeding its young with its blood, because the Egyptian story of the vulture wounding its thigh has nothing analogous to the natural-history fact of the flamingo, while the fable of the pelican pouring from its self-inflicted wound the life-restoring blood which reanimates its offspring is still further from the mark."

In a short criticism upon the subject in the same number of *Land and Water*, Mr. H. J. Hancock is inclined to believe that some confusion has arisen in the translation from the original Hebrew. "The word קָאַת (*Kàh-ath*'), which is rendered πέλεκαν in the Septuagint, and Pelican, or Onocrotalus, in the Vulgate, is derived from the verb קָא 'to vomit,' and signifies 'a vomiter.' This name, evidently a general one, may have been intended by the Hebrew writers to apply either to such birds as, like the pelican and many others, possess the power of disgorging their food on being disturbed or alarmed, or to such birds as are accustomed to nourish their young from their own crops; and, in the latter case, the curious bloody secretion of the flamingo may well have given rise to the superstition concerning the pelican. I may observe, as an evidence that the translators did not consider the Hebrew word to be other than a general name, that *Kà-ath*' is sometimes rendered 'cormorant' (Isa. xxxiv. 11; Zeph. ii. 14). For further information concerning this point, I would refer your readers to the 'Hebrew and Chaldee Concordance,' p. 1083; Bate's 'Hebrew Dictionary,' p. 538; and Parkhurst's 'Hebrew Dictionary,' pp. 631, 632."

Shakespeare, doubtless, had not investigated the subject so narrowly, but was content to accept the common story as he found it, and to apply it metaphorically as occasion required.

The majority of the birds mentioned in this chapter are not natives of the British Islands, but, strange as it may appear, there is evidence to show that the pelican, or, to speak more correctly, a species of pelican, once inhabited the English fens.

The peat-bogs of Cambridgeshire have yielded of late years a large number of bones of birds, and amongst these has been discovered the wing-bone of a pelican. This interesting discovery was made known by M. Alphonse Milne-Edwards, in an able article in the "Annales des Sciences Naturelles,"* a translation of which subsequently appeared in *The Ibis*.† The author thus anticipates the objections of the sceptical :—

"We may be inclined, perhaps, to wonder that a single bone, belonging (as it does) to a young animal, and consequently not presenting all its anatomical characters, should permit the exact recognition of the genus and species of bird to which it belongs. So precise a determination would not be always possible, but in the present case there need be no doubt; for I have shown, in another work,‡ that the wing-bone in the genus *Pelicanus* offers extremely clear distinctive peculiarities, which do not allow of its being confounded with that of any other bird."

The only species of pelican which has been recorded to have occurred in England in recent times, is the great white pelican, *P. onocrotalus*.

* Cinquième série, tom. viii. pp. 285-293.
† *Ibis*, 1868, pp. 363-370.
‡ "Oiseaux Fossiles de la France," p. 230.

Latham has stated,* on the authority of Sir Thomas Brown, that a pelican of this species was killed in Horsey Fen in 1663. This statement was copied by Montagu,† and subsequently by Dr. Fleming,‡ but there is no evidence to show that the bird was a wild one. On the contrary, it is probable, as suggested by Sir Thomas Brown, that it may have been one of the King's pelicans which was lost about that time from St. James's Park.

He says§:—"An *onocrotalus*, or pelican, shot upon Horsey Fen, May 22, 1663, which, stuffed and cleaned, I yet retain. It was three yards and a half between the extremities of the wings; the chowle and beak answering the usual description; the extremities of the wings for a span deep brown; the rest of the body white; a fowl which none could remember upon this coast.

"About the same time, I heard one of the king's pelicans was lost at St. James's; perhaps this might be the same."

Latham was further assured by Dr. Leith, that in the month of May he saw a brown pelican fly over his head on Blackheath, in Kent. Montagu, however, suggests that the bird was an immature swan.

In *The Zoologist* for 1856 (p. 5321), the Rev. H. B. Tristram has recorded, that on the 25th of August, 1856,

* "Synopsis," iii. p. 577 (1785).
† "Suppl. Orn. Dict." (1813).
‡ " Hist. Brit. An." p. 118 (1828).
§ "Works:" Wilkin's ed. vol. iv. p. 318.

the remains of a pelican were picked up on the shore at Castle Eden, Durham. Such are the scanty records of the appearance of a pelican in England in modern times.

The bone found in Cambridgeshire may have belonged to *P. onocrotalus*, a native of South and South-Eastern Europe, and which is stated to be "common on the lakes and watercourses of Hungary and Russia, and also seen further south in Asia and in Northern Africa." M. Milne-Edwards, however, has not quite determined the species, for, on comparison with the bones of other recognized and existing species, it appears to differ rather remarkably in its greater length.

Enough has probably been said, however, to show the interest which attaches to the discovery, and to suggest further research.

With the pelican ends the long list of birds mentioned in the works of Shakespeare.

The reader who has had the patience or the curiosity to follow us thus far will, doubtless, ere this have formed a just estimate of Shakespeare's qualifications as a naturalist, and will have drawn the only conclusion which the evidence justifies.

It is impossible to read all that Shakespeare has written in connection with ornithology, without being struck with the extraordinary knowledge which he has displayed for the age in which he lived; and our admiration for him as a poet must be increased tenfold on perceiving that the beauteous thoughts, which he has clothed in such beauteous language, were dictated by a pure love of nature, and by a study of those great truths which appeal at once to the heart and to reason, and which infuse into the soul of the naturalist the true spirit of poetry.

APPENDIX.

A TABLE

OF

ORNITHOLOGICAL ALLUSIONS

IN THE ORDER IN WHICH THEY OCCUR:

THE PLAYS AND POEMS BEING ALPHABETICALLY ARRANGED.

All's Well that Ends Well: PAGE
   Act I.   Sc. 1—[Hawking-eye]   55
    „   „   3—Cuckoo .   .   . 154
    „ II. „   5—Lark .   .   . 136
    „   „   Bunting   . 136
    „ III. „   5—Limed   . 160
    „ IV. „   1—Chough   . 117
    „   „   Woodcock . 231
    „   „   3—Crow .   . 110

Antony and Cleopatra:
   Act II. Sc. 2—Eagle   .   . 26
    „   „   3—Cocks   . 172, 219
    „   „   Quails   .   . 219
    „   „   6—Cuckoo .   . 154
    „ III. „   2—[Swan]   . 201
    „   „   [Kite].   . 44

Antony and Cleopatra (continued):

				PAGE
Act III.	Sc.	10—Mallard	. . . . .	238
,,	,,	13—Kite	. . . . .	44
,,	,,	Seel	. . . . .	70
,,	,,	Dove	. . . . .	195
,,	,,	Ostrich	. . . . .	195
,, IV.	,,	8—[Nightingale]	. . . .	123
,,	,,	12—[Swallow]	. . . .	276
,, V.	,,	2—Seel	. . . . .	70

As You Like It:

Act I.	Sc.	2—Pigeons	. . .	180, 185
,,	,,	3—Juno's Swans	. . .	206
,, II.	,,	3—Ravens	. . . .	106
,,	,,	Sparrow	. . .	106, 146
,,	,,	5—Eggs	. . . . .	32
,,	,,	7—[Goose]	. . . .	197
,,	,,	[Cock]	. . . . .	168
,, III.	,,	3—Falcon	. . . .	61
,,	,,	Bells	. . . . .	61
,,	,,	Pigeon	. . .	180, 185
,,	,,	4—Goose	. . . .	197
,, IV.	,,	1—[Pigeon]	. . . .	180
,,	,,	Parrot	. . . .	272
,,	,,	3—Moss'd	. . . .	34
,, V.	,,	4—Stalking-horse	. . .	238

Comedy of Errors:

Act II.	Sc.	1—[Stale]	. . . . .	245
,,	,,	2—Owls	. . . . .	96
,, III.	,,	1—Crow	. . . . .	114
,, IV.	,,	2—Lapwing	. . . .	221

Coriolanus:

Act I.	Sc.	1—Cormorant	. . .	260
,,	,,	Goose	. . . .	197
,,	,,	4—Geese	. . . .	197
,, III.	,,	1—[Crow]	. . . .	110
,,	,,	[Eagle]	. . . .	23
,,	,,	Cry havoc	. . .	(note) 57
,,	,,	Quarry	. . . .	57
,,	,,	5—[Kite]	. . . .	43

APPENDIX.   301

Coriolanus (continued):

				PAGE
Act III.	Sc.	5—[Crow]		110
,, IV.	,,	5—Daw		119
,,	,,	7—Osprey		42
,, V.	,,	3—[Dove]		180, 191
,,	,,	[Gosling]		197
,,	,,	6—[Eagle]		23
,,	,,	[Dovecote]		180

Cymbeline:

Act I.	Sc.	2—Eagle		28, 45
,,	,,	Puttock		28, 45
,,	,,	3—[Crow]		110
,,	,,	4—Fowl		235
,, II.	,,	2—Philomel		125
,,	,,	[Raven]		99
,,	,,	3—Lark		132
,,	,,	4—[Watching]		45
,, III.	,,	1—Crows		112
,,	,,	3— ,,		112
,,	,,	Eagle		27
,,	,,	4—Jay		121
,,	,,	Swan's nest		206
,,	,,	6—Owl		83
,,	,,	Lark		136
,, IV.	,,	2—Ruddock		141
,,	,,	Wren		144
,,	,,	The Roman Eagle		28
,, V.	,,	3—Crows		111
,,	,,	4—Eagle		30
,,	,,	Prune		31
,,	,,	Cloys		31
,,	,,	5—The Roman Eagle		29

Hamlet:

Act I.	Sc.	1—Cock		167
,,	,,	3—Woodcocks		229
,,	,,	5—The falconer's call		55
,, II.	,,	2—Aiery		39, 58
,,	,,	Kites		43
,,	,,	Hawk		75, 223
,,	,,	Hernshaw		75, 223

Hamlet (*continued*):

			PAGE
Act II. Sc.	2—Pigeon-liver'd		185
,, ,,	Kites		43
,, ,,	French falconers		56
,, ,,	Eyases		58
,, III. ,,	2—[Raven]		99
,, ,,	Recorder	(note)	129
,, IV. ,,	5—Owl		88
,, ,,	Pelican		286
,, ,,	[Dove]		180
,, ,,	7—Check		60
,, V. ,,	1—Dove		180
,, ,,	2—[Chough]		115
,, ,,	Lapwing		222
,, ,,	Bevy		218
,, ,,	Sparrow		146
,, ,,	[Woodcock]		229
,, ,,	Quarry		56

Henry IV.—Part I.:

Act I. Sc.	3—Popinjay		273
,, ,,	Starling		274
,, II. ,,	1—Turkies		177
,, ,,	2—Chuffs		118
,, ,,	Wild-Duck		237
,, ,,	4—[Wild-Geese]		246
,, ,,	Sparrow		147
,, ,,	[Cuckoo]		147
,, III. ,,	1—[Raven]		99
,, ,,	[Goose]		197
,, ,,	Redbreast-teacher		142
,, ,,	2—Cuckoo		155
,, IV. ,,	1—Estridge		286
,, ,,	Bated		286
,, ,,	Eagles		36, 286
,, ,,	Dove		180
,, ,,	2—Caliver		240
,, ,,	Wild-Duck		240
,, ,,	Scare-crows		115
,, V. ,,	1—Gull		148
,, ,,	Cuckoo's bird		148

APPENDIX. 303

Henry IV.—Part I. (continued):

				PAGE
Act V.	Sc.	1—Sparrow	. . .	148
,,	,,	[Vultures]	. .	41

Henry IV.—Part II.:

Act III.	Sc.	1—Seel	. . .	70
,,	,,	2—Ouzel	. . .	139
,,	,,	Dove	. . .	196
,,	V. ,,	1—Cock and pye	. .	172
,,	,,	Pigeons	. .	180, 196
,,	,,	Hens	. . .	196
,,	,,	Wild-Geese	. .	246
,,	,,	4—Vultures	. .	41

Henry V.:

Act I.	Sc.	2—Eagle	. . .	32
,,	,,	Eggs	. . .	32
,, II.	,,	1—Kite	. . .	43
,,	,,	Crow	. . .	111
,,	,,	2—Cloy	. . .	31
,, III.	,,	6—Gull	. .	149, 266
,,	,,	7—Hawk	. . .	73
,,	,,	Lark	. . .	133
,,	,,	Hooded	. . .	62
,,	,,	Bate	. . .	62
,, IV. Prologue—Cocks			. .	168
,,	Sc.	1—Mounted	. . .	63
,,	,,	Stoop	. . .	63
,,	,,	2—Carrions	. . .	104
,,	,,	Crows	. . .	104

Henry VI.—Part I.:

Act I.	Sc.	2—Halcyon days	. .	275
,,	,,	Mahomed's Dove	. .	194
,,	,,	[Eagle]	. . .	23
,,	,,	4—Scare-crow	. .	115
,,	,,	5—Doves	. . .	180
,, II.	,,	2—Turtle-doves	. .	180, 191
,,	,,	4—Hawks	. . .	73
,,	,,	Pitch	. . .	73
,,	,,	Daw	. . .	119

APPENDIX.

Henry VI.—Part I. (continued):   PAGE
Act III. Sc. 3—Peacock . . . 175
„ IV. „ 2—[Owl] . . . 83
„ „ 3—[Vulture] . . . 40
„ V. „ 3—Swan . . . 204
„ „ Cygnets . . . 204

Henry VI.—Part II.:
Act I. Sc. 2—[Hawk] . . . 72
„ „ 3—Limed . . . 161
„ „ 4—Screech-Owls . . .85, 97
„ II. „ 1—Flying at the brook . 50, 51
„ „ Old Joan . . . 50
„ „ Point . . . 50, 51
„ „ Falcon . . . 50
„ „ Pitch . . . 50, 51
„ „ Hawks . . . 50
„ „ Tower . . . 50, 51
„ „ Fowl . . . 51
„ „ 4—Limed . . . 161
„ III. „ 1—Dove . . . 180
„ „ [Raven] . . . 101
„ „ [Eagle] . . . 23
„ „ Kite . . . 44
„ „ 2—Raven . . . 101
„ „ Wren . . . 101, 144
„ „ Partridge . . . 44, 216
„ „ Puttock . . . 44, 216
„ „ [Kites] . . . 43
„ „ [Screech-Owl] . . . 85
„ „ 3—[Lime-twigs] . . . 160
„ IV. „ 1—[Eagle] . . . 23
„ „ 10—Ostrich . . . 285
„ „ Crows . . . 113
„ V. „ 2—Kites . . . 43, 112
„ „ Crows . . . 112

Henry VI.—Part III.:
Act I. Sc. 1—Eagle . . 38
„ „ Tire . . 38
„ „ Hawk's bells 61
„ „ 4—Swan . . 205

APPENDIX.   305

Henry VI.—Part III. (continued):

				PAGE
Act I.	Sc.	4—Dove		54, 195
,,	,,	Falcon		54
,,	,,	Woodcock		232
,,	II.	,,	1—Eagle's bird	25
,,	,,	Night-Owl		.88, 94
,,	,,	2—Doves		91, 195
,,	,,	6—[Screech-Owl]		85
,,	V.	,,	2—The princely Eagle	33
,,	,,	4—Owl		85
,,	,,	6—Limed		160
,,	,,	Owl		86
,,	,,	[Raven]		102
,,	,,	Night-Crow		102
,,	,,	Pies		121

Henry VIII.:

Act II.	Sc.	3—[Lark]	136
,, III.	,,	2—Larks	136
,, IV.	,,	1—The bird of peace	180

Julius Cæsar:

Act I.	Sc.	3—Bird of night	89
,, V.	,,	1—Eagles	27
,,	,,	Raven	99–110
,,	,,	Crows	112
,,	,,	Kites	43
,,	,,	3—[Eagles]	27
,,	,,	[Kites]	43
,,	,,	Ravens	104

King John:

Act I.	Sc.	1—Sparrow	145
,, II.	,,	2—Cry havoc	(note) 57
,, IV.	,,	3—Raven	103
,, V.	,,	1—[Crow]	110
,,	,,	2—Eagle	38
,,	,,	Aiery	38
,,	,,	Towers	38
,,	,,	Souse	38
,,	,,	7—Cygnet	201
,,	,,	Swan	201

R R

APPENDIX.

King Lear :

				PAGE
Act I.	Sc.	4—Hedge-Sparrow		147
,,	,,	Cuckoo		147
,,	,,	Kite		44
,, II.	,,	2—Wagtail		156
,,	,,	Goose		198
,,	,,	Halcyon		275
,,	,,	4—Wild-Geese		246
,,	,,	Vulture		41
,,	,,	Owl		97
,, III.	,,	4—The five wits		95
,,	,,	Pelican		287
,,	,,	6—[Nightingale]		123
,, IV.	,,	6—Crows		116
,,	,,	Choughs		116
,,	,,	Crow-keeper		114
,,	,,	Wren		144
,,	,,	Lark		135

Love's Labour's Lost :

Act I.	Sc.	1—Cormorant		260
,,	,,	Green-Geese		197
,, III.	,,	1—Goose		197
,, IV.	,,	1—Owl		95
,,	,,	3—Green-Goose		198
,,	,,	Woodcocks		229
,,	,,	Raven		109
,,	,,	[Turtle]		191
,,	,,	Eagle-sighted		25
,,	,,	Bird-bolts		162
,, V.	,,	1—Pigeon		180
,,	,,	2—Pigeons		180
,,	,,	Owl		95
,,	,,	[Cuckoo]		147
,,	,,	[Lark]		130
,,	,,	[Turtle-dove]		191
,,	,,	Rook		121
,,	,,	Daw		119

Macbeth :

Act I.	Sc.	2—Sparrow		147
,,	,,	[Eagle]		23
,,	,,	5—Raven		102

Macbeth (continued):

				PAGE
Act I.	Sc.	6—Martlet		277
,, II.	,,	1—Owl		84
,,	,,	2—"Obscure bird"		85
,,	,,	4—Falcon		39, 51
,,	,,	Towering		39, 51
,,	,,	Owl		51
,, III.	,,	2—[Crow]		110–115
,,	,,	4—Maws		46
,,	,,	Kites		46
,,	,,	Magot-pies		120
,,	,,	Choughs		120
,,	,,	Rooks		120
,, IV.	,,	1—Owlet		84
,,	,,	2—Wren		91, 143
,,	,,	Owl		91, 143
,,	,,	3—Vulture		40
,,	,,	[Quarry]		57
,,	,,	[Kite]		43
,, V.	,,	3—Loon		258
,,	,,	[Geese]		197

Measure for Measure:

Act I.	Sc.	4—Lapwing		221
,, II.	,,	1—Scare-crow		115
,, III.	,,	1—Enmew		64–66
,,	,,	Falcon		64
,,	,,	Fowl		64
,,	,,	2—Sparrows		146

Merchant of Venice:

Act I.	Sc.	2—Throstle		137
,, II.	,,	2—Doves		196
,,	,,	6—Venus' Pigeons		190
,,	,,	9—Martlet		278
,, III.	,,	2—Swan		201
,, V.	,,	1—Crow		143
,,	,,	Lark		135, 143
,,	,,	Nightingale		128, 143
,,	,,	Goose		128, 143, 197
,,	,,	Wren		128, 143
,,	,,	Cuckoo		150

Merry Wives of Windsor:

				PAGE
Act I.	Sc.	1—Cock and pye	. .	171
,,	,,	3—Bully-rook .	. .	121
,,	,,	[Raven] .	. .	99
,,	,,	Vultures .	. .	41
,,	,,	[Dove] .	. .	190
,,	II. ,,	1—Cuckoo-birds	. (note)	148
,,	III. ,,	3—Eyas-musket	. .	74
,,	,,	Birding .	. .	72
,,	,,	[Hawk] .	. .	73
,,	,,	4—[Geese] .	.	197
,,	,,	5—Birding .	. .	72
,,	IV. ,,	2—Birding .	. .	72
,,	,,	Birding-pieces	. 72,	164
,,	V. ,,	1—Goose .	. .	197
,,	,,	5—Swan .	.	207
,,	,,	Goose .	.	207

Midsummer Night's Dream:

Act I.	Sc.	1—Doves of Venus .	190
,,	,,	Lark . .	133
,,	,,	2—Dove . .	195.
,,	,,	Nightingale .	195
,,	II. ,,	1—Crows . .	110
,,	,,	[Dove] .	180
,,	,,	[Bolt] . .	162
,,	,,	2—Owl . .	89
,,	,,	Philomel .	125
,,	,,	Raven .	108
,,	,,	Dove . .	108
,,	III. ,,	1—[Wild-fowl] .	. 235
,,	,,	Ousel-cock .	139
,,	,,	Throstle .	137
,,	,,	Wren . .	142
,,	,,	Finch .	144
,,	,,	Sparrow .	147
,,	,,	[Lark] . .	130
,,	,,	Cuckoo .	150
,,	,,	2—Wild-Geese	246
,,	,,	Fowler	246
,,	,,	Choughs	119
,,	,,	[Crow]	110

APPENDIX.

Midsummer Night's Dream (continued):

				PAGE
Act IV.	Sc.	1—Lark		131
„ V.	„	1—Recorder		129
„	„	Goose		197
„	„	2—Screech-Owl		86

Much Ado about Nothing:

Act I.	Sc.	1—Parrot-teacher	272, 273
„	„	Bird-bolt	162
„	„	Crow	114
„	„	Wise and warm	95
„ II.	„	1—Partridge	218
„	„	Fowl	237
„	„	3—Raven	101
„	„	Fowl	238
„	„	Daw	119
„	„	Gull	269
„ III.	„	1—Lapwing	221
„	„	Haggards	59
„	„	Limed	160
„	„	4—[Hawk]	73
„ V.	„	1—Woodcock	229

Othello:

Act I.	Sc.	1—Daws	120
„	„	3—Seel	70
„	„	Snipe	233
„ II.	„	1—Birdlime	161
„	„	3—Speak Parrot	272
„ III.	„	Watch	45
„	„	Haggard	57
„	„	Jesses	57
„	„	Seel	71
„ IV.	„	1—Raven	100
„ V.	„	1—" Cry on "	(note) 56
„	„	2—[Gull]	239, 267
„	„	Swan	201

Pericles:

Act III. Introd.	—[Duck]	222–224, 237
„ IV.	„ [Night-bird]	99
„	„ Dove	113, 191
„	„ Crow	113

Pericles (continued):

			PAGE
Act IV.	Sc.	3—Wren	144
,,	,,	[Eagle]	23
,,	,,	6—Coistrel	74

Richard II.:

Act I.	Sc.	1—Pitch	51
,,	,,	3—Falcon	54
,,	,,	Cloy	31
,,	II. ,,	1—Cormorant	259
,,	,,	Pelican	287
,,	,,	Imp	69
,,	III. ,,	3—Eagle	24
,,	,,	Night-Owls	85
,,	,,	Lark	136

Richard III.:

Act I.	Sc.	1—[Eagle]	23, 45
,,	,,	Kites	45
,,	,,	Buzzards	45, 47
,,	,,	3—Wren	144
,,	,,	[Eagle]	23
,,	,,	[Mew'd up]	64
,,	,,	Aiery	39
,,	IV. ,,	4—Owls	86
,,	V. ,,	2—Swallow	277
,,	,,	3—Lark	133
,,	,,	Cock	167
,,	,,	"Cry on"	(note) 56

Romeo and Juliet:

Act I.	Sc.	2—Swan	114, 206
,,	,,	Crow	114, 206
,,	,,	3—Dove-house	180
,,	,,	4—Crow-keeper	114
,,	,,	Soar	50, 51
,,	,,	Pitch	50, 51
,,	,,	5—Cock-a-hoop	169
,,	,,	Dove	113, 194
,,	,,	Crows	113, 194

APPENDIX. 311

Romeo and Juliet (continued):

				PAGE
Act II.	Sc.	2—Falconer	. . .	54
,,	,,	Lure . .	. .	54
,,	,,	Tassel-gentle	. .	54
,,	,,	4—Goose . .	. .	197
,,	,,	5—Dove . .	.	180
,,	III.	,,	2—Hood . .	. . 62
,,	,,	Unmann'd .	. .	62
,,	,,	Bating	. . .	62
,,	,,	Raven .	. .	108, 109
,,	,,	4—Mew'd up .	. .	64
,,	,,	5—Nightingale .	. .	124
,,	,,	Lark . .	.	124, 131, 134
,,	,,	Eagle . .	. .	25
,,	IV.	,,	4—Watch .	. . 46
,,	,,	Watching .	.	46
,,	V.	,,	1—[Dove]. .	. 194
,,	,,	3—Maw .		46

Taming of the Shrew:

Induct.	Sc.	1—[Nightingale]	.	123
,,	,,	2—Hawking .	.	72
,,	,,	Hawk .	.	72
,,	,,	Lark . .	.	72
,,	,,	1—Mew .	.	64, 65
Act I.	,,	2—Woodcock .	.	229
,,	II.	,,	1—Nightingale .	. 124
,,	,,	Buzzard		47
,,	,,	Turtle . .		47
,,	,,	Wise and warm .		95
,,	III.	,,	1—Stale . .	. 245
,,	,,	2—Dove .	.	180
,,	IV.	,,	1—Falcon .	62
,,	,,	Stoop .	.	62
,,	,,	Lure .		55, 62
,,	,,	Man .		45, 62
,,	,,	Haggard		45, 62
,,	,,	Watch .		45, 62
,,	,,	Kites .		45, 62
,,	,,	Bate .	.	45, 63
,,	,,	Peacock	. (note)	175
,,	,,	2—Haggard	. .	59

Taming of the Shrew (continued):

				PAGE
Act IV.	Sc.	3—Jay		122
,,	,,	Lark		122
,, V.	,,	2—Hawk		73

The Tempest:

Act I.	Sc.	2—Raven's feather		107
,, II.	,,	1—Bat-fowling		157
,,	,,	Chough		117
,,	,,	2—Duck		238
,,	,,	Goose		197
,,	,,	Jay's nest		122
,,	,,	Sea-mells		122, 269
,, IV.	,,	1—Sparrows		146
,,	,,	Barnacles		246
,,	,,	Peacock	(note)	175
,, V.	,,	1—Owls		96

Timon of Athens:

Act I.	Sc.	1—Eagle	26
,, II.	,,	1—[Gull]	267
,, III.	,,	6—Swallow	277
,,	,,	Tiring	38
,, IV.	,,	3—Eagle	34

Titus Andronicus:

Act II.	Sc.	2—Swallows		277
,,	,,	3—Philomel		125
,,	,,	Owl	94,	105
,,	,,	Raven		105
,,	,,	Lark		136
,, III.	,,	1—[Raven]		99
,,	,,	Lark		136
,, IV.	,,	1—Philomel		125
,,	,,	Swan		205
,,	,,	2—Swallow		276
,,	,,	3—Pigeon	180,	183
,,	,,	4—Pigeons		184
,,	,,	Eagle		33
,, V.	,,	2—Vulture		40
,,	,,	[Philomel]		125
,,	,,	3—Fowl		236

Troilus and Cressida:

				PAGE
Act I.	Sc.	1—Cygnet's down		206
,,	,,	2—[Eagles]		23
,,	,,	[Crows]		110
,,	,,	Daws		119
,,	II.	,,	1—Sparrows	146
,,	,,	[Owl]		83
,,	,,	2—Cormorant		260
,,	,,	3—[Raven]		99
,,	III.	,,	1—Doves	196
,,	,,	2—Sparrow		145
,,	,,	Watch'd		45
,,	,,	Falcon		54
,,	,,	Tercel		54
,,	,,	Ducks		54
,,	,,	Plantage		192
,,	,,	Turtle		180, 192
,,	,,	3—Peacock		175
,,	IV.	,,	2—Lark	131
,,	,,	Crows		131
,,	V.	,,	1—Finch-egg	144
,,	,,	Quails		219
,,	,,	Owl		83
,,	,,	Puttock		44
,,	,,	2—Raven		100
,,	,,	Parrot		272
,,	,,	11—[Screech-Owl]		85
,,	,,	[Goose]		197

Twelfth Night:

				PAGE
Act I.	Sc.	3—Coystril		74
,,	II.	,,	3—Gull	149, 267
,,	,,	Woodcock		229
,,	,,	5—Stanniel		73
,,	,,	Check		60, 73
,,	,,	Gull-catcher		267
,,	,,	Turkey-cock		180
,,	,,	Woodcock		231
,,	,,	Bird-bolts		163
,,	,,	Stone-bow		163
,,	III.	,,	1—Haggard	60
,,	,,	Check		60

APPENDIX.

Twelfth Night (continued):
                                                        PAGE

Act III. Sc.	2—Wren			144
,, ,,	[Gull]			267
,, ,,	4—[Nightingale]			123
,, ,,	Daws			119
,, ,,	Limed			161
,, IV. ,,	2—Wild-fowl			232, 257
,, ,,	Woodcock			232, 257
,, V. ,,	1—Raven			108
,, ,,	Dove			108
,, ,,	Gull			267

Two Gentlemen of Verona:

Act II. Sc.	1—Robin-Redbreast		142
,, III. ,,	1—Nightingale		128
,, IV. ,,	4—Geese		198
,, V. ,,	4—[Nightingale]		123

The Winter's Tale:

Act II. Sc.	3—Kites		107
,, ,,	Ravens		107
,, III. ,,	2—[Crow]		110
,, IV. ,,	2—Lark		130
,, ,,	Thrush		137
,, ,,	Kite		46
,, ,,	Woodcock		230
,, ,,	3—Jay		121
,, ,,	Falcon		64
,, ,,	Swallow		277
,, ,,	Crow		113
,, ,,	Dove		185
,, ,,	Turtles		180, 192
,, ,,	Choughs		118
,, ,,	Pheasant		210
,, ,,	4—Dove's down		194
,, V. ,,	3—[Turtle]		180

Lucrece:

Venus' doves	190
Limed	160
Cloy'd	31
Owls	97

APPENDIX. 315

Lucrece (continued):

Dove	190
[Night-Owl]	83
Falcon	61
Fowl	61
Vulture	41
[Hawk]	72
Cuckoos	149
Sparrows	149
Ravens	110
[Crow]	110
Swan	201
[Eagles]	23
Philomel	125
[Fowls]	235

The Passionate Pilgrim:

Dove	180
Philomela	125
Lark	130
Nightingale	125

The Phœnix and Turtle:

Eagle	23
Swan	201
Crow	110
Turtle	191

Sonnets:

XXIX.	Lark	132
LXX.	Crow	110
LXXXVI.	Gulls	269
XCI.	Hawks	72
CII.	Philomel	125
CXIV.	Crow	110
	Dove	180

Venus and Adonis:

Doves	180, 190
Eagle	38

Venus and Adonis (continued):

	PAGE
Tire	38
Dive-dapper	258
Crows	113
Owl	98
Vulture	41
Falcon	56
Lure	56
Lark	131
Doves of Paphos	190

INDEX.

A.
Adder, 13, 15, 16, *Intro.*
Aiery, 39.

B.
Badger, 12, *Intro.*
Bandoleers, 243.
Bat, 13, 14, *Intro.*
Bat-fowling, 157-160.
Barnacle Goose, 247.
Barnacles, 247-256.
Bating, 62.
Bee, 17, 18, 19, *Intro.*
Beetle, 17, 20, *Intro.*
Bells, 60.
Bird-bolts, 163.
Bird-catching, 4, 157.
Birding, 72.
Birding-pieces, 72, 164, 239.
Bird of Jove, 28, 29.
Bird-lime, 160.
Bird-traps, 162.
Birds of song, 123.
Birds under domestication, 167.
Blackbird, 139.
Black Ouzel, 139.
Brock, 12, *Intro.*
Bunting, 136.
Butterfly, 17, *Intro.*
Buzzard, 47.

C.
Cadge, 63.
Cadger, 64.
Caliver, 239.
,, derivation of, 240.
,, description of, 240.
,, figure of, 242.
,, price of, 243.
Camelot, 198, 199.
Caterpillar, 17, *Intro.*
Chase, Wild-goose, 199.
Chough, 115.
,, and Crow, 116.
,, language of, 117.
,, red-legged, 119.
,, russet-pated, 119.
Cloys, 31, 32.
Cock, 167.
,, ancestry of domestic, 174.
Cock-a-hoop, 169, 170.
Cock and pye, 171.
Cock-crow, 168.
Cock-fighting, 172-174.
Coistrel, 74.
Cormorants, 259.
,, fishing with, 260.
,, the King's, 261-264.
,, home of the, 265.
Coursing, 12, *Intro.*
Coystril, 74.
Cricket, 17, *Intro.*
Crow, 99.
,, black as a, 113.
,, food for, 112.

Crow, habits of, 111.
,, -keeper, 114.
,, Night-, 102.
,, Scare-, 114.
,, to pluck, 114.
Crows and their relations, 99.
Cry havoc, 57.
Cuckoo, 147-156.
,, habits of, 150.
,, note of, 151.
,, songs, 152-156.
Cygnet, 201-206.

D.
Daw, 119.
Deer-hunting, 8, *Intro.*
,, -shooting, 4, *Intro.*
,, -stealing, 6, *Intro.*
,, wounded, 10, *Intro.*
Dive-dapper, 258.
Divers, 258.
Dove, 191.
,, of Paphos, 191.
,, of Venus, 191.
,, Rock-, 190.
,, Turtle-, 191.
Dove-house, 180.
Dove, Mahomed's, 193.
,, timidity of, 195.
Doves, dish of, 196.
Dormouse, 13, *Intro.*
Drone, 17, 19, *Intro.*
Duck, 237.
,, -hunting, 237.

E.
Eagle, 23-40.
,, age of, 35.
,, eggs of, 32.
,, eye, 25.
,, eyrie of, 38.
,, longevity of, 33-35.
,, omen of victory, 27.
,, power of flight, 25, 26.
,, power of vision, 24.

Eagle trained for hawking, 36, 37.
,, the Roman, 28-30.
Enmew, 64, 66.
Eyas-musket, 74.
Eyesses, 57, 58.
Eyrie, 39, 57.

F.
Falcon, 52.
,, docility of the, 54.
,, -gentle, 53.
,, Haggard-, 57-59.
,, and Tercel, 52.
Falconer, 54.
,, qualities of a good, 55.
,, call of the, 55.
,, wages of, 80.
Finch, 144.
Fishing, 3, *Intro.*
Fly, Blow-, 17, *Intro.*
,, Gad-, 17, *Intro.*
,, House-, 17, 20, *Intro.*
,, small Gilded-, 17, *Intro.*
Flying at the brook, 51.
Forester, 6, 10, *Intro.*
Fowl, 235.
,, flight of, 236.
,, Sea-, 235.
,, Wild-, 235-237.
Fowling, 4, *Intro.*
Fox, 11, *Intro.*

G.
Game-birds, 209.
,, former value of, 212.
,, laws, 215.
,, preserving, 209-214.
Gin, the, 231.
Glowworm, 17, *Intro.*
Gnat, 17, *Intro.*
Goose, 197.
,, a green-, 197.
,, a stubble-, 198.
,, former value of a, 197.
,, Wild-, 246.

INDEX.

Grasshopper, 17, *Intro*.
Grebe, 258.
,, Great-crested, 258.
,, Little, 258.
Guinea-fowl, 179.
Gull, 266.
,, -catchers, 267.
,, -gropers, 268.

H.

Haggard, 57-59.
Halcyon, 275.
,, days, 275.
Hare, 11, *Intro*.
Hawks, 49.
,, how to seel, 70.
,, keep of, 79.
,, trappings of, 58-64.
,, value of, 77, 78.
,, unmann'd, 62.
Hawking, age of, 50.
,, sundries, 80-82.
,, terms, 51.
Hedgehog, 13, *Intro*.
Hernshaw, 75, 223.
Heron, 223.
,, -hawking, 224-228.
,, in bills of fare, 228.
Hood, 61.
Hounds, 8, 9, *Intro*.
Hunting, 4, *Intro*.

I.

Jackdaw, 119.
Jay, 121.
Jesses, 58, 59.
Imping, 67, 68.
Jove's bird, 28, 29.

K.

Kestrel, 73.
Kingfisher, 275.
Kite, 43-47.
,, habits of, 46.

Kite, nest of, 47.
,, ill-omened, 45.

L.

Lang-nebbit things, 228.
Lapwing, 221.
,, decoying from nest, 221.
Lark, 130.
,, at heaven's gate, 132.
,, herald of morn, 131.
,, soaring and singing, 135.
,, song of the, 130-134.
,, method of taking, 136.
,, the ploughman's clock, 133.
Lime, 160.
Loon, 258, 259.
Lure, description of the, 55.
,, use of the, 56.

M.

Magpie, 120.
Mallard, 238.
Marten, 33.
Martin, 277.
Martlet, 277, 278.
Mole, 13, *Intro*.
Moth, 17, *Intro*.
Mew, 64.
,, origin of the word, 65.
Mews, the Royal, 65, 66.
Musket, 74.

N.

Night-crow, 102.
Nightingale, 124.
,, lamenting, 125.
,, recording, 129.
,, singing against a thorn, 126, 127.
,, singing by day, 128.
,, song of, 124.

O.

Owl, 83-98.
,, its associations, 83.
,, its character maligned, 93.

Owl, its comrades, 97.
,, its fame in song, 96.
,, its five wits, 95.
,, its habits misunderstood, 86.
,, its utility to the farmer, 87.
,, its use in medicine, 84.
,, its note, 90.
,, its retiring habits, 94.
,, robbing nests, 91.
,, of ill-omen, 85.
Osprey, 41.
,, its power over fish, 43.
Ostrich, 286.
Ouzel, 139.

P.

Parrot, 272.
,, -teacher, 273.
Partridge, 216.
,, in kite's nest, 216.
,, -hawking, 217.
,, netting-, 218.
Peacock, 175.
,, introduction of, 176.
,, value of, 175.
,, variety of, 176.
Peewit, 222.
Pelican, 286.
,, fable of the, 287.
,, explanation of fable, 288–294.
Pelicans in England, 295.
Pheasant, 210.
,, introduction of, 211.
,, -hawking, 217.
Pigeon, 180.
,, Barbary-, 189.
,, Carrier-, 183.
,, domesticated, 181.
,, -fanciers, 182.
,, feeding young, 186.
,, -liver'd, 185.
,, -post, 184.
,, price of, 196.
Pitch, 51.

Plantage, 192.
Point, 51.
Prune, 31.

Q.

Quail, 218.
,, -fighting, 219.
,, note of the, 220.
Quaint recipes, 71.
Quarry, 57.

R.

Rabbit, 12, *Intro.*
,, -netting, 12, *Intro.*
Raven, 100.
,, of ill-omen, 101.
,, deserting its young, 106.
,, feathers of, 107.
,, food of, 105.
,, presence on battle-fields, 104.
,, supposed prophetic power, 103.
,, variety of, 109.
Recipes, quaint, 71.
Redbreast, 139.
,, -teacher, 142.
Robin, 139.
Rock-dove, 190.
Rook, 121.
Ruddock, 140.
,, covering with leaves, 141.

S.

Sea-fowl, 235.
Sea-gulls, 266.
Sea-mells, 270.
Seel, 69.
Seeling, 69.
Slow-worm, 16, *Intro.*
Snake, 13, 15, *Intro.*
Snipe, 233.
,, -netting, 234.
Souse, 38, 39.
Sparrow, 144.
,, fall of a, 146.
,, hedge-, 147.

Sparrow, Philip, 145.
,, value of a, 146.
Sparrowhawk, 73.
Springes, 229.
,, how to make, 230.
Stag, wounded, 10, *Intro.*
Stale, 244.
,, how to make a, 245.
Stalking, 238.
Stalking-horse, 238.
Starlings, 274.
,, talking, 274.
Stoop, 63.
Swallow, 277.
Swallow's herb, 279.
,, stone, 283.
Swan, 201.
,, habits of the, 204.
,, nest of the, 204.
,, song of the, 202.
Swan's down, 206.
Swans of Juno, 206.
,, warrant for, 207.
Squirrel, 13, *Intro.*

T.

Tassel-gentle, 54.
Tercel, 53.
,, and Falcon, 52.
Throstle, 137.
,, song of the, 138.
Tire, 38.

Tower, 39, 51.
Towering, 39, 51.
Toad, 13, 15, *Intro.*
Tradition, a curious, 88.
Trout, 3, *Intro.*
Turkey, 177.
,, introduction of, 177.
Turkey-fowl, 179.
Turtle-dove, 191.

V.

Vulture, 40.
,, repulsive habits of, 41.

W.

Wagtail, 156.
Wasp, 17, *Intro.*
Watching, 45.
Weasel, 13, 32.
Wild-cat, 13, *Intro.*
Wild-duck, 237.
Wild-fowl, 235, 257.
Wild-goose, 246.
Wild-goose chase, 199.
Winter-ground, 141.
Wren, 142.
,, courage of, 143.
,, pugnacity of, 143.
,, song of, 143.
Woodcock, 228, 271.
,, springe for a, 229.
Woodcock's head, the, 232.

T T

Woodfall and Kinder, Printers, Milford Lane, Strand, London, W.C.

www.ingramcontent.com/pod-product-compliance
Lightning Source LLC
Chambersburg PA
CBHW031853220426
43663CB00006B/604